API Management

An Architect's Guide to Developing and Managing APIs for Your Organization

Second Edition

Brajesh De

Apress®

API Management: An Architect's Guide to Developing and Managing APIs for Your Organization

Brajesh De
Bangalore, Karnataka, India

ISBN-13 (pbk): 979-8-8688-0053-5
ISBN-13 (electronic): 979-8-8688-0054-2
https://doi.org/10.1007/979-8-8688-0054-2

Managing Director: Welmoed Spahr
Acquisitions Editor: Celestin Suresh John
Development Editor: James Markham
Project Manager: Jessica Vakili
Copyeditor: Kim Burton

Cover image designed by Freepik (www.freepik.com)

Distributed to the book trade worldwide by Springer Science+Business Media New York, 1 NY PLaza, New York, NY 10004. Phone 1-800-SPRINGER, fax (201) 348-4505, e-mail orders-ny@springer-sbm.com, or visit www.springeronline.com. Apress Media, LLC is a California LLC and the sole member (owner) is Springer Science + Business Media Finance Inc (SSBM Finance Inc). SSBM Finance Inc is a **Delaware** corporation.

For information on translations, please e-mail booktranslations@springernature.com; for reprint, paperback, or audio rights, please e-mail bookpermissions@springernature.com.

Apress titles may be purchased in bulk for academic, corporate, or promotional use. eBook versions and licenses are also available for most titles. For more information, reference our Print and eBook Bulk Sales web page at http://www.apress.com/bulk-sales.

Any source code or other supplementary material referenced by the author in this book is available to readers on the Github repository: https://www.apress.com/gp/services/source-code.

Paper in this product is recyclable

In loving memory of my parents whose spirits and blessings continue to guide me

Table of Contents

About the Author

Brajesh is Sr. Director with **Blue Altair**, leading their API Management and Integration practice. He has more than 25 years of industry experience specializing in API Management and Cloud Integration space. He has led many large-scale Digital Transformation projects helping enterprises across industries in laying out API First strategy and executed some of them on multi-cloud platforms. His innovations are patented and granted across four countries in areas like API Assessment and data veracity. He is a Google-certified Cloud Security architect and MIT-certified Application Security Architect. Before **Blue Altair** he worked with Accenture, Apigee, and Wipro as a Global API capability lead, Principal Architect, and Lead integration architect.

About the Technical Reviewers

Chandresh Pancholi is SDE-3 at nnnow.com (Arvind Internet group). Prior to that, he worked with Flipkart Internet Pvt. Ltd. as a senior software developer. He has worked on multiple back-end frameworks like Spring, Dropwizard, Flask, Golang, and Spring Boot. Chandresh graduated from LNMIIT, Jaipur, and received a master's degree from BITS, Pilani. He is also a keen contributor to Apache open source foundations projects.

Rajesh Doda is a digital transformation expert and API strategist with a stellar track record guiding enterprises toward modernization. With decades of experience, he's designed digital platform strategies and implemented scalable API management platforms. Outside of his professional pursuits, Rajesh enjoys hiking and practicing yoga and is an avid book club member.

CHAPTER 1

Introduction to APIs

An Application programming interface (API) exposes a business service or an enterprise asset to the application developers. Applications can be installed and accessed from a variety of devices, such as smartphones, tablets, kiosks, gaming consoles, connected cars, and so forth. Google Maps APIs for locating a place on a map, Facebook APIs for gaming or sharing content, and Amazon APIs for product information are some examples of APIs. Developers use these APIs to build cool and innovative apps that enrich the user experience. For example, developers can use APIs from different travel companies to build an app that compares and displays each travel company's price for the same hotel. A user can then make an informed decision and book the hotel through the company providing the best offer. This saves users from comparing on their own—thus improving the overall experience. APIs thus provide an improved user experience.

An API is a software-to-software interface that defines the contract for applications to talk to each other over a network without user interaction. When you book a hotel room online from a travel portal with your credit card, the travel portal/application sends your booking information to the hotel's reservation system to block the room. It also sends the credit card information to a payment application. The payment application interacts with a remote banking application to validate the credit card details and process the payment. If the processing is successful, the hotel room is reserved for you. The interaction of the travel portal with the hotel's reservation system and the payment application both use APIs.

B. De, *API Management*, https://doi.org/10.1007/979-8-8688-0054-2_1

As a user, you see only one interaction to collect the booking and credit card information. But behind the scenes, the applications work together using APIs. An API does this by "exposing" some of the business functions to the outside world in a limited fashion. That makes it possible to share business services, assets, and data so that other applications can easily consume without sharing the code base. APIs can be thought of as *windows to the code base*. They clearly define how a program interacts with the rest of the software application—saving time and resources and avoiding potential legal entanglements. The API contract defines how the service is provided by the provider and consumed by a consumer. The contract can include the definition and terms of service, SLAs like uptime/availability, licensing agreements for service usage and pricing, and the support model.

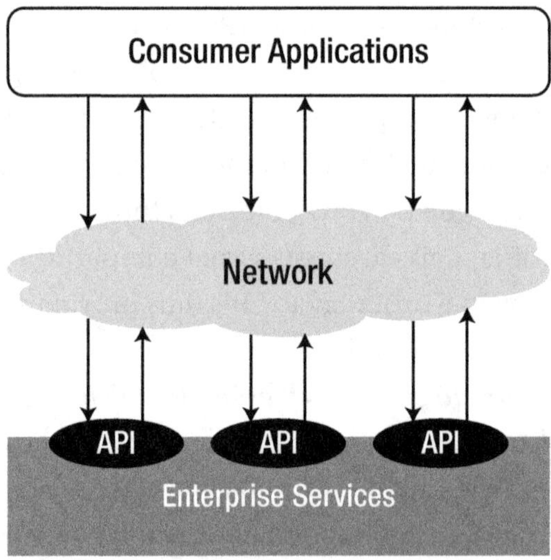

***Figure 1-1.** An API provides an interface for consumer applications to interact with enterprise services over a network*

The contract defines the protocol, the input and output formats, and the underlying data types for the software components to interact. It defines the functionality independent of the component's underlying implementation technologies. The underlying implementation may change, but the contract definition should remain constant. The contract increases the confidence and thus the use of a component. An API with a well-defined contract provides all the building blocks needed for different software applications to communicate easily with each other. The contract for an API defines the methods and data formats that applications can use to request and exchange information or perform specific actions.

This chapter covers the following topics.

- The evolution of APIs
- The difference between web APIs and websites
- The characteristics of an API
- The types of APIs (using some popular examples)
- The difference between web APIs, web services, and service-oriented architecture
- An API value chain
- Various business models for APIs

APIs for Dummies

APIs can be best explained with the analogy of a restaurant. In the restaurant, you look at the menu to select what you want to eat. You then call the waiter to order the item on the menu. You may specify special instructions to prepare the item, such as the spice level, or to include any special vegetables. The waiter writes down the order with your instructions and delivers it to the chefs in the kitchen. Once the chef prepares the order as requested, the waiter picks it up from the kitchen and takes it to the table. As a customer, you review the dish to ensure it is made to your specifications and then eat it. You may later provide a review or feedback on the service provided.

- **You are the consumer of API.** Sending the request for the item in the menu to the kitchen team.
- **The waiter is the API.** He takes your request to the chef in the kitchen since you cannot directly go to the kitchen and order. The waiter then transports the prepared food, which is the response, from the kitchen to your table. The waiter acts as the data messenger and the delivery mechanism to interact with the chefs in the kitchen.
- **The menu is the API documentation.** It tells what you can ask of the API, the waiter. It has information about the food that can be prepared by the chefs in the kitchen and its price. The waiter only understands the information that is on the menu.
- **The kitchen is the API server.** It serves the request by preparing the food requested from the menu. The chef in the kitchen knows how to prepare the food, which is the business logic that is being processed by the server. But you do not know the name or address of the chef. The kitchen, as the API server, serves the dish while maintaining confidentiality and security. The dish is prepared per the standard recipe and instructions, ensuring compliance.

Like a waiter, an API receives the request from the consumer, takes it to the server, fetches the requested information from the database in the server, and delivers the response with the data to the consumer.

The Evolution of APIs

The term *API* may mean different things to different people, depending on the context. There are APIs for operating systems, applications, and the Web. For example, Windows provides APIs used by system hardware and applications. APIs are at work when you copy text or a picture from Microsoft PowerPoint to Word. Most operating environments provide an API so programmers can write applications consistent with it. Today, you probably refer to web APIs built using REST technologies when discussing APIs. Hence, web APIs are synonymous with REST APIs. Web APIs allow you to expose your assets and services in a form easily consumed by another application remotely over HTTP(s).

The following describes the evolution of the modern-day web API.

> In 2000, Roy Thomas Fielding's dissertation, "Architectural Styles and Design of Network-Based Software Architectures," was published.
>
> **February 2000**: APIs are first demonstrated by Salesforce during the launch of its XML APIs at the IDG Demo 2000.
>
> **November 2000**: eBay launched the eBay API and the eBay Developers Program. It was made available to many licensed eBay partners and developers.
>
> **July 2002**: Amazon Web Services is launched. It allows third parties to search and display Amazon.com products in an XML format.
>
> **February 2004**: Marks the beginning of the social media era, with Flickr launching its popular photo-sharing site.
>
> **August 2004**: Flickr launches its API, which helps it to become the most preferred image platform. The Flickr API allows users to easily embed their Flickr photos into their blogs and social network streams.

> **June 2005**: The Google Maps API launched, allowing developers to integrate Google Maps into their websites. Over a million websites use the Google Maps API today, making it one of the most heavily used web application development APIs.
>
> **August 2006**: Facebook launched its Developer API platform, allowing developers access to Facebook friends, photos, events, and profile information.
>
> **September 2006**: Twitter introduced its APIs to the world in response to the growing usage of people scraping its website or creating rogue APIs.

By 2006, web APIs were demonstrating the power of the Internet. They were being used to share content and made available to social networks. However, they were still not considered fit for mainstream businesses. This year also marked the beginning of the *cloud computing* era.

> **March 2006**: Amazon S3 is launched. It provides a simple interface to retrieve and store any amount of data at anytime from anywhere on the Web.
>
> **September 2006**: Amazon launched EC2—the Elastic Compute Cloud platform. It provided resizable computing capacity in the cloud, allowing developers to launch different sizes of virtual servers within Amazon data centers.

With cloud computing, web APIs witnessed their real power. APIs can now be used to deploy global infrastructure. APIs move from being used only for social fun and interaction to actually running real businesses. The emergence of mobile devices, smartphones, and app stores became the next big game changer.

March 2009: Foursquare is launched to provide a local search-and-discovery service mobile app. It provided a personalized local search experience for its users. By considering the places a user goes, the things they have told the app that they like, and the other users whose advice they trust, Foursquare aims to provide highly personalized recommendations on the best places to go near the user's current location. By March 2013, the Foursquare API had more than 40,000 registered developers building a new generation of apps using Foursquare's location-aware services.

June 2009: Apple launched the iPhone 3G. iPod Touch and iPhone owners could download apps onto their devices through iTunes desktop software or the App Store. The APIs emerged as the driving force for the growth of the app economy.

October 2010: Instagram launched its photo-sharing iPhone app.

By 2012, APIs had evolved significantly, driven by business needs and technological advancements in social media, mobile, analytics, and the cloud. REST APIs dominated the API landscape due to its simplicity and scalability. JSON became the de facto standard for all data exchange in APIs.

In 2015, Facebook introduced GraphQL as an alternative to RESTful APIs. GraphQL allows clients to request precisely the data they need, reducing over-fetching and under-fetching of data. It gained popularity for its flexibility and efficiency. Advancements in cloud native technologies and the growth of microservices led to an increase in no. of APIs within organizations. Serverless platforms, like AWS Lambda and Google Cloud

Functions, provided new ways to deploy and manage APIs without worrying about infrastructure management. Open API and Async API provided improved standards to define API interfaces for synchronous and asynchronous communications. The COVID-19 pandemic accelerated digital transformation efforts, increasing reliance on APIs for remote work, healthcare, e-commerce, and other sectors.

APIs Are Different from Websites

Websites publish information that users can consume, but websites do not have contracts. A website's layout, content, and look and feel can change without prior notice to users. There is no contract around a website's structure and content. When a website changes its content, visitors see the update; perhaps it has a new look and feel. When a website is dramatically redesigned, the only impact is users getting accustomed to the new layout. Users might initially find it difficult to find their favorite information at a particular place or in a particular form, but most get used to the changes over time.

An API, on the other hand, has a well-defined contract. Other applications depend on this contract to use it. Unlike humans, programs are not flexible. So, if the contract of the API changes, there is a ripple effect on the apps built using the contract. The effect could be potentially large. This does not mean that an API cannot change. Changes necessary to meet evolving business needs are inevitable. Changes could be in the business logic, the back-end infrastructure, or the API contract interface. Changes to the implementation of the infrastructure do not necessarily require changes to the API interface. Such changes can happen frequently. However, any change to the API interface impacts the applications using them and should be versioned and backward compatible.

Defining an API and Its Characteristics

In technical terms, an API defines the contract of a software component in terms of the protocol, data format, and endpoint for two computer applications to communicate with each other over a network. In simple terms, APIs govern how two applications can talk to each other.

An API provides a framework for building services that can be consumed over HTTP by a wide range of clients running on different platforms, such as iPhones, tablets, smartphones, browsers, kiosks, connected cars, and so forth. These applications can be web applications or apps running on devices.

An API provider should provide the following information about the API.

- The actions that the API can perform to provide business functionality
- The location where the API can be accessed (A URI is normally used to specify the location.)
- The API's input and output parameters, including parameter names, message format, and data types (The message format can be JSON or XML.)
- The network protocol that the client must use to call the API (Common network protocols include HTTP/ HTTPS, FTP/ SFTP, and JMS.)
- The API security information that must be followed and presented by the client to access the APIs (An API may be protected using basic and multi-factor authentication, mTLS, input validation, IP filtration, and more.)

- The service-level agreement (SLA) the API provider adheres to, such as response time, throughput, and availability
- The technical requirements about the rate limits control the number of requests an app or user can make within a given period
- Any legal or business constraints on using the API (This can include commercial licensing terms, branding requirements, fees and payments for use, and so on.)
- Documentation to aid the understanding of the API

Optionally, the API provider may provide the following to aid developers in building and monitoring their apps.

- A portal on which developers can register themselves and their apps before using the APIs
- Example programs and tutorials for using the APIs
- A developer community forum and blogs to support developers and help them collaborate
- Tools to expose and test the APIs
- Health and usage information on the APIs used by developer apps

Types of APIs

APIs can be broadly classified into public and private (see Figure 1-2). Going by the name, public APIs are open to all for use. Private APIs, on the other hand, are accessible only to a restricted group. Private APIs may be for B2B partner integrations or internal use. Those used for partner integration are also known as *partner APIs*. Those for internal use are referred to as *internal APIs*. An internal API can ease and streamline internal application integrations. Internal developers can also use it to build mobile apps for an organization's use.

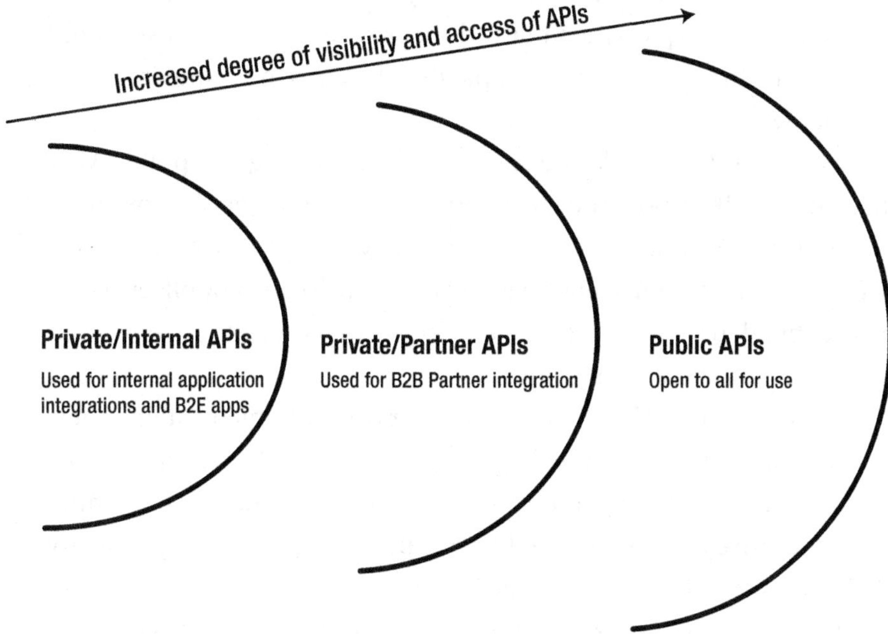

Figure 1-2. *Types of APIs: internal, partner, and public*

The interface of a public API is designed to be accessible by a wider developer community for building mobile and web apps. Internal app developers can access public APIs within an organization and the outside developer community that wants to build apps using them. Public APIs can help an organization add value to its core business through innovation by being open to a wider audience of app developers. Open developers use their imagination to build cool apps using public APIs. Public APIs also increase the use of company assets and add business value without direct investment in app development. Public APIs can generate new business ideas and decrease development costs. The success of a public API depends on its ability to attract developers and help them create truly great apps. A well-designed, well-documented, clean, and intuitive interface allows developers to quickly understand the functionality of an API and how to use it.

However, public APIs can significantly add a lot of management overhead. For example, when many third-party apps actively use an API, upgrading the interface without impacting the apps in production is challenging.

Increased security risks are another major challenge for public APIs. Since public APIs expose the back-end systems of an organization through the enterprise firewall that all can access, they open doors for hackers to intrude into the system. Hence, when an enterprise uses public APIs, it needs to build in additional layers of security to protect its systems from hacker attacks via these APIs.

Private APIs are behind the closed doors of your organization. They are mostly intended for internal app integration or B2B integration with partners or for developing mobile and web apps for internal consumption. Every enterprise developing a public API probably first developed a private API. Be it Facebook, Twitter, Google, or any enterprise—their public APIs, websites, and mobile apps are all powered by their private APIs behind the scenes. The visible public APIs are only the tip of the iceberg. Private APIs form the large underwater mass of the iceberg. Most of these APIs are private and internal to companies, used exclusively by their developers or partners with contractual agreements. These APIs are not exposed to the external developer community but drive the entire API economy. Sometimes, the internal use of a company's private APIs for business transformation can derive more business benefits than public APIs. Hence, the importance of building private APIs should never be underestimated.

How do you make an API private? One simple way is to host it on a public network but not publicize its existence and documentation to the developer community. This approach can work initially but can lead to problems in the future. Developers have a habit of trying out uncanny things and could accidentally discover your unpublicized, private API and start using it for app development. If the app becomes popular and the API publisher decides to modify or retire their private API, it can lead to public outcry. A better approach is to provide security and access control to your APIs and restrict their use to a limited set of known developers and partners. Approaches to secure your APIs are discussed later in this book.

Examples of Popular APIs

The history of web APIs dates back to 2005. Since then, the growth in the number of APIs has been exponential. Many large organizations from different industry sectors have created and published their APIs for public consumption. Some APIs are used experimentally, while others are used in mainstream business to implement innovative use cases and have become popular. However, with the emergence of new technologies and the evolution of human preferences, the popularity of APIs can change over time. The following are some popular APIs across different categories.

- **Social media and messaging APIs**: Social media giants like Facebook, Instagram, LinkedIn, and X (formerly Twitter) use APIs to get social information, pictures, videos, and news that other users post. Developers can build more engaging and interesting applications using these APIs' social connections, user data, and profile information.
- **Mapping and geolocation APIs**: Google Maps API, Mapbox API, OpenStreetMap API, and MapMyIndia provide APIs to start with maps and locations. These APIs can be embedded within JavaScript apps to provide value-added and innovative consumer services. Companies like Uber, FedEx, and Urban

Company use these mapping APIs to provide their consumers with efficient routing and precise location information.

- **Finance and payment APIs**: Stripe, PayPal, Google Pay, and Razor Pay are some of the most popular API providers for online payment processing, billing, invoicing, and financial transaction services. They provide APIs to handle payments, subscriptions, and point-of-sales transactions for in-person and online payments. Some also provide digital wallet services with options for global payment integration. Businesses use these APIs to integrate payment processing into their applications and websites.
- **Communication and collaboration APIs**: APIs like Twilio, Slack, Zoom, and Microsoft Teams offer services for SMS, email, voice, video communication, and collaboration features. These APIs are integrated with various applications for chatting, sending messages via SMS, or for alerting purposes.
- **E-commerce and marketplaces APIs**: Platforms like Amazon, eBay, Shopify, and Etsy use APIs for e-commerce integration and provide an online marketplace. They provide APIs for customer management, product management, cart management, order processing, and more that are needed for e-commerce integrations. Developers use these REST APIs to easily integrate and extend their online stores' functionality.

- **Health and medical data APIs**: Cerner APIs, Allscripts APIs, and OpenFDA Drug APIs are popular APIs that provide patient monitoring, medical management, and health data exchange. Hospitals and healthcare providers use these APIs to exchange digital records of a patient's medical history, information about medicines and dosages, and track patient's health-related information from connected wearable and medical devices.
- **Travel and transportation APIs**: APIs from providers like Uber, Lyft, Amadeus, and Skyscanner provide services for booking, transportation, routing, and travel planning services. Many apps use these APIs to access real-time travel data and assist their customers in planning trips. Skyscanner APIs provide services for flight search, hotel search, and car rental search. These APIs can be used to search and compare travel options. Google Maps and OpenTripMap APIs provide information about tourist attractions, places of interest, and directions to plan the trip.
- **Government and civic APIs**: There are many popular APIs from government agencies across the globe providing public data and information about census, health, education, government laws, city services, infrastructure, economic and social conditions, global issues, and more. Some popular APIs are the UN Data API, NASA API, Census Bureau API, World Bank API, and the Data.gov API, to name a few. App developers are using these APIs to access public data and government services, facilitate transparency, enhance civic engagement, and provide valuable information and tools to the public.

- **Media and entertainment APIs**: Some of the popular APIs in the field of media and entertainment are YouTube API, Spotify APIs, and SoundCloud APIs. IMDb APIs. Developers can use these APIs to integrate media content, streaming services, and entertainment-related features into apps to provide a more engaging experience. Users can get access to music and video catalogs, create, and update their playlists, update user profiles, and enable audio/video playback features using these APIs. Vimeo provides APIs that allow users to upload videos, manage content, and embed them into their applications.
- **Educational APIs**: Educational institutions and EdTech companies are building various apps using the education and learning APIs to provide innovative experiences to their students. Coursera API, Khan Academy API, Wikipedia APIs, Google Books, and Classroom APIs are some of the most popular educational APIs. These APIs can be integrated into apps to provide course information and enrolment options, access and manage course content, create and assess assignments, view learner's activities and progress, and much more. These APIs can offer innovative learning experiences and create custom study tools.
- **Weather and environmental data APIs**: AccuWeather API, OpenWeather API, World Air Quality Index (WAQI) API, and PurpleAir API are popular APIs for weather and air quality information. Weather APIs provide weather data services that include current conditions, forecasts, severe weather alerts, and

historical data for locations across the globe. APIs for air quality provide information about the pollution levels and air quality indices for worldwide locations. These APIs can be used to build apps that assist with travel and vacation planning, agriculture and farming, home automation for automatic temperature control, fitness and health apps to provide recommendations for outdoor activities, environmental monitoring, and many more.

- **Cloud service APIs**: AWS, Azure, and Google Cloud provide APIs that allow developers to manage and deploy various cloud resources programmatically. These APIs can manage and secure cloud services like virtual machines, databases, storage, networks, serverless computing, and more.
- **Content delivery and storage APIs**: Dropbox, Google Drive, and Amazon S3 APIs provide capabilities to store, organize, and retrieve data on the cloud. With proper authentication and authorization, these data can be shared with others who want to access them.
- **Search and discovery APIs**: Google custom search APIs allow customers to build a custom search engine powered by Google's search index. These APIs can be used to implement site-specific search capabilities in websites. The Yelp Fusion API and the Foursquare API let users search for local businesses and places of interest and have access to user ratings and reviews for the same. Zomato APIs provide information for food and dining restaurants around the globe with access to menus, ratings, and reviews. News API provides access

to news articles and headlines from various sources across the globe. Many more API providers provide advanced search and content discovery capabilities to address different use cases and client needs. All these APIs can be integrated into different apps to provide useful and innovative customer experiences.

- **Machine learning and AI APIs**: TensorFlow API, Open API, Google Cloud AI APIs, and the scikit-learn API are some of the most popular APIs for machine learning and AI. They provide capabilities for natural language processing, visual recognition, chatbots, data mining, and machine learning tasks like classification, regression, clustering, and more.
- **ChatGPT APIs**: OpenAI has exposed APIs that enable you to integrate the advanced language processing capabilities of ChatGPT with apps and services. This allows you to integrate generative AI capabilities into your applications to provide improved and innovative user experiences. Generative AI can provide personalized recommendations for customers through human-like interactive assistance. Shopify has recently added ChatGPT into its Shop app to help customers identify and find items they want using interactive prompts.

The Difference Between a Web Service and a REST API

Wikipedia defines a *web service* as "a method of communication between two electronic devices over a network." It is a software function provided at a network address over the Web, with the service always on—as in the concept of utility computing. The W3C defines a *web service* as "a software system designed to support interoperable machine-to-machine interaction over a network."

Going by these definitions, an API and a web service can be considered related concepts. The W3C Web Services Architecture Working Group states that a *web service architecture* requires specific implementation of a web service. In this, a web service "has an interface described in a machine-processable format (specifically WSDL). Other systems interact with the web service described using SOAP (Simple Object Access Protocol) messages, typically conveyed using HTTP with an XML serialization in conjunction with other web-related standards."

SOAP web services typically use HTTP as a transport protocol, which is not mandatory. SOAP can be over JMS/FTP/SMTP or any layer 7 protocol. The SOAP message structure consists of a SOAP envelope inside the SOAP headers and the SOAP body. The SOAP body contains the actual information you want to send. It is based on the standard XML format, designed to transport and store structured data. SOAP is a mature standard that is heavily used in many systems but does not use many functionalities built into HTTP.

On the other hand, an API is a broader concept that refers to a set of rules, protocols, and tools that allow different software components, whether web services or not, to interact with each other. RESTful APIs use HTTP as the transport protocol for communications. REST is an architectural pattern (resource-oriented), an alternative to SOAP. Unlike SOAP, RESTful applications use the HTTP built-in headers (with a variety of media types) to carry meta-information and use the GET, POST, PUT, and DELETE verbs to perform CRUD operations. REST is resource-oriented and uses clean URLs (or RESTful URLs). The body can be JSON or XML, the former preferred due to its simple structure. The principles of RESTful APIs are discussed later in the book.

So far, web services have been synonymous with SOAP web services. With the advent of REST, APIs are commonly referred to as RESTful web services. SOAP is preferred for service interactions within enterprises. Conversely, REST is the choice for exposed services, such as public APIs using HTTP(s).

In terms of performance, SOAP-based web services are heavyweight, requiring additional processing of extra SOAP elements in the payload. REST-based web services are simpler, with lightweight requests and responses in JSON format, which provides a performance advantage and reduces network traffic. RESTful services have better cache support and are preferred for mobile and web apps. Since JSON is lighter, apps run faster and more smoothly.

How Are APIs Different from SOA?

What is the difference between APIs and *service-oriented architecture* (SOA)? Most enterprises are already using SOA. Are APIs still needed? If yes, why? Then, what is the real difference between the two? There is a lot of confusion about whether APIs are different or similar to SOA. Let's look at their characteristics to understand it better.

The core concept of SOA is service. A service can be defined as "a logical representation of a repeatable activity that has a specific outcome." Service-oriented architecture defines the architecture and principles for designing services for an application to increase its reuse. Services are well-contained and have a well-defined interface that defines the contract between the service provider and the consumer.

From a technical perspective, APIs also share the same characteristics. But they are more open, developer-centric, easily consumable, and support human-readable formats like JSON. APIs are designed with consumer needs in mind. What makes APIs different from SOA is the objective behind them. SOA helps with the agility and pace of the delivery of a service, whereas APIs help in the pace of innovation for building apps. SOA emerged as a means to shield service consumers from back-end changes. With the growing need for omnichannel front-end application channels, there is also a need to protect these services. APIs can provide a layer to shield the services from the rapidly changing demands of front-end apps. With APIs and SOA, you can create a calm eye in a hurricane of change.

Services are how providers codify the base capabilities of their domains. APIs are how those capabilities are repackaged, productized, and shared in an easy-to-use format. In that fashion, APIs and services are complementary rather than contradictory and applied together, dramatically increasing the overall effectiveness of enterprise innovation.

At a technology level, SOA is related to XML and SOAP, whereas APIs are related to REST and JSON. SOA services are described using WSDL, whereas APIs are described using Open API Specification or RAML. SOA services are normally published in a UDDI registry that is internal to the organization. APIs are published by an API provider in a portal that developers normally use for onboarding and finding information about the APIs.

Keeping the technical differences aside, the real difference between SOA and APIs centers on scope and governance. SOA is more focused on building reusable enterprise services that enable integration within the enterprise. It provides controlled access to the services for trusted and well-known partners, whereas APIs open services for developers to access them on the public internet using REST principles. APIs are managed as a product that app developers can consume. RESTful design, a JSON data format, and a simple versioning approach complemented with the well-documented and human-readable interface make it easier for developers to adopt and consume APIs.

API technology focuses on consuming the back-end services created using SOA principles. Hence, APIs can be considered an evolution of SOA, imbibing many of the same concepts and principles of creating and exposing reusable services. The main difference between them is that

APIs are focused more on making consumption easier. In contrast, SOA is focused on control and has an extensive and well-defined description language (see Figure 1-3).

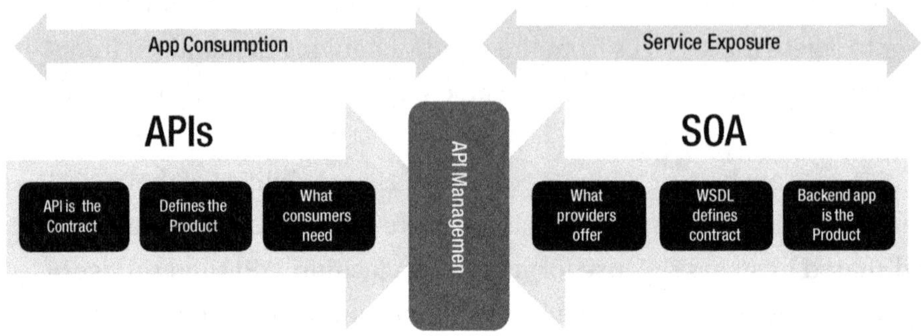

Figure 1-3. *APIs vs. SOA*

APIs provide an agile, flexible, and robust approach to building mobile apps. SOA cannot provide the agility and flexibility to meet growing customer demands. SOA does not match the preferred design for today's mobile apps. API management has become necessary to build, manage, and scale apps for the digital economy. With the help of an API tier to connect your systems of record to your systems of engagement, you can extend your SOA capabilities to match the data requirements of a digital economy.

From a governance perspective, SOA is managed through a governance model that is more formal, heavyweight, and prescriptive. Data schemas and interface specifications have been a strong focus of SOAP services. Any change in the SOA services data type must go through rigorous governance approval, which makes SOA slow. API initiatives, on the other hand, are more agile and focused on developer adoption and usage. The success of an API is measured by the agility it offers to application delivery.

The API Value Chain

APIs provide a means to expose business assets to the end user. To understand the API value chain, you must understand what happens when a business provides an API and identify the actors involved at each step (see Figure 1-4).

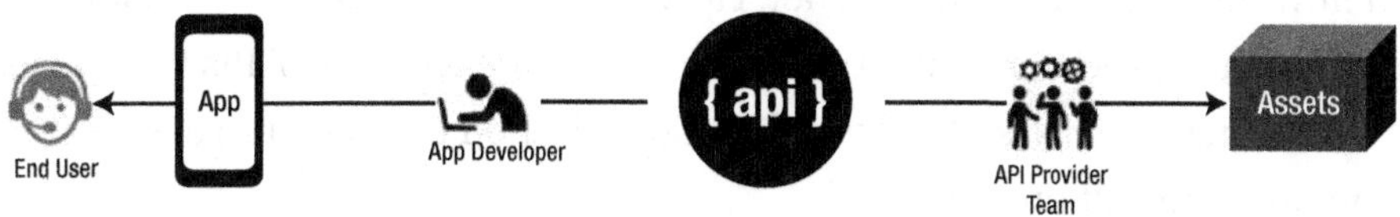

Figure 1-4. *API value chain*

The *business asset* marks the beginning of the API value chain. The business identifies the asset and its value and makes it available to others. The business asset can be any data or business functionality. It can range from product catalogs to customer information, Twitter feeds, postal tracking information, and payment and banking services. The value derived through the use of the asset depends on multiple factors. The following questions foster an understanding of the value of an asset.

- What business asset is being exposed as an API, and what is the value to its owner?
- What benefits would the provider get by creating a channel for using the assets via API?
- Who are the potential users of the asset, and how would the end users get access to the assets?
- What benefits would the end user get by using the asset? Of what potential value could these assets be to the others?
- How easily can the end user access and use it?

The value of the asset determines the success of the API. Exposing the assets to others should also benefit the owner.

Once an asset has been identified, the next step is to create an API to expose the business assets. The **API provider**'s job is to design the API so that the intended audience can easily use it. In most cases, the asset owners are themselves the API providers. In this case, the benefits of the API flow directly to the asset owner. However, in some cases, the owner may have an agreement with another organization to create APIs to expose its assets. In such cases, the rewards get distributed between the asset owner and the API provider.

The **app developers** then assess the APIs and create apps using them. Developers can be an individual entity or a group belonging to an organization. They are may be referred to as *company developers* if they belong to an organization.

The **apps** created by the developers can be mobile apps or web apps. These apps should be made available to the end user to add value to the business. An app store is the most popular channel for distribution. But there may also be other channels for distribution and marketing. Apps can be either freely downloadable or paid.

The **end users** are the final actors in the API value chain. They are the users of the app. They can use the app on their mobile devices, smartphones, tablets, iPhones, or desktops or from other connected devices, such as connected cars, kiosks, and so forth.

The success of the API strategy depends on the various links in the API value chain. It depends on the involvement and commitment of the key stakeholders in the value chain. It is important to get them all involved for the success of your API. There has to be a proper handshake among all the stakeholders. The API provider needs to understand the value of the business asset and decide on the best interface to expose it. The developer must understand the business asset and its interface and create an app that meets the end user's needs and adds value for them. All the stakeholders should understand the core business needs and the value of creating the API. The app built using the API should be easy to use, and the average person should easily understand its purpose and value. Only then can the API strategy be successful.

API Business Drivers

APIs form the foundation of digital business. Adopting the business model depends on the asset being exposed as an API. The asset can be the *data* or the *business logic*. The following are some business drivers for building APIs.

- Growing new business capabilities and opportunities
- Opening new marketing channels and lines of business
- Improving customer reach and loyalty
- Innovating at the edge of business
- Accelerating time to market
- Advancing operational efficiency and control
- Driving traffic and accelerating internal projects

API Business Models

APIs drive business agility and growth and open new channels for revenue. There are many business models to monetize APIs. The model to choose from depends on the organization's business goal, the API's value proposition, the target audience, industry trends, and the competitive landscape. The most common business models for APIs are as follows.

- **Free or open APIs (freemium)**: APIs are offered for free to drive broader adoption. Customers are for higher usage limits and to access enhanced features.

- **Pay-as-you-go (usage-based)**: Consumers are charged for what they consume based on the number of API calls, business transactions, or data used.
- **Subscription**: API provider earns revenue through recurring subscription fees, which can be a fixed monthly/yearly fee or tiered subscription level based on usage limits and features.
- **Transaction fee**: The API provider earns revenue from a portion of the business transaction fee or a fixed fee charged from the consumer for every successful transaction via the APIs.
- **Data licensing/syndication**: Revenue is generated by licensing the data or charging for access to premium data sets provided by the APIs, generally for research and analysis purposes.
- **Affiliate and referrals**: In this model, the API provider earns revenue by referring API users to their partners' programs in exchange for a commission or incentive. The API provider earns for each successful sign-up with the partner.

Some API providers may combine one or more of these models to diversify their revenue streams and cater to different customer segments. The various monetization models are discussed later in the book.

CHAPTER 2

API Management

Customers today want access to enterprise data and services through a variety of digital devices and channels. To meet customer expectations, enterprises need to open their assets in an agile, flexible, secure, and scalable manner. APIs form the window into an enterprise's data and services. They allow applications to easily communicate with each other using a lightweight protocol like HTTP. Developers use APIs to write applications that interact with the back-end system. Once an API has been created, it must be managed using an *API management platform*.

An API management platform helps organizations publish APIs to internal, partner, and external developers to unlock the unique potential of their assets. It provides the core capabilities to ensure a successful API program through developer engagement, business insights, analytics, security, and protection. An API management platform helps businesses accelerate outreach across digital channels, drive partner adoption, monetize digital assets, and provide analytics to optimize investments in digital transformation (see Figure 2-1).

B. De, *API Management*, https://doi.org/10.1007/979-8-8688-0054-2_2

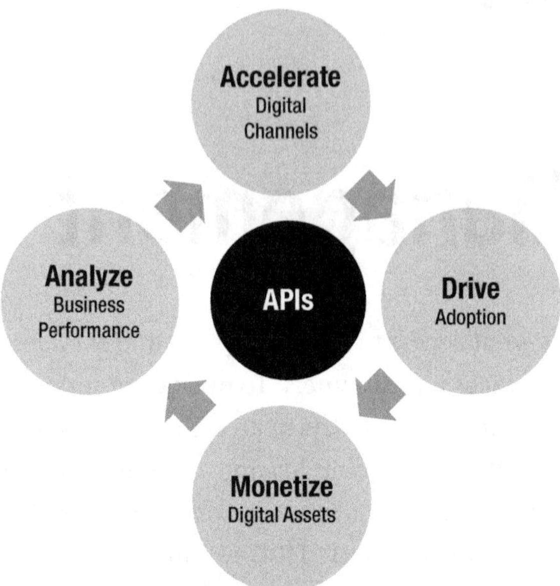

Figure 2-1. *API management offerings*

An API management platform enables you to create, analyze, and manage APIs in a secure and scalable environment (see Figure 2-2). An API management platform should provide the following capabilities.

- Developer enablement for APIs
- Secure, reliable, and flexible communication
- API lifecycle management
- API auditing, logging, and analytics

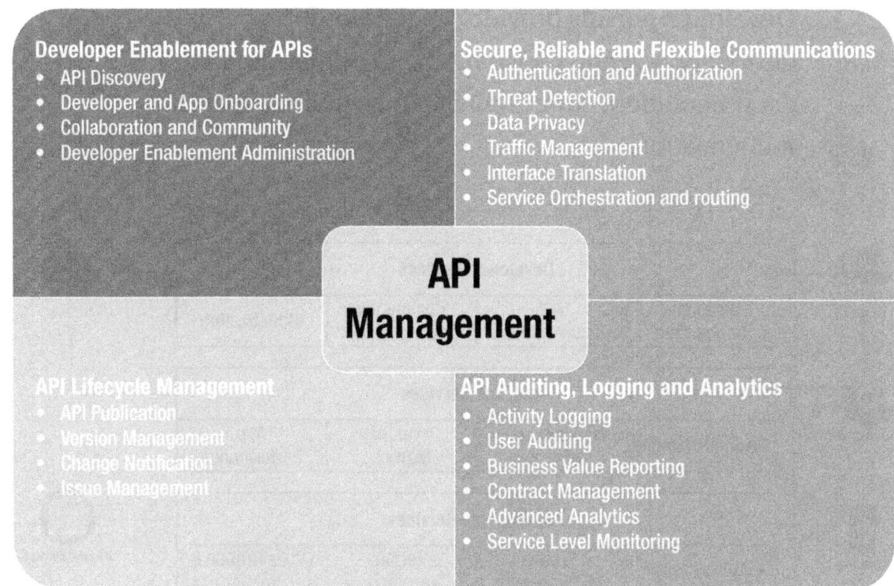

Figure 2-2. *API management capabilities*

API management capabilities can be delivered by any API management vendor in a public cloud as a hosted service or deployed on-premise in a private cloud. A hybrid approach can also be followed, with some components of the API management platform being offered as a hosted solution and others deployed on-premise for increased security and control.

An API management platform provides these capabilities as three major types of services (as illustrated in Figure 2-3).

- **API gateway services** allow you to create and manage APIs from existing data and services. They allow you to add security, traffic management, interface translation, orchestration, and routing capabilities to your API.
- **Analytics services** monitor traffic from individual apps and provide businesses with insight and operational metrics, API and app performance, and developer engagement metrics.

- **Developer portals** provide capabilities for developer and app registration and onboarding, API documentation, community management, and API monetization.

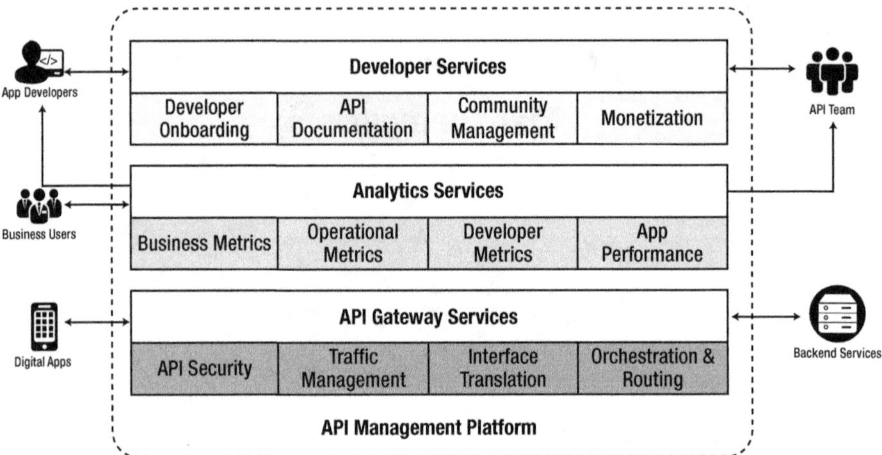

Figure 2-3. *API management platform services*

This chapter introduces you to the different capabilities required for an API management platform and shows how the different services provided by the platform enable these capabilities. In the process, it also introduces the various concepts and technologies for API management.

Secure, Reliable, and Flexible Communication

APIs let digital apps communicate with back-end services. Communication forms the core of APIs. Communication can use REST, SOAP, Plain Old XML (POX), or other protocols. REST is the most preferred communication protocol for APIs due to its inherent characteristics, which are described later in this book. An API management platform must provide a framework that allows secure, reliable, and flexible communication channels. The *API gateway* within the API management platform provides the services that form the core capabilities required for API communications.

The API Gateway

An API gateway forms the heart of any API management solution that enables secure, flexible, and reliable communication between the back-end services and digital apps (see Figure 2-4). It exposes, secures, and manages back-end data and services as RESTful APIs. It provides a framework to create a facade in front of the back-end services. This facade intercepts the API requests to enforce security, validate data, transform messages, throttle traffic, and finally route it to the back-end service. The static response may be cached to improve the performance. The API gateway can optionally orchestrate requests between multiple back-end services and connect to databases to service the request. These functionalities can be implemented in a gateway through configurations and scripting extensions.

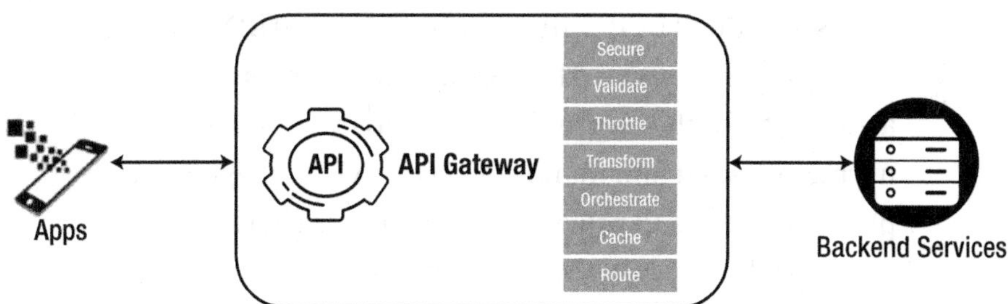

Figure 2-4. *API gateway capabilities*

The main features of an API gateway include—but are not limited to—the following.

API Security

APIs provide access to valuable and protected data and assets. Therefore, security for APIs is paramount to protect the underlying assets from unauthenticated and unauthorized access. Due to the programmatic nature of APIs and their accessibility over the public cloud, they are also prone to different threat attacks. Therefore, the API management platform should address the following aspects of API security.

- **Authentication**: Authentication is the process of uniquely determining and validating a client's identity. An *app* acts like a client making an API call. It is software that consumes an API to access enterprise assets, data, and services. It can run on the Internet, a computer, smartphones, tablets, or any other electronic device.

  Apps are usually made available by their developers through a distribution platform, such as Apple's App Store, Google Play, or the Windows Phone Store. Every app is identified by its *name,* and a unique UUID is known as the *app key.* The app key often serves as an identity for the app making a call to the API. It is normally issued and managed via the API management platform of the API provider. An app key is also known as an *API key,* an *app ID,* or a *client ID.*

  The API management platform must be able to issue, track, and revoke the app key. Authentication services may also require integration with identity management systems that control user access to applications and other services.

- **Authorization**: Authorization controls the access level provided to an app making an API call. It controls which API resources and methods an app can invoke. When an app makes an API call, it normally passes an OAuth *access token* in the HTTP headers. This token is generated as part of the OAuth handshake and is associated with *scopes* that determine the APIs that can be accessed using the token.

  An access token can be associated with one or multiple scopes. Each access token may have an expiry duration that controls the validity of the token. If the token is expired, a new access token must be generated. An app can do this automatically by presenting a *refresh token*. The refresh token may be exchanged for a new access token with a renewed validity period. Using a refresh token by an app to regenerate the access token improves the overall user experience.

- **Identity mediation**: APIs normally use OAuth protocols for implementing security. However, the back-end services may be secured using SAML or WS-Security headers. Hence, the API management platform must be able to integrate with back-end IDM platforms and do identity mediation. OAuth to SAML is a very common identity mediation requirement.

- **Data privacy**: APIs expose data that may be sensitive; such data should be visible only to its intended recipient. Any sensitive data in transit should be encrypted. If such data gets logged anywhere, it must be masked. The API management platform must, therefore, possess data privacy capabilities. Data privacy can be achieved through encryption and data masking. Sensitive data should be encrypted with digital certificates in transit.

The API management platform should have support for SSL/TLS. Additional encryption of specific elements within the payload may also be required for some use cases. Masking sensitive data at rest within audits and log files is another data privacy requirement that an API management platform should provide.

- **Key and certificate management**: The API management platform should also provide the capability to manage keys and certificates required for data privacy.
- **Denial-of-service (**DoS**) protection**: APIs open valuable data and assets outside the enterprise's firewalls. This increases the attack surface and makes them more prone to attacks. Hackers may try to bring down back-end systems by pumping unexpectedly high traffic through the APIs. DoS attacks are very common on APIs. Hence, the API management platform should be able to detect and stop such attacks.
- **Threat detection**: The likelihood of bad actors making attacks using malicious content is high for public APIs. Content-based attacks can be malformed XML or JSON, malicious scripts, or SQL within the payload. Such attacks can also happen to private and enterprise APIs. The API management platform should be able to identify malformed request formats or malicious content within the payload and then protect against such attacks. Error visualization capability can also detect hackers attempting to find an exploitable weakness in APIs.

API Traffic Management

Depending on the nature of the data and services the API provides, traffic management offers a different business value to different classes of customers. Each customer class may be willing to pay differently for access. For example, some app developers prefer to try out APIs for free. The API provider may allow such users to make several API calls in a day/week/month. Paying customers, however, want access to a higher or an unlimited number of API calls. Again, the API provider may allow customers a different level of access depending on their location or the time of the day; for example, internal enterprise users may get unlimited access to a high-performing API, whereas public Internet users may have limited access. More API calls may be allowed during off-peak hours, but a limited number is allowed during peak business hours. The API provider may have different requirements to throttle and manage the API traffic. The API platform should provide the following capabilities for traffic management.

- **Consumption quota**: Defines the number of API calls an app can make to the back end over a given time interval. Calls exceeding the quota limit may be throttled or halted. The quota allowed for an app depends on the API's business policy and monetization model. A common purpose for a quota is to divide developers into categories, each with a different quota and, thus, a different relationship with the API. For example, free developers who sign up might be allowed to make a small number of calls. But paid developers (after their verification) might be allowed to make more calls.

- **Spike arrest**: Identifies an unexpected rise in the API traffic. It protects back-end systems not designed to handle a high load. The API management platform may drop API traffic volume exceeding the spike arrest limit to protect back-end systems in the event of DoS attacks.
- **Usage throttling**: Provides a mechanism to slow down subsequent API calls. This can improve the overall performance and reduce impacts during peak hours. It helps ensure that the API infrastructure is not slowed down by high volumes of requests from a certain group of customers or apps.
- **Traffic prioritization**: Helps the API management platform determine which class of customers should be given higher priority. API calls from high-priority customers should be processed first. Not all API management platforms support this capability. Hence, an alternative approach or design may be required for traffic prioritization.

Interface Translation

When an enterprise creates an API to expose its data and services, it needs to ensure that the API interface is intuitive enough for developers to easily use. APIs should be created with an API-first approach, which promotes API creation with a consumer focus. Hence, the interface for the API is most likely different from that of the back-end services that it exposes. The API gateway should, therefore, be able to transform the API interface to a form that the back end can understand. The API gateway should support the following to support interface translation.

- **Format translation**: The back-end system might expect data in SOAP, XML, CSV, or any other proprietary format. The API consumer cannot easily consume such data formats. Hence, the API gateway should be able to easily transform from one format to another. Most API management platforms can transform data from XML to JSON (and vice versa) with a one-to-one mapping of the data elements. Mapping from JSON to any other data format may be supported through customization.

- **Protocol translation**: Most back-end systems that host services provide a SOAP interface for consumers. However, SOAP is not a protocol suitable for APIs to build apps for digital devices. API management platforms must be able to perform a protocol transformation from SOAP to REST to provide a lightweight interface for consumers. Support for other protocol transformations—like HTTP(s) to JMS/FTP/JDBC—may be a nice-to-have feature in the API management platform.
- **Service and data mapping**: An API management platform should provide a graphical representation of the different back-end service component that maps to provide an API service. It should incorporate service mapping tools that enable the discovery and description of existing service delivery assets so that they can be wired into your API design.

Caching

Caching is a mechanism to optimize performance by responding to requests with static responses stored in-memory. An API proxy can store back-end responses that do not change frequently in memory. As apps make requests on the same URI, the cached response can be used to respond instead of forwarding those requests to the back-end server. Thus, caching can improve an API's performance through reduced latency and network traffic.

Similarly, some static data required for request processing may also be stored in-memory. Instead of referring to the main data source each time, such data can be retrieved from the cache for processing the request. An expiry date/time can be set for the cached data, or the data can be invalidated based on defined business rules. If the data is expired, new data is retrieved from the source, and the cache is refreshed with the updated data.

Service Routing

APIs must route consumer requests to the right back-end service providing the business functionality. There may be one more back-end system providing the back-end functionality. Hence, the API management platform should be able to identify and route the request to the correct instance of the back end. The API management platform should support the following routing capabilities.

- **URL mapping**: The incoming URL's path may differ from that of the back-end service. A URL mapping capability allows the platform to change the path in the incoming URL to that of the back-end service. This URL mapping happens at runtime, so the consumer retrieves the requested resource via service dispatching.
- **Service dispatching**: It allows the API management platform to select and invoke the right back-end service. In some cases, multiple services may have to be invoked to orchestrate and return an aggregated response to the consumer.

- **Connection pooling**: The API management platform should be able to maintain a pool of connections to the back-end service. Connection pooling improves overall performance. Also, it may be required for traffic management purposes to ensure that only a fixed maximum number of active connections are opened at any point in time to the back-end service.
- **Load balancing**: It distributes API traffic to the back-end services. Various load-balancing algorithms may be supported. Based on the selected algorithm, the requests must be routed to the appropriate resource hosting the service. Load balancing capabilities also improve the overall performance of an API.

Service Orchestration

In many scenarios, the API gateway may need to invoke multiple back-end services in a particular sequence or in parallel and then send an aggregated response to the client. This is known as *service orchestration*. The service orchestration capability helps create a coarse-grained service by combining the results of multiple back-end service invocations. This improves the client's overall performance by reducing latency introduced due to multiple API calls. Service orchestration capability may require the API gateway to maintain states between API calls. However, the API gateway should be as light and stateless as possible. Hence, it is recommended that the API gateway only be involved in orchestrating non-transactional read-only services.

API Auditing, Logging, and Analytics

Businesses need insight into the API program to justify and make the right investments to build the right APIs. They need to understand how an API is used, know who is using it, and see the value generated from it. With proper insight, businesses can decide how to enhance their value by changing or enriching the API. An API gateway should provide the capability to measure, monitor, and report API usage analytics. Good business-friendly dashboards for API analytics measure and improve business value. A monetization report on API usage measures business value; hence, it is another desirable feature of an API management platform.

API Analytics

Analytics provide you with information to make future decisions about your API. When you see an increase in API traffic, you need to know whether this indicates the success of your API program or whether it is being used maliciously, resulting in inflated traffic. How do you determine the adoption of your API? Is there an increased interest in your APIs within the developer community? Is there an increase in the number of apps built using your APIs? How has the performance of the APIs been in terms of response time and throughput? What are the different kinds of devices being used to access the APIs? How have the APIs been adopted across the globe? As an API provider and consumer, you need to know the answer to these questions and many others. The more you know, the better you can determine what's going on. You need metrics to decide which features should be added to your API program. API analytics is the answer to all queries.

The API management platform should be able to provide the following capabilities required for analytics.

Activity Logging

Activity logging provides basic logging of API access, consumption, performance, and any exceptions. The platform should capture and provide information on who is using an API, what types of apps and devices the API is being called from, and which geographical region is the source of the API traffic. It should log the IP address of the clients, as well as the date and time when a request was received and the response was sent. The gateway within the API management platform should log which API and method are being invoked by the client. Various metainformation, such as URI, HTTP verb, API proxy, developer app, and other information, can be logged into the gateway for every API call. The platform can process this information later to provide meaningful reports for API analysis. API performance metrics and response/error codes should also be logged as part of activity logging.

User Auditing

User auditing can help an API administrator review historical information to analyze who accesses an API, when it is accessed, how it is used, and how many calls are made from the various consumers of the API.

Business Value Reports

Business value reports gauge the monetary value associated with the API program. Monetization reports of API usage provide information on the revenue generated from the API. The API gateway should be able to provide API usage monetization reports. Some APIs may be directly monetized, but many have an indirect model for monetization. Hence, additional value-based reporting should also be possible within an API management platform to measure customer engagements. Engagements can be measured by the number of unique users, the number of registered developers, the number of apps built using the APIs, the number of active apps, and many other items.

Advanced Analytics

The API management platform should be able to extract and log custom variables from within the message payload for advanced analytics reporting. It should provide API administrators and product managers the capability to create pluggable and custom reports from the captured information.

Service-level Monitoring

The API management platform should provide performance statistics that track the latency within the platform and the latency for back-end calls. This helps the API administrator find the source of any performance issues reported on any API. The platform should be able to report errors raised while processing the API traffic within the platform or those received from the back end. Classifying the errors by type, frequency, and severity gives API administrators a valuable aid for troubleshooting.

Developer Enablement for APIs

An API program cannot be successful without the active involvement of a developer community. Application developers use APIs to build mobile apps or custom integration between two or more applications. Hence, developers need to know which APIs are available, their functionalities, and how they can be used. Developers should have a playground to experience and test APIs to effectively use them in their applications. An API management platform should provide services that enable developers to build apps using the APIs. A developer portal can provide these services.

Developer Portal

A *developer portal* is a customized website that allows an API provider to provide services to the developer community. It is a content management system that documents the APIs—their functionalities, interfaces, getting-started guides, terms of use, and much more. Developers can sign up through the portal and register their applications to use the APIs. They can interact with other developers in the community through blogs and threaded forums. The portal can also be used to configure and control the monetization of the APIs. Monetization gives developers self-service access to billing and reports, catalogs and plans, and monetization-specific settings.

An API management platform developer portal should include the capabilities described in the following sections.

API Catalog and Documentation

As an API provider, you need a platform to publicize and document your APIs. Developer enablement services should allow an API provider to publish a discoverable catalog of APIs. An API catalog is also sometimes referred to as an *API registry*. Developers should be able to search the catalog based on various metadata and tags. The catalog should document the API functionality and interface, how-to guides, terms of use, reference documents, and so forth. Information about the API versions available should also be included in the documentation.

Developer Support

Properly designed REST APIs are normally very intuitive for developers to understand. App developers can easily start using them for app development. Still, the API provider should provide resources that developers can use to build innovative apps. Good API documentation and accelerators in the form of test and development kits can speed up the adoption of APIs. API documentation should describe the API interface and provide how-to guides for interacting with the APIs. The developer portal can provide embedded test consoles that developers can use to play with an API and get a feel for it. Sample code that demonstrates the use of APIs can act as a quick start guide and be very helpful to app developers. App developers often look for device-specific libraries to interact with the services exposed by the APIs, such as downloadable SDKs within the developer portal.

Developer Onboarding

To start consuming the APIs, developers must register with the API provider to get access credentials. Developers can either sign up independently or as part of a company. The signup process should be simple and easy. Developers should be able to go through a self-registration process and view the APIs available from the API provider. Developers can then select an API product and register their apps to use it. After successful registration and approval, an API key and a secret to uniquely identify the app are generated. The API key is also called an *app key* or a *client ID*. The approval process may be automatic or manual, based on the terms and conditions and the monetization model setup. In a manual approval, a member of the API management team approves the registration request. The API key is generated only after successful approval of the app. In some cases, developers may form part of a company. In such scenarios, a key management capability is important so API consumers can add, modify, or revoke the API keys within their organization.

Community Management

App developers often like to know the views of other developers in the community. They may want to collaborate and share their API usage experiences. Blogs and forums form a major part of collaboration and community management. Developers may share their experiences with API usage via blog posts; such posts may need to be moderated by the API provider before they become visible to everyone. An API provider may also create a blog to share updates and plans with the API consumer community. Advice and best practices on API usage may also be shared on blogs and discussion forums. A developer should also be able to report any issues with an API or its usage to the API provider's support team. The developer portal may have a link to raise support tickets. Integrated blogs and forums can build a truly dynamic community to enhance the use of the provider's APIs.

API Lifecycle Management

API lifecycle management can control how an API is developed and released to consumers. Consumers can use published APIs to build apps. They can report problems or raise a request for a new API feature. An API management platform should provide the following capabilities required for API lifecycle management.

API Creation

An API acts as a facade to interact with the back-end services. The API team should be able to design the REST interface for the API and create an *API proxy* to interact with the back-end services. An API proxy is a facade to securely expose the back-end services to consumers. Policies attached to the flow paths of the API proxy should be able to implement security, traffic management, message translation, encryption, filtering, caching, orchestration, and routing. Once the development is complete, the API team must be able to deploy and test the API through a console. An embedded console to test APIs can be handy and reduce development time. The API management platform should provide tools that enable the creation of the APIs and subsequently deploy and test them on an environment before they are published for production.

API Publication

Once an API has been created, it must be published to an environment before it can be discovered and consumed. The API management platform must provide tools that can be used to migrate the APIs from lower environments and deploy them to production. Once it is deployed to production, the API specifications and other details should be published in the developer portal for consumers to discover and use in their apps. In case of any incorrect deployment, the platform must provide the ability to roll back to a previously deployed version of the API.

Version Management

APIs evolve with newer business requirements. Hence, managing multiple versions of an API to support existing consumers is an important capability that the API management platform must provide. Version management should also provide the ability to smoothly deprecate and retire older versions. When an API version is marked as deprecated, the existing consumers should be notified through deprecation warnings. Deprecated APIs may continue to serve traffic from existing consumers. However, new consumers should not be able to sign up to use deprecated APIs. With proper notice and period, deprecated APIs should be retired and removed from the platform to avoid maintenance overheads. The API management platform should provide the capability to manage the retirement of an API.

Change Notification

Changes to an API may adversely affect its consumers. Hence, consumers must be notified of any planned changes to the API. Developers using the APIs should be aware of any API changes. The API management platform must provide a mechanism to notify API consumers of any API upgrades or outages. Notification can be made via email, SMS, or social media. Release notifications can provide updates about new releases and features added to the API. API consumers should be notified about planned or unplanned downtimes. An API developer portal can be used to send release and availability notifications to subscribed users.

Issue Management

The API management platform should provide API consumers with the facility to log issues found in the APIs. App developers consuming APIs must be able to report any issues or shortcomings related to their APIs. They should be able to raise support tickets and seek assistance with API usage. The issues can be reported through the developer portal. The API management platform should provide the capability to integrate defects reporting and issue management capabilities in existing systems within the enterprise.

CHAPTER 3

Designing a RESTful API Interface

REpresentational State Transfer (REST) is an architectural style. It is not a strict standard but provides certain guidelines and constraints. American computer scientist Roy Fielding originally described these constraints in his doctoral dissertation.

REST relies on stateless, cacheable, and client-server communication protocols like HTTP. By following the principles of REST and applying them to stateless protocols such as HTTP, developers can build API interfaces that can be used from any device or operating system. Well-designed REST APIs attract developers to build apps that use them. An API interface should be easy to understand and intuitive to the developers. Creating a well-crafted, aesthetically designed REST API is a must-have for the success of any enterprise API program. This chapter looks at the different constraints REST advocates and how they can be used to design a truly RESTful API interface.

B. De, *API Management*, https://doi.org/10.1007/979-8-8688-0054-2_3

REST Principles

REST is a set of design principles for building scalable web services. Roy Fielding described the following six constraints in his PhD dissertation for building a RESTful architecture.

- Uniform interface
- Client-server
- Stateless
- Cache
- Layered system
- Code on demand

Let's look at each of these constraints in more detail.

Uniform Interface

A uniform interface defines the communication contract between client and the server. It helps decouple the architecture. Client and server applications can be developed independently as long as they abide by the interface. The interface defines the mechanism and format for interaction—where and how the client can access a server resource. A resource URI identifies resources. Each resource has its own unique URI. However, the physical resources are themselves separate from their representation; for example, the server does not send information about the back-end database storing the product information. Instead, it sends an XML or JSON representation of a product or a collection of products to the client.

Client-Server

The client-server constraint builds a loosely coupled and scalable web architecture. If the client and the server follow a uniform interface, they can be developed independently, using any language or technology. The client need not be worried about the database used for the server to store data and assets. Similarly, the server need not be worried about the client implementation technologies or the user interface or user state. It promotes separation of concerns and build simpler and scalable architecture.

Stateless

Statelessness is one of the key principles of a RESTful service. It dictates that a web server is not required to remember the state of the client application. All relevant contextual information should be sent by the client application in the request to the server for all its interactions. The state information can be included as part of the URI as a variable or it can be included as a query parameter, header parameter, or in the body. Once the request is processed by the server, the updated state of the resource is sent back in the response via headers and the body. If the state must span multiple requests, the responsibility of resending the state information lies with the client. This reduces the burden of the server to maintain, update, and communicate the state information of each of its client, thus increasing the server scalability. Additionally, even load balancers do not have to worry about the session affinity for stateless systems.

Cache

Caching is yet another REST constraint that increases the scalability and overall performance of the server application. The cache may reside anywhere between the client and server in the network path. It can reside in the server, an external location like the CDN, or inside the client application. By following the caching constraint, the server can specify whether a particular response can be cached. If the response is cacheable, the server may specify the lifetime of the cached response. Based on the lifetime, the client can decide whether to use a cached response or make a separate request to get the live data. Caching the response data can reduce the client-perceived latency and increase the overall availability and reliability of the application. Providing a cached response from the API layer can also reduce the load on the back-end systems, which may not have been originally designed for high loads. Well-managed caching can eliminate some client-server interactions, further improving scalability and performance.

Layered Systems

The layered system principle enables a network intermediary to be installed between the client app and the actual back-end server. The layered system can be a proxy or a gateway that acts as a facade for the back-end system. It can be used to implement security, caching, rate limiting, load balancing, and so forth. The client never gets to know if it is connected directly to the source of the service or to an intermediary. The caching and load balancing implemented on the intermediary node can improve the scalability of the system.

Code on Demand

The code-on-demand constraint enables a web server to transfer executable programs to a client. This constraint tends to establish a technology coupling between the client and the web server. The client must be able to understand and execute the code it downloads on demand from the server. This is the only optional constraint for the REST architectural style. Examples of code on demand are Java applets, scripts, plug-ins, and Flash.

Designing a RESTful API

Now that you understand the fundamentals of REST principles, let's look at the various considerations for designing a REST API interface.

A uniform interface is one of the fundamental principles of the RESTful architectural style. Web components interoperate consistently within the uniform interface's four constraints, which Fielding identified as follows.

- Identification of resources
- Manipulation of resources through representation
- Self-descriptive messages
- Hypermedia as the engine of application state (HATEOS)

Identification of Resources

Before you can identify a resource, you need to understand that a *resource* is any web-based concept that can be referenced by a unique identifier and manipulated via the uniform interface. While designing a REST API for a travel portal, your resources could be customer, reservation, ticket, hotel, flight, bus, car, and so forth. A resource can be a single entity or a collection of entities. According to Roy Fielding's dissertation: "The key abstraction of information in REST is a resource. Any information that can be named can be a resource: a document or image, a temporal service (e.g., today's weather in Los Angeles), a collection of other resources, a non-virtual object (e.g., a person), and so on."

A resource is identified by a URI (Uniform Resource Identifier). A URI provides the name and the network address of a resource. All the information that a server provides can be identified as a resource. For example, the URI `http://www.foo.com/v1/customers` identifies a resource by name— `"customers"`. To manipulate a resource, the client connects to the server address specified in the URI (in this case `www.foo.com`) using a method like GET and access it using the relative path (/v1/customers). If the request is successfully executed, the response is a collection of customers. Again, resources can be related to each other; for example, a customer may have multiple reservations for different dates and hotels in different places. A reservation is related to the customer as a subresource; for example, http://www.foo.com/v1/customers/12345/reservations.

The resources themselves are conceptually separate from the representations that are returned to the client. For example, the resource may be residing in some database, but when the server responds to a request for a resource, it does not send the database itself; rather it responds with some representation of the resource that represents a record in the database. For example, the record of a resource instance may be represented in XML, JSON, or HTML format, when it is returned to the client. The following is an example of a *customer* resource representation in JSON format with a *reservation* subresource.

```
{
    "firstName": "Mark",
    "lastName": "Johnson",
    "CustId": "John123",
    "age": 26,
    "address":
    {
        "streetAddress": "28 2nd Street",
        "city": "New York",
        "state": "NY",
        "postalCode": "10021"
    },
    "reservations":
    [
        {
          "type": "official",
```

```
            "number": "212-555-4321",
            "date": "03-12-2016"
          },
          {
            "type": "personal",
            "number": "646-555-9765",
            "date": "02-06-2015"
          }
      ]
}
```

Manipulation of Resources through Representation

Clients modify a representation of a resource. The same exact resource may be represented in different ways for different clients. For example, for a UI client, it might be represented in HTML format; whereas for application clients, it might be represented in either JSON or XML format. The representation is a way for clients to interact with the resource, but it is not the resource itself.

Self-Descriptive Messages

Each message (request/response) must be self-descriptive. That mean that the message may contain additional information to tell the recipient how to process it. Information such as format (JSON/XML), size, payload itself, and other metadata information included in the message can be used by the recipient for processing. An HTTP message provides headers to organize the various types of metadata into uniform fields. For example, `Content-Type` can specify the format of the message; `Content-Length` can be used to specify the size of the payload. Many such HTTP headers can be included in the message to describe to the recipient on how they should process the message.

Hypermedia as the Engine of Application State (HATEOAS)

A resources' state information may include links to other resources. These links provide information on what to do next and how to traverse through other related resources in a meaningful manner; for example, after getting information about the *account*, you may want to deposit, withdraw, or transfer money. So the response of a RESTful service providing the account information may include links for the next action that the customer may want to do, as follows.

```
GET /account/12345 HTTP/1.1
HTTP/1.1 200 OK
{"account_number":"12345",
 "balance":"100.0",
 "currency":"USD",
 "links": [ {
        "rel": "deposit",
        "href": "http://localhost:8080/account/12345/deposit"
    },
        {
        "rel": "withdraw",
        "href": "http://localhost:8080/account/12345/withdraw"
    },
        {
        "rel": "transfer",
        "href": "http://localhost:8080/account/12345/transfer"
    }]
}
```

The presence or absence of a link in a resource representation is an important part of resource's current state.

While designing a REST API interface, you should keep all of these constraints in mind. The next few sections look at how to build a REST API interface by following these constraints.

Resource Identifier Design Using URIs

In a RESTful API, designing the resource is one of the most important tasks for its success. A well-designed resource makes the API intuitive, simple to understand, and easy to use. Let's look at some of the best practices for designing RESTful APIs.

Resource Naming Conventions

Every resource should have a meaningful name to identify itself. Name a resource using a noun as opposed to a verb or an action. The URI for the resource should refer to a thing rather than an action. CRUD function names should not be used in the URI or resource names; for example, while designing resource for a customer's entity, the resource URI should be named `/customers` instead of `/getCustomers`.

Modeling Resources and Subresources

According to Roy Fielding's dissertation a resource is "*any concept that might be the target of an author's hypertext reference must fit within the definition of a resource.*" It can be single instance of an object or a collection of objects. Even business processes and capabilities can fit the definition of a resource according to Roy Fielding. Resources form the core of REST API design. The starting point of modeling resources is to analyze the current business domain and identify all the relevant objects in it that can be named. The focus for identifying resources and modeling them should be from the consumer's point of view. It is important to select the right resources and model them at the right level of granularity.

For example, a resource can be a collection of customers in an online store or it can be a single customer. You can identify a collection of customers using `/customers`, while a single instance of a customer can be identified using `/customers/{customerId}`. Each customer may further have multiple orders. The URI to refer to the subcollection of orders is modeled as `/customers/{customerId}/orders`. A single instance of the order may be identified by `/customers/{customerId}/orders/{orderId}`. By following a logical grouping or resources and their hierarchy, you can model the resource URI path to access a collection of resources or an individual resource.

Best Practices for Identifying REST API Resources

The following are some of the best practices for identifying resources for RESTful API design.

- Resources should not be too fine-grained because they lead to chatty communication between the consumer and the provider. Chatty communication degrades overall performance of the app that is using the API; hence, it should be avoided.
- Resources should not be too course-grained because this leads to APIs that are too difficult to use and maintain.
- Resources should be designed such that they do not lead to migration of control flow business logic to the API consumer side; for example, if updates to the

customer information requires multiple fields to be updated in a specific sequence that depends on some logic, then the API to update the customer information should be designed so that the client is not responsible for executing the required flow logic.

The responsibility of executing the logic should lie with the resource server hosting the resource. Shifting the logic to the consumer side has the risk of putting the resource data in an inconsistent state, especially in the event of failure. Fine-grained APIs that perform CRUD operations may put the business logic on the client side, creating tight coupling between the API consumer and the provider. Any change in business logic at the provider end would require corresponding changes on the API consumer side. They may not be possible in many cases, where consumers do not want to make frequent changes to the applications on their side.

- Resource selection should be independent of the underlying domain implementation details. Hence, even a business process can be modeled as a resource if the process involves the operation of multiple low-level resources. For example, the process of setting up a customer in a bank may be modeled as a resource. So there can be a resource created for a customer account setup—such as `/accountSetup`–that needs to call operations on related resources for entities such as customer and account. By modeling a business process as a resource, the API consumer does not need to apply the business logic in the code.

URI Path Design

Every collection and resource in an API has its own URL. It is recommended to design URLs using an alternate combination of collection/resource path segments, relative to the API entry point. Table 3-1 explains the concept better, with guidelines on how to define the top-level resource and related subresources.

Table 3-1. *Top-Level Resources and Related Subresources*

URL	Description
/api	The entry point for the API. Also sometimes referred as 'basePath'. `Eg:/api`
/api/{ResColName}	Resource name of a top-level collection `Eg:/api/customers`
/api/{ResColName}/{ResId}	The ResId inside collection of resources `Eg:/api/customers/Customer1234`
/api/{ResColName}/{ResId}/{SubResColName}	Sub resource collection under resource ResId `Eg:/api/customers/Customer1234/orders`
/api/{ResColName}/{ResId}/{SubResColName}/{SubResId}	SubResId inside sub resource collection `Eg:/api/customers/Customer1234/orders/order-123`

There may be arbitrary levels of nesting for subresources. However, limiting the depth to two or three, if possible, is recommended because longer URLs are more difficult to work with.

A URI design that follows a predictable pattern with a hierarchical approach to traverse through the resources eases developer adoption; for example, `/stores/{storeId}/products/{productId}`. This helps developers to guess the URI for a given resource; and hence, it can make direct calls without going through links.

URI Format

Let's now look at the recommended format of a URI and learn how this format can be effectively used for designing an API. As per RFC 23964: "a Uniform Resource Identifier (URI) is a compact string of characters for identifying an abstract or physical resource." This identifier can be realized in one of two ways: as a Uniform Resource Locator (URL) or a Uniform Resource Name (URN).

URLs (e.g., `http://www.foo.com/users/mike`) are used to identify the online location of an individual resource; whereas URNs (e.g., `urn:user:mike`) are intended to be persistent, location-independent identifiers. The URN functions like a person's name; whereas a URL is like that person's street address. In other words, the URN defines an item's identity (the user's name is Mike) and the URL provides a method for finding it (Mike can be found at `www.foo.com/users/`).

The syntax of a URI is a hierarchical sequence of components as follows.

```
scheme:[//authority][/]path[?query][#fragment]:
```

- **Scheme name** identifies the protocol (e.g., FTP, HTTP, HTTPS, IRC:)
- **Authority** refers to the actual DNS resolution of the server. It consists of the hostname or IP address of the server, optionally along with the port number. The credentials to access the server can also be included as part of the authority as follows: *[user:password@]host[:port].*
- **Path** pertains to a sequence of segments separated by a forward slash (/).
- **Query** contains additional non-hierarchical identification information and is often separated by a question mark (?).
- **Fragment** provides direction to a secondary resource within the primary one identified by the authority and path, and separated from the rest by a hash (#).

Naming Conventions for URI Paths

Keep URIs short and simple because it helps you write, remember, and spell it easily. The following are some of the recommended naming conventions for URI paths.

- Name a collection resource with a *plural noun*; for example, `http://www.foo.com/api/customers`.
- Name a singular resource with a *singular noun*; for example, `http://www.foo.com/api/customers/customer1234`.
- Name a controller resource using a *verb*; for example, `http://www.foo.com/api/customers/customer1234/register`.
- Avoid using CRUD operation names in URIs. For example, do not use URIs such as `http://www.foo.com/api/getcustomers`.
- Use lowercase letters for naming URIs. Avoid mixed and uppercase letters in URIs. Mixed case is harder to type and read.
- Use hyphens instead of a space or an underline. They are more aesthetic and easier to read. Spaces in URLs get transformed into URL encoded `%20s`, further degrading readability. For example, use URIs such as `http://www.foo.com/api/about-us`.
- Avoid using characters that require URL encoding, such as spaces.

HTTP Verbs for RESTful APIs

Once the resources have been identified, the following are next set of questions to ask.

- What would a consumer like to do with the resource?
- What aspects of the resource would be of interest to a consumer?

The answers to these questions identify the HTTP verbs to be used for each of the identified resources.

HTTP verbs form an important part of a RESTful API design. They identify the actions to be performed on a resource. A consumer's actions with a resource can be mapped to an HTTP verb in most cases; for example, creating a product can be done using the HTTP verb POST. The primary and most commonly used HTTP verb are POST, GET, PUT, and DELETE. These verbs perform the CRUD operations on the resource as follows.

- POST creates a new instance of the resource.
- GET is used to read.
- PUT is used to update.
- DELETE is used to delete.

There are other verbs—such as HEAD, OPTIONS, TRACE, and CONNECT—in the HTTP 1.1 spec. Let's look at the detailed usage of these verbs in the design of a REST API interface in the next few sections of this chapter.

GET

The GET verb is used by the client to retrieve information about the requested resource entity identified by the request URI. Requests using GET should only retrieve data and should never modify the data in any way. The GET request is considered *safe*. GET is a read-only method and does not make any changes to the resource data. Hence, it can be used without risk of data modification or corruption. Also, calling the GET method on a resource once has the same effect as calling it multiple times. Hence, the GET verb is *idempotent* and *safe*.

If the request has been executed successfully, the server returns the requested data normally in XML or JSON, depending on the format requested by the client. The HTTP `Accept` header is used by the client to specify the expected format of the response. The request may contain additional HTTP headers that can control the data returned by the server in response to the GET request. For example, if the request message includes headers such as `If-Modified-Since`, `If-Unmodified-Since`, `If-Range`, `If-Match`, or `If-None-Match`, it is processed as a conditional GET method. The server responds with the entity only if the conditions described by the header field(s) are satisfied.

The conditional GET method is used to reduce unwanted network usage. The server inspects these conditional headers to determine whether the client is already in possession of some of the data it is requesting. Data is returned only if the condition is satisfied; otherwise, no data is transferred in the response. Thus, conditional GET headers reduces network traffic.

On successful execution of the GET request, the server responds with HTTP response code of *200 OK*. In the event of an error, the server usually responds with the *404 Not Found* or *400 Bad Request* status code.

The following are examples of GET request for a resource.

```
GET https://www.foo.com/customers
GET https://www.foo.com/customers/{customerId}
```

POST

The POST verb is normally used to create a new resource. In particular, it is used to create a subresource, which is subordinate to the parent resource identified by the request URI. To create a new resource, send a POST request to the URI of the parent resource and the server takes care of creating the new resource as a subresource of the parent, based on the information provided in the payload. Each new resource created is assigned a name or an ID to uniquely identify it. This identifier may be used to retrieve the resource information using a GET request at a later time.

On successful execution of the POST request, the origin server should respond with a *201 Created status* code. The response payload should contain the details of the resource created in a format expected by the client. The response should also contain a `Location` header to specify the location of the newly created resource. If the resource cannot be created, the server may respond with a *204 No Content* status code.

POST is neither *safe* nor *idempotent*. It is therefore recommended for non-idempotent resource requests. Making two identical POST requests usually results in two resources containing the same entity.

The following is an example of a POST request to create a customer resource.

```
POST http://www.foo.com/customers HTTP/1.1
{
  "customers": {
    "customerId": "12345",
    "customerName": "Brajesh De",
    "Address":{
      "AddressLine1":"206 Lane 1",
      "AddressLine2":"22 Cross",
      "City":"Bangalore",
```

```
        "State":"Karnataka"
        }
  }
}
```

PUT

The PUT method is generally used to update an existing resource entity identified by the request URI. If the resource identified by the request URI exists, then the message payload should be considered as the changed version of the existing resource entity. If the resource does not exist, and the URI is capable of being defined as a new resource, the server can create a new resource with the information provided in the message payload.

On successful execution of the PUT request, if a new resource is created, the server must respond with a *201 Created* status code. If an existing resource is modified, the server must respond with either the *200 OK* or the *204 No Content* status codes to indicate successful execution of the request. In the event of errors in modifying or creating a PUT request, the server should respond with an HTTP error response status code and an error message that indicates the nature of the problem.

PUT is *idempotent* but not *safe*. This means invoking the PUT method multiple times with the same request payload has the same effect on the resource—it continues to exist in the same state. But since the PUT method updates the resource entity, this method is not safe.

The following is an example of a PUT request.

```
PUT http://www.foo.com/customers/12345 HTTP/1.1
{
  "customers": {
    "customerId": "12345",
    "customerName": "Brajesh De",
    "Address":{
```

```
        "AddressLine1":"206 Lane 1",
        "AddressLine2":"22 Cross",
        "City":"Bangalore",
        "State":"Karnataka"
        }
    }
}
```

The Difference Between PUT and POST

It is recommended to use POST for creating new resources and PUT for updating an already existing resource. Use POST if the *server* is responsible for creating the resource name or ID and hence is the URI of the new resource. PUT may be used for creating a new resource only when the *client* is responsible for deciding the new URI (via its resource name or ID) for the resource. A POST verb should be used if the client doesn't or shouldn't know the resulting URI of the new resource before creation. If the resource is already created, PUT should be used to update the resource.

DELETE

The DELETE verb is used to delete the resource represented by the request URI.

On successful execution, the server responds with 200 OK or 204 No Content status codes. If the 200 OK status code is returned, it may also contain the representation of the deleted resource. Since additional bandwidth requirements for the response payload may impact the overall performance, it is recommended to respond with HTTP 204 No Content on successful deletion of the resource.

The DELETE verb is idempotent and not safe. The resource is removed or marked as deleted in the database on successful execution of the DELETE request.

Repeatedly calling DELETE on a resource ends up the same: the resource is gone. However, there is a caveat about DELETE idempotence. Calling DELETE on a resource a second time often returns a 404 (NOT FOUND) since it was already removed and hence can no longer be found. This makes DELETE operations no longer idempotent. However, this is an appropriate compromise if resources are removed from the database instead of being simply marked as deleted.

The following is an example of a DELETE request.

```
DELETE http://www.foo.com/customers/12345 HTTP/1.1
```

PATCH

The PATCH method was added to HTTP specs in March 2010. This method is similar to the PUT method and can be used to update an existing resource definition. The difference between PUT and PATCH is that PATCH can be used to do a partial update of an existing resource definition; whereas PUT does a complete update. With the PATCH method, only certain attributes of the resource can be specified for update.

The following is an example of a PATCH request.

```
PATCH http://www.foo.com/customers/12345 HTTP/1.1
{
  "customers": {
    "Address":{
      "AddressLine1":"205 Lane 2"
      }
  }
}
```

OPTIONS

The OPTIONS verb allows the client to determine the options and/or requirements for interacting with a resource or a server. The OPTIONS verb determines the HTTP methods and headers allowed for interacting with a resource. It indicates to the client the capabilities of a server without actually performing any of the CRUD operations. The client can specify a URL for the OPTIONS method to refer to a specific resource. An asterisk (*) should be used if the client is interested in knowing or testing the capabilities of the entire server. Responses of this method cannot be cached.

This is an optional method that is not always supported by all service implementations. Many popular sites do not support this method; for example, GitHub responds with a 500, Google Maps with 405 Method Not Allowed. If this method is supported, the response should be 200 OK and have an `Allow` header containing a list of HTTP methods that may be used on this resource.

The client can use the OPTIONS method to support cross-origin resource scripting (CORS) implementation. Chapter 7 looks at how to implement CORS for building secure web APIs.

The following is an example of an OPTIONS request.

```
OPTIONS * HTTP/1.1
```

HEAD

The HEAD method is identical to GET. The difference is that with HEAD method, the server responds only with a response line and headers. The response to the HEAD method does not contain the entity-body. The metainformation contained in the HTTP headers in response to a HEAD request is identical to the information sent in response to a GET request. This gets only the metainformation about the resource entity, without actually transferring the resource entity-body in the response payload. It reduces network bandwidth usage. This method is often used for testing recent modifications, the validity of hypertext links, and accessibility.

Idempotent and Safe Methods

Some HTTP methods can be called multiple times without any change in the result or the state of the resource. This brings in the concept of a method being idempotent and/or safe. An *idempotent* HTTP method can be called many times without getting a different outcome. It does not matter if the method is called one time or 100 times—the result is going to be the same. A point to note is that idempotency refers to the result of the method execution and not to the resource itself. For example, calling a GET method on a particular resource always gives the same result unless the resource has been changed in some other way. An HTTP method is considered safe if it does not modify the state of the resource. For example, calling a GET or HEAD method on a resource URL never modifies the resource itself; hence, it is considered safe.

Table 3-2 summarizes whether an HTTP method is idempotent and/or safe.

Table 3-2. *Idempotent and/or Safe HTTP Methods*

HTTP Verb Name	Idempotent	Safe
GET	Yes	Yes
POST	No	No
PUT	Yes	No
DELETE	Yes	No
HEAD	Yes	Yes
OPTION	Yes	Yes
PATCH	No	No

HTTP Status Code

The HTTP response communicates the status of the request processing. The response contains certain metadata and optional payloads. The `Status-Line` part of the HTTP response message is used to inform clients of their request processing results in the following format.

```
Status-Line = <HTTP-Version> SP <Status-Code> SP <Reason-Phrase> CRLF
```

HTTP defines 40 status codes to communicate the execution results of a client's request. The status code is divided into the following five categories.

- **1xx Informational** communicates transfer protocol level information.
- **2xx Success** communicates that the request from the client was successfully received, understood, and accepted.
- **3xx Redirection** communicates that additional action needs to be taken by the user agent to fulfill the request.
- **4xx Client Error** indicates errors caused by the client.
- **5xx Server Error** indicates that server is aware that an error occurred while processing the request and cannot process it further.

Normally, 2xx and 3xx status codes are treated as success codes. Any 4xx or 5xx status code is treated as an error code.

Table 3-3 lists the most commonly used success codes.

Table 3-3. *The Most Commonly Used Success Codes*

Status Code	Reason-Phrase	Meaning
200	OK	It indicates that the request has been processed successfully.
201	Created	It indicates that the request has been processed and a new resource has been created successfully.
202	Accepted	It indicates that the server has received the request and is being processed asynchronously.
204	No Content	It indicates that the response body has been purposely left blank.
301	Moved Permanently	It indicates that a new permanent URI has been assigned to the client's requested resource.
303	See Others	It indicates that the response to the request can be found in a different URI.
304	Not Modified	It indicates that the resource has not been modified for the conditional GET request of the client.
307	Use Proxy	It indicates that the request should be accessed through a proxy URI specified in the Location field.

Table 3-4 lists the most commonly used error codes.

Table 3-4. *The Most Commonly Used Error Codes*

Status Code	Reason Phrase	Meaning
400	Bad Request	It indicates that the request had some malformed syntax error due to which it could not be understood by the server. Probable reason is missing mandatory parameters or syntax error.
401	Unauthorized	It indicates that the request could not be authorized, possibly due to missing or incorrect authentication token information.
403	Forbidden	It indicates that the server understood the request, but it could not be processed due to some policy violation or the client cannot access the requested resource.
404	Not Found	It indicates that the server did not find anything matching the request URI.
405	Method Not Allowed	It indicates that the method specified in the request line is not allowed for the resource identified by the request URI.
408	Request Timeout	It indicates that the server did not receive a complete request within the time it was prepared to wait.
409	Conflict	It indicates that the request could not be processed due to a conflict with the current state of the resource.
414	Request URI Too Long	It indicates that the request URI length is longer than the allowed limit for the server.
415	Unsupported Media Type	It indicates that the server does not support the request format.

(*continued*)

Table 3-4. (*continued*)

Status Code	Reason Phrase	Meaning
429	Too Many Requests	It indicates that the client sent too many requests within the time limit than it is allowed to.
500	Internal Server Error	It indicates that the request could not be processed due to an unexpected error in the server.
501	Not Implemented	It indicates that the server does not support the functionality required to fulfill the request.
502	Bad Gateway	It indicates that the server, while acting as a gateway or proxy, received an invalid response from the back-end server.
503	Service Unavailable	It indicates that the server is currently unable to process the request due to temporary overloading or maintenance of the server. Trying the request at a later time might result in success.
504	Gateway Timeout	It indicates that the server, while active as a gateway or proxy, did not receive a timely response from the back-end server.

Resource Representation Design

A REST API resource entity representation is used to convey the state of the resource. The message body of the request/response is used to convey the state of the resource entity. The client sends the resource entity to the server in the request message payload of a POST, PUT, or PATCH message. The server sends the resource entity state in the response message payload for a GET, POST, PUT, or optionally, DELETE request.

A text-based format is normally used to represent the resource state. JSON and XML are the most commonly used text formats for representing the state of the resource entity. JSON is lightweight and provides a simple way to represent a resource. Due to the seamless integration of JSON with the browser's native runtime environment, JSON is the preferred choice for data representation in the design of a REST API. XML, on the other hand, is verbose, hard to parse, hard to read, and its data model is not compatible with many programming languages. This makes JSON a preferred choice over XML for representing the resource entity for a REST API. Many popular API providers have already moved away from XML to the JSON format. However, if the API consumer base consists of a large number of enterprise customers, you still have to support the XML data format for your APIs.

As a general guideline, it is advisable to support JSON data format by default and provide additional support for the XML format, if required. With support for both JSON and XML formats, how does the client specify the preferred format for the response? There are the following options.

- Use the `Accept` header.
- Append `.json` or `.xml` extensions to the endpoint URL.
- Include a query parameter in the URL to specify the response format.

Using the `Accept` header to specify the response message format is most preferred of the three options. The following are some of the basic best practices for the JSON format representation of the resource entity.

- JSON should be in a well-formed format, with the variable names and their values enclosed in double quotes.
- JSON names should use mixed lowercase and uppercase letters. Special characters should be

avoided whenever possible. JSON names like `fooName` are preferred over `foo-Name` because they allow the use of the cleaner dot notation for property access in JavaScript.

- The `Content-Type` header in the message should be set to `application/json` when a JSON format payload is included.

Hypermedia Controls and Metadata

HTTP headers in the request/response convey metadata about the messages and the resource entity in the message. HTTP specification defines a set of standard headers that can be used for various purposes. The specification also allows extension mechanisms to include custom HTTP headers. HTTP headers are classified into four types.

- **Entity headers** provide metainformation about the entity body or resource in the message. Information such as the allowed HTTP methods, the media type, size, location of the resource entity or cache expiration date-time, and so forth, are some examples of `Entity Header` types.
- **General headers** provide information that can apply to both request and response messages. Caching directive, connection information, message origination date-time, and any message transformation applied to the whole message are some examples of `General Header` types.
- **Client request headers** are included *only* in the request message sent by the client or browser to the server. Authorization information, user agent information, information about the character set,

encoding, or language that the client can accept, are some examples of information provided by `Client Request` headers.

- **Server response headers are** included *only* by the server in the response sent to the client. Some examples of `Server Response` headers are information about the age of the response generated by the origin server, ETag information for caching purposes, and the duration for which the server is unavailable for the requesting client.

Let's continue to look at the most common HTTP headers and how they can be used to design a better RESTful interface.

Accept (Client Request Header)

The `Accept` header is used in the request message to specify the media types that the client accepts for the response. It is a mechanism for the client application or browser to indicate to the server which MIME types it expects.

The client can specify a range of media types using an asterisk (*) or multiple media types using comma-separated values. Specific media ranges or specific media types can override media ranges. If more than one media range applies to a given type, the most specific reference has precedence.

For example, `Accept: text/*, application/xhtml+xml, application/xml;q=0.9, */*`, has the following precedence.

1. `application/xml;q=0.9`
2. `application/xhtml+xml`
3. `text/*`
4. `*/*`

The client can specify its relative preference for a media type using an optional q parameter. The following is an example.

```
Accept: audio/*; q=0.3, audio/basic
```

These examples indicate that audio/basic is preferred, but any audio type is also acceptable if it is the best available after a 70% markdown in quality.

If no Accept header field is specified, then it is assumed that the client accepts all media types. If an Accept header field is present, but the server cannot send a response that is acceptable according to the Accept field value, then the server should respond with an HTTP status code of *406 Not Acceptable.*

Accept-Charset (Client Request Header)

The client uses the Accept-Charset request header to specify the character sets it understands and, therefore, can be included by the server in the response. As with the Accept header, the client can specify multiple charsets in a comma-separated list. A q value on a scale of 0 to 1 can also be included to specify the acceptable quality level for non-preferred character sets.

If the client does not include an Accept-Charset header in the request, it is assumed that any character set is acceptable. If an Accept-Charset header is present, the server cannot send an acceptable response according to the Accept-Charset header. The server should send an error response with the *406 Not Acceptable* HTTP status code, but sending an unacceptable response is also allowed per the HTTP specs.

The following is an example of the Accept-Charset header.

```
Accept-Charset: iso-8859-5, unicode-1-1;q=0.8
```

Authorization (Client Request Header)

The client uses the `Authorization` header to include authentication information needed to access a server resource. If the server needs authentication and the `Authorization` header is not present in the request or has an incorrect value, the server should send an error response with a 401 Unauthorized HTTP status code. The server should also include the `WWW-Authenticate` header in the response, indicating the required authentication scheme(s): Basic or Digest Access.

The following is an example of the `Authorization` header.

```
Authorization: BASIC Z3Vlc3Q6Z3Vlc3QxMjM=
```

Host (Client Request Header)

The `Host` request header specifies the server address and the port of the resource requested. A `Host` without any port information implies the default port. The default port is 80 for HTTP and 443 for HTTPS.

The following is an example of the `Host` header.

```
Host: http://www.foo.com
```

Location (Server Response Header)

The server uses the `Location` response header to redirect the recipient to a URI other than the request URI for completion. The server returns this header in the following two scenarios.

- When a new resource is created after the successful execution of a POST or a PUT request, the `Location` header contains the location information of the newly created resource, and the HTTP response status code should be *201 Created.*

- When the resource has moved temporarily or permanently or is the result of a request execution, it is available at a different location. In this scenario, the `Location` header contains the redirected URI, and the HTTP response status code should be 3xx. The `Location` information is then used by the browser to load a different web page, as specified in the header, thus aiding in automatic redirection.

The following is an example of a `Location` header.

```
Location: http://www.foo.com/http/index.htm
```

ETag (Server Response Header)

The `ETag` (entity tag) response header provides a mechanism for the server to send information about the current state of the entity. It is an alphanumeric string that uniquely identifies a specific version of the resource. If the resource has changed, the `ETag` value changes. Hence, the `ETag` value can be compared to determine whether the cached resource entity on the client side matches that on the server.

It is a mechanism used for web cache validation that allows a client to make conditional requests. It makes caches more efficient and saves bandwidth because the server does not need to send the full response if the content has not changed.

The following is an example of the `ETag` header.

```
ETag: "686897696a7c876b7e"
```

Cache-Control (General Header)

The `Cache-Control` general header field specifies instructions on caching response information by the client and/or any intermediary along the request/response chain. Directives contained in this header provide information about the cacheability of the response. It specifies if the response can be cached or not. If yes, can it be cached in a public or private cache? It also specifies if the cache can be archived and stored. This header also contains information about the maximum duration the response can be cached.

The following is an example of a `Cache-Control` header.

```
cache-control: private, max-age=300, no-cache
```

Content-Type (General Header)

The `Content-Type` header specifies the media type of the payload included in the message.

The following is an example of the `Content-Type` header.

```
Content-Type: text/html; charset=ISO-8859-4
```

Header Naming Conventions

Earlier sections looked at the best practices for naming resources and URIs. For good API design, even the HTTP headers should be named according to a convention. This section looks at some of the recommended best practices for naming headers.

HTTP specifications provide names for all standard HTTP headers and their syntax. It also provides extension mechanisms to include custom headers if required. The following conventions are recommended for naming custom HTTP headers.

- Historically, `X-` has been used as a prefix for naming non-standard custom headers. RFC 6648 has deprecated the use of this convention because it causes more problems than it solves. Hence, do not prefix custom header names with `X-` or similar constructs.

- Name custom headers meaningfully and with the assumption that all custom headers may become standardized, public, commonly deployed, or usable across multiple implementations.
- Use hyphens in header names if required; for example, `My-Header-Name`.
- Do not use spaces in header names.

Versioning

Versioning is one of the most important considerations for web API design. Regardless of the approach followed, REST APIs should always be versioned. It supports developing APIs using an iterative approach.

There are multiple approaches for versioning an API. The following are some questions to ask when thinking about API versioning.

- Which versioning approach should be used?
- When should a new version of the API be created?
- How and where to indicate the version of the API?
- How many versions should be maintained?
- How long should the older versions of the API be maintained?
- What are the deprecation mechanisms for older versions?

Many other considerations and approaches for API versioning are discussed later in this book.

Querying, Filtering, and Pagination

Enterprises use REST APIs to expose their data and services. The resource collection returned by REST API may be huge. Transmitting the entire payload over the network is heavy on the bandwidth. Additionally, processing an entire collection on the client side would be processor-intensive. Since a UI can display only a limited amount of data, this also becomes important from a UI processing standpoint; for example, 20 results per page. Hence, the need arises to be able to query, filter, and paginate the response. The API should provide a mechanism for the consumer to specify the query parameters and filter criteria. They should also be able to specify a range of data to be returned in the response. The range can be in terms of the number of elements, a date and time range, or offset and a limit.

It is important to note that providing support for querying, filtering, and pagination is not mandatory for all REST APIs. This is a resource-specific requirement and, by default, is not required to be supported on all resources. Consider designing the API to support filtration and pagination only if the number of entities in the resource collection that can be returned by default is high. The API documentation should specify if these complex functionalities are available for any specific service.

Limiting via Query-String Parameters

Filtering and pagination for an API are best implemented by designing the API interface with `offset` and `limit` query-string parameters. The `offset` parameter indicates the beginning item number in a collection, and the `limit` specifies the maximum number of items to return.

The following is an example.

```
GET http://www.foo.com/products?offset=0&limit=25
```

In this example, the `offset` value 0 and `limit` value 25 indicate the return of the first 25 items in the list. If the number of items fetched from the back end is more than 25, only the first 25 are returned. To retrieve the next set of items, the client has to make another call with a changed value for `offset` (=25) and `limit` (=25). If the number of items in the list is less than 25, all the items are returned in the response. This approach implements pagination support in the API.

It is important to understand that `offset` and `limit` are query-string parameters and are not dictated by standards or specifications. Hence, different API providers may implement the same concept using different parameter names. `start`, `count`, `page`, and `rpp` (records per page) are other query-string parameters that can be used to implement pagination. An API designer can name to suit the business context.

Filtering

Filtering is an approach to restrict the results returned in the response by specifying additional search criteria. These search criteria must be met on the data returned in the result. The filtering can become complex if the API has to support a complicated set of search criteria. The filtering criteria are based on the resource attribute. The complexity increases if filtering involves a complex combination of comparison operators. However, filtration can be achieved by supporting simple criteria, such as `starts-with` or `contains`, and so forth.

The filtering criteria can be specified using the `filter` query string containing a delimiter-separated list of name/value pairs. The delimiters that have conventionally worked are the vertical bar (`|`) to separate individual filter phrases and a double colon (`::`) to separate the names and values. This approach supports a wide range of use cases for filtering and makes the filter criteria user-readable. The following is an example.

```
GET http://www.foo.com/customers?filter="name::matt|ci
ty::delhi"
```

Note that the property names in the name/value pairs match the names of the properties returned by the service in the payload. Wild cards can also be included in the filter values using the asterisk (*).

Filtering can be implemented for an API using one of the following approaches.

- Map the filter criteria to the back-end database SQL queries and implement filters at the database layer. This would retrieve the data matching the criteria from the data store; the same can be passed to the client with minimal messaging.
- Implement filter criteria in the service implementation layer. The service accepts the filter criteria as inputs and applies them to the data fetched from the data store. This may be required when the search criteria are complex or require some business logic to be executed on the data set returned from the data store.
- Implement filter criteria on the API's intermediary layer. If there is no change to the database or service implementation layer, the filtering is done on the intermediary API node that is generally introduced for creating and exposing REST APIs. Implementing the filter on the intermediary API node might be complex due to these tools' limited programming support.

When deciding which approaches to adopt, it is recommended to implement filtering as close to the resource data store as possible.

The Richardson Maturity Model

The Richardson Maturity Model defines the levels to assess the maturity of a REST API service. It defines the following four levels (0–3) based on services support for URI, HTTP verbs, and hypermedia.

- Level 0: Swamp of POX
- Level 1: Resources
- Level 2: HTTP verbs
- Level 3: Hypermedia controls

Figure 3-1 shows the three core technologies with which Richardson evaluates service maturity. Each layer builds on top of the concepts and technologies of the layer below. The higher up the stack an application sits, and the more it employs the technologies in each layer, the more mature it is.

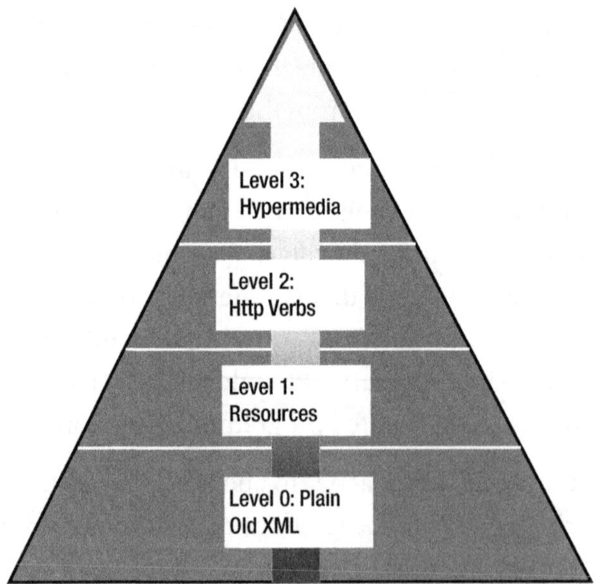

Figure 3-1. *Richardson's Maturity Model for REST APIs*

Let's look at each of these levels in detail.

Level 0: Swamp of POX (Plain Old XML)

This is the most basic level of maturity. The service has a single URI as the entry point at this level. HTTP is used as the transport system for remote interactions. The payload content can be described in XML, JSON, YAML, key-value pairs, or any format you choose. Normally, the POST method sends the request to the server. SOAP and XML RPC are examples of services at level 0 maturity. Figure 3-2 shows a client requesting an appointment service to get the availability of slots for a given date and doctor. The search parameters are sent in POX format using a POST request.

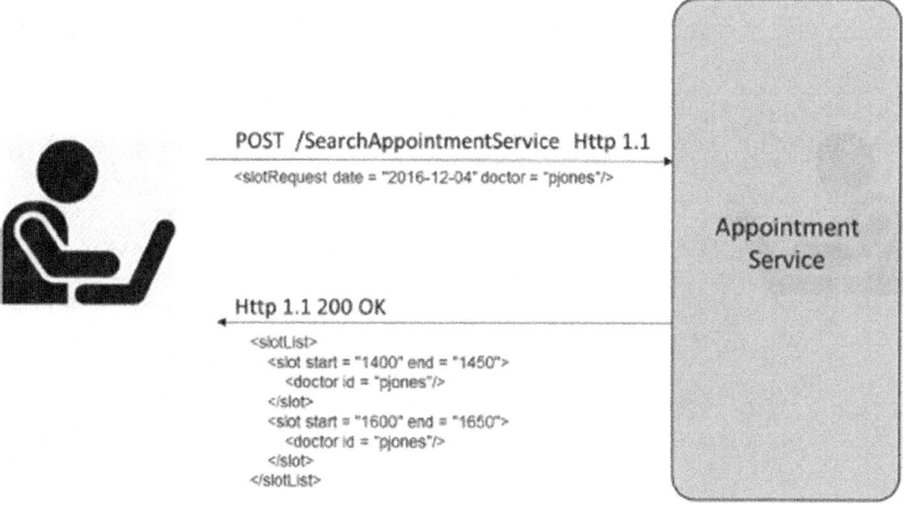

***Figure 3-2.** Level 0: POX way of communication*

Level 1: Resources

The first step toward RESTful maturity is the introduction of resources. At this level, instead of having a single URI as an endpoint for all services, you start interacting with individual resources through separate URIs. So instead of going through an endpoint like `http://www.foo.com/searchAppointmentService`, you use resource URIs like `http://www.foo.com/api/doctors/{doctorId}`. Here `doctors` is a resource, and you can access an individual doctor's information using `{doctorId}`. At this level, you still use POST as the only HTTP method for your communication. Figure 3-3 shows a client requesting an appointment service to get the availability of slots for a given date and doctor. The URL used to get the slot availability of the doctor is resource-oriented.

Figure 3-3. *Level 1: Using resources for communication*

Level 2: HTTP Verbs

At levels 0 and 1, the applications use the POST method for all communication. Level 2 maturity moves toward using the HTTP verbs more closely to how they are used in HTTP itself. To fetch the slot availability of a particular doctor, it should be using the HTTP verb GET at this level. As you've seen, the GET verb is safe because it is read-only and does not make any significant changes to the state of the resource. Hence, you can use the GET verb any number of times, in any order, and still get the same result every time unless the resource has been modified using a different method. If you have to create a new appointment, you can use the POST method. If you want to update an existing appointment, you may use the PUT method.

In addition to using HTTP verbs, level 2 introduces HTTP response codes to indicate the status of an operation on a resource. The service returns with HTTP response code 201 if a resource was successfully created. If the operation on a resource was successful, the 200 status code is used in the response. If the operation on a resource resulted in an error, an appropriate 4xx or 5xx response code should be used in the response. Figure 3-4 shows a client requesting an appointment service to get the availability of slots for a given date and doctor. The GET HTTP verb is used to access the resource-oriented URL to get the appointment slots of the doctor. HTTP response code 200 OK is returned to indicate a successful response.

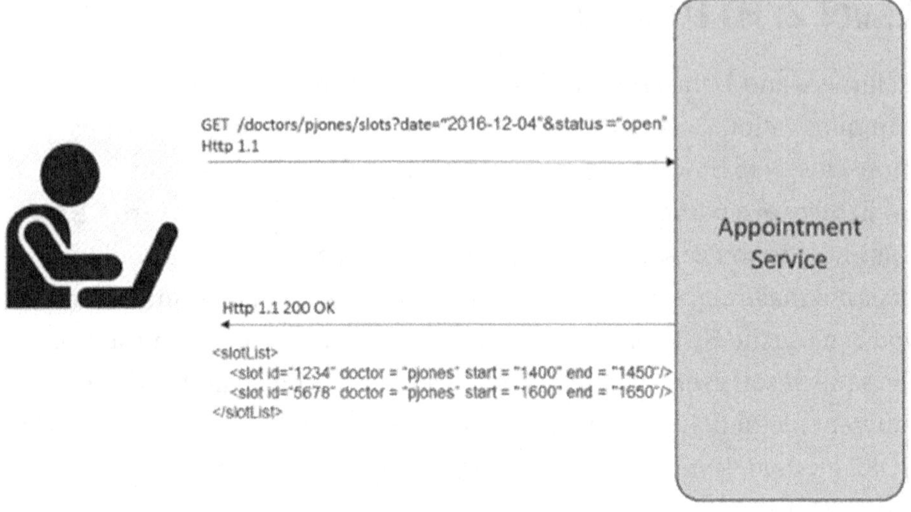

Figure 3-4. *Level 2: Using resources and verbs for communication*

Level 3: Hypermedia Controls

This is the final level for REST maturity, where HATEOS enters the picture. It addresses the question of what to do next. After receiving the response for a service invocation, what are the next logical steps for the client? What are the possible branches for traversal in a tree at a given node? This helps the client be more intelligent and decide or prompt the user for the necessary actions.

At level 3 maturity, the response of a REST service may contain a list of URIs. These URIs are the resources that the client wants to act upon as the next course of action. So rather than the client having to know where to post the next request, the hypermedia controls in the response tell how to do it. Figure 3-5 shows a client requesting an appointment service to get the availability of slots for a given date and doctor. The response returned for the GET request contains hyperlinks for the next possible actions that the client can do to book a slot.

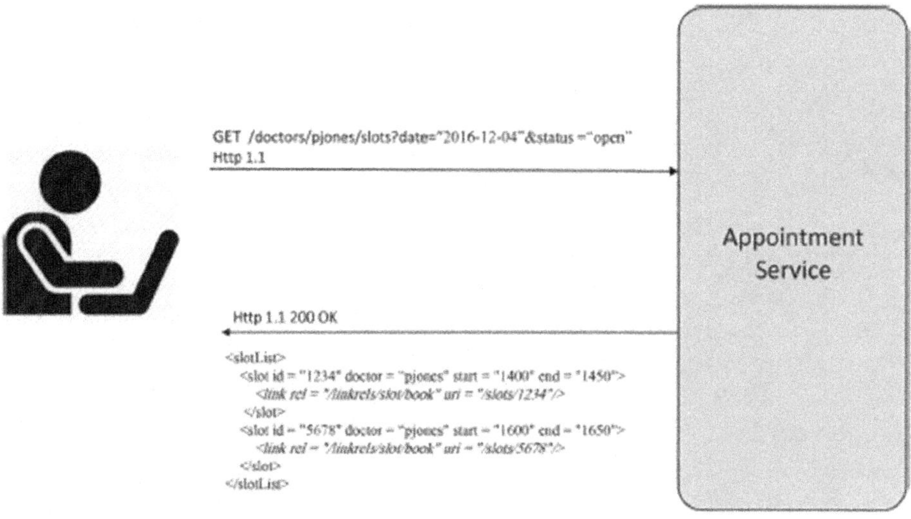

Using Resource, Verb and HATEOAS for communication

***Figure 3-5.** Using resources, verbs, and HATEOAS for communication*

An obvious advantage of hypermedia controls is that it allows the server to change its URI scheme without breaking clients. It also helps client developers expose the protocol. The link gives client developers a hint on the next possible options. It may not provide all the information, but it at least gives developers a starting point to think about more API information and look for a similar URI in the API documentation. Currently, there are no absolute standards on how to represent hypermedia controls. It is up to the service implementation team to decide how to implement HATEOS in their service.

According to Martin Fowler's article on the Richardson Maturity Model (`https://martinfowler.com/articles/richardsonMaturityModel.html`), RMM provides a good way to think of the different elements of a RESTful service. But it is not a definition of levels of REST itself. Roy Fielding has made it clear that level 3 RMM is a precondition of REST.

CHAPTER 4

API Documentation

Documenting an API is important for its successful adoption. APIs expose data and services that consumers want to use. An API should be designed with an interface that the consumer can understand. API documentation is key to the app developers comprehending the API. The documentation should help the developer learn about the API functionality and enable them to use it easily.

This chapter looks at the aspects of documenting an API and some tools and technologies available for API documentation, including RAML, OpenAPI, API Blueprint, and others.

The Importance of API Documentation

As an API provider or developer, you may master your API. You have inside knowledge about its functionality, what it is supposed to do, how it will be used, its security, limitations, error scenarios, and so forth. As an API provider, you have gradually learned everything about the API through various discussions, documentation, and references. However, this is not the case for the consumers of your API. The app developer community or API consumers look at the API's interface and wonder what the API does, how it should be used, what to expect when an error occurs, what security credentials to use, how and where to get the security credentials to use the API, and so forth. Hence, what is easy and simple to the API developer

B. De, *API Management*, https://doi.org/10.1007/979-8-8688-0054-2_4

may not be intuitive to the API consumer. Good API documentation can help bridge the gap and make the API successful. API documentation communicates a vast amount of information about the API.

As enterprises move along in the digital transformation journey, there has been exponential growth in public and private APIs. In this competitive world, another API provider may likely expose the data and services your API exposes. Today, APIs are being seen as a product. Just as any product has a user guide, APIs must have detailed documentation for their consumers. The importance increases if the APIs are being monetized. User-friendly API documentation is key to its successful adoption. An API document is like an entrance into your API and provides a warm welcome to the API's consumers.

The API documentation should

- Get users started quickly
- Include useful and relevant information
- Provide sample code
- Document a list of REST endpoints
- Document the message payload
- Provide Response status code and error messages

The Audience for API Documentation

API documentation is used for various reasons. It is like a user manual for a product. Like a user manual, API documentation should have a quick-start guide, which quickly makes the first API call and lets consumers have a feel for it. At the next level, it should document the API's features, the resources, the APIs to access them, and the error conditions for troubleshooting. Hence, the API documentation can be used primarily by the following types of audiences.

- A **CTO** evaluates similar and competing APIs from a business, technology, and monetization perspective.
- **Business stakeholders** namely business executives, product managers, and decision-makers would be interested in the API documentation to know the capabilities of the APIs and how they meet the business needs. They would like to refer to the API documentation to understand its value proposition and the potential use cases where they can be applied.
- An **app** or **integration architect** explores the API to match the requirements for building an app or an integration solution.
- An **app developer** wants to get started using the API with a quick-start guide and a detailed tutorial. Sample SDKs and API calls in the API documentation are immensely useful to an app developer.
- A **quality assurance engineer** looks at ensuring the quality and published SLAs of the API. They look at the documentation to understand the expected functional and non-functional behavior of the APIs and validate them.
- An **IT support specialist** supports the app and is interested in the error and troubleshooting information for debugging any issues with the app. Operations and support team members would also be interested in information on the APIs' deployment, monitoring, and security configurations.

- The **legal team** and **compliance officers** refer to the API documentation to ensure that the APIs meet the country's and industry's legal and compliance requirements. They would be interested to know about the API's data usage and storage requirements to ensure that PII and sensitive information are handled per the compliance guidelines.

Model for API Documentation

A good API document communicates all information about the usage of the API—for both humans and machines. The API document should provide all necessary information to app developers or API consumers in a human-readable format. The documentation should help them assess its suitability in their client app. It should provide information about its licensing policy, usage requirements, input and output parameters, message format, error messages, and more. Similarly, the API interface should be documented such that its interface can be parsed by a machine to generate client stubs and server-side skeleton code that can be further developed. If an API has multiple active versions, the documentation must highlight the same and elaborate on the functional differences between the versions. To make API documentation effective, it should include the following aspects of the API.

- Title
- Endpoint
- Method
- URL parameters
- Version information
- Message payload

- Header parameters
- Response code
- Error code
- A sample request and response
- Tutorials and walkthrough
- Service-level agreement
- Functional description of the API

Figure 4-1 shows an example of API documentation using OpenAPI.

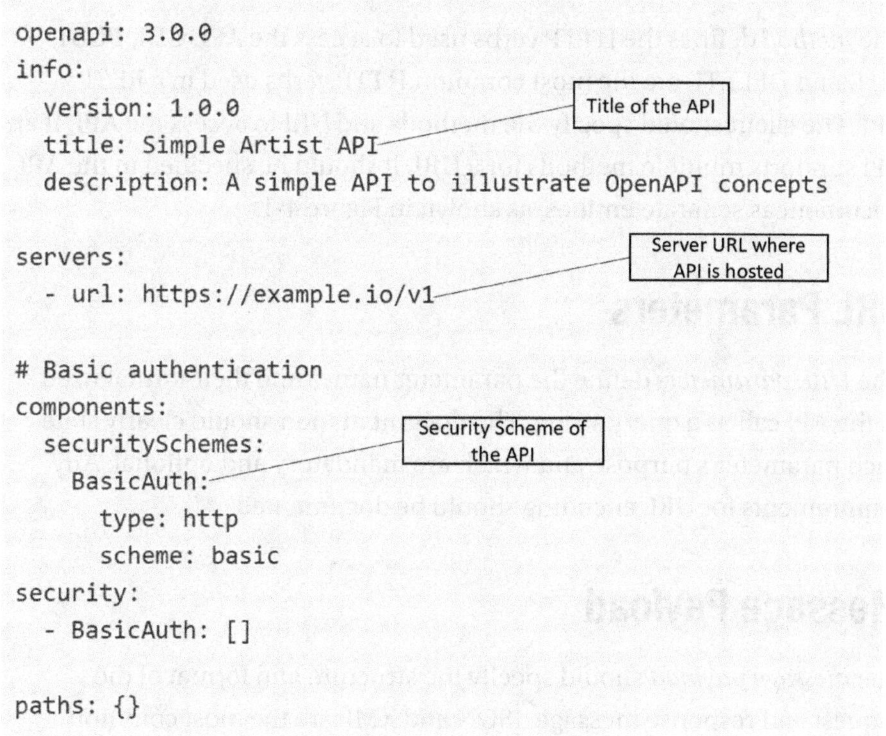

openapi: 3.0.0
info:
version: 1.0.0
title: Simple Artist API
description: A simple API to illustrate OpenAPI concepts
servers:
- url: https://example.io/v1
Basic authentication
components:
securitySchemes:
BasicAuth:
type: http
scheme: basic
security:
- BasicAuth: []
paths: {}
Title of the API
Server URL where API is hosted
Security Scheme of the API

Figure 4-1. *API documentation using OpenAPI*

Title

The *title* should provide the name of the API, which can be used for its identification.

Endpoint

The *endpoint* is the entry point for the API. It defines the URL that clients need to use to invoke the API.

Method

The *method* defines the HTTP verbs used to access the API. GET, POST, PUT, and DELETE are the most common HTTP verbs used in a REST API. The client should specify the methods and URI to access the API. If an API supports multiple methods for a URI, it should be specified in the API document as separate entities, as shown in Figure 4-1.

URL Parameters

The *URL parameters* define the parameter names and their format used in the API call as a query string. The documentation should clearly state each parameter's purpose and which are mandatory and optional. Any requirements for URL encoding should be documented.

Message Payload

The *message payload* should specify the structure and format of the request and response message. JSON and XML are the most common formats used for a REST API. Other formats can be used as well. The message structure should specify the schema of the message payload. Any data constraints in the request payload should be documented. Including a table that provides the name, data type, description, and any remarks is a good practice. Figure 4-2 shows a snippet of an OpenAPI specification of an API, with the message format for a request and response payload.

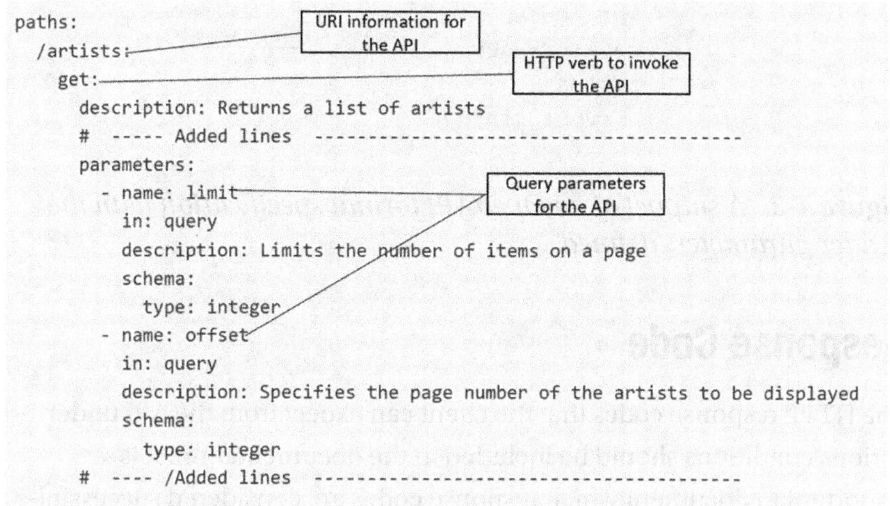

Figure 4-2. *A snippet of an OpenAPI format specification with the message format for a request with query parameter*

Header Parameters

The *header parameters* should specify the standard and custom HTTP headers included in the request and response headers. At a minimum, all mandatory headers should be specified here. Any specific format for the header values must be included.

Figure 4-3 shows a snippet of API documentation in OpenAPI specification with the header parameters defined.

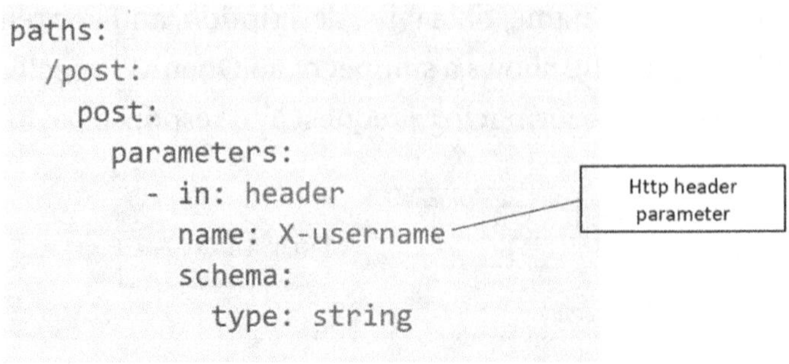

```
paths:
  /post:
    post:
      parameters:
        - in: header
          name: X-username
          schema:
            type: string
```

Http header parameter

***Figure 4-3.** A snippet of an OpenAPI format specification with the header parameters defined*

Response Code

The HTTP response codes that the client can expect from the API under various conditions should be included in the documentation. It is important to document which response codes are considered successful and which are considered errors. All possible response codes, their meaning, and their root causes should be specified. This helps the API consumer more easily troubleshoot issues.

Error Codes and Responses

Normally, 4xx and 5xx HTTP response status codes are considered errors. HTTP specifications define the purpose of these status codes. Not all HTTP response status codes may have been implemented for an API. The API documentation should include the HTTP response status codes that the API consumer can expect in different error scenarios. The sample error response payload and the HTTP response status code should also be specified. This helps the consumer application parse error messages. The error response payload may include specific business error codes and descriptive error messages that offer information about the exact cause of the error. All error codes and error messages should be defined in the API documentation.

Figure 4-4 shows a snippet of an OpenAPI specification in an API document, with the response code and error codes defined.

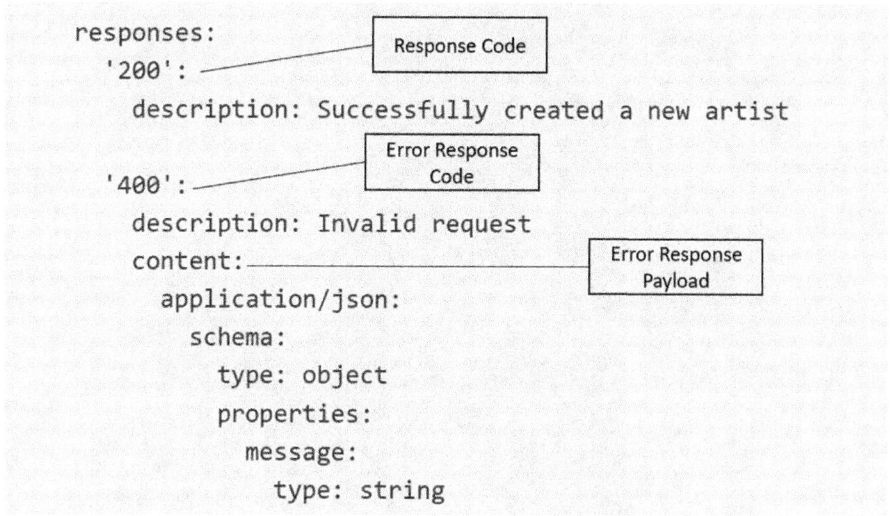

Figure 4-4. *A snippet of an OpenAPI specification in an API document, with the response code and error codes defined*

Sample Calls

As part of the documentation, include sample HTTP calls with all parameters and expected sample responses. This gives the developer a visual sense of what the message structure should look like. Include samples for all the various message formats supported, such as XML and JSON. Sample calls can be included in a wiki format or as interactive smart docs. Figure 4-5 is an example of a sample GET call for an API.

```
GET http://myapi-prod.mycomp.com/api/echo/v1/test-path/{id} HTTP/1.1
Host: myapi-prod.mycomp.com
Accept: */*
Accept-Encoding: gzip,deflate,sdch
Accept-Language: en-US,en;q=0.8,fa;q=0.6,sv;q=0.4
Cache-Control: no-cache
Connection: keep-alive
Origin: http://editor.swagger.io
Referer: http://editor.swagger.io/
User-Agent: Mozilla/5.0 (Windows NT 10.0; WOW64) AppleWebKit/537.36 (KHTML, like Gecko)
Chrome/54.0.2840.99 Safari/537.36
```

Figure 4-5. *A sample GET call for an API*

Tutorials and Walk-throughs

An example is always better than tons of documentation. Hence, a tutorial with example code on how the API can be called from an app is always very helpful to the developer community. Sample SDKs for making API calls in some of the most popular languages—such as Java, Node.js, C#, PHP, Ruby, and Python—help developers quickly adopt the API. Including SDKs for different digital platforms, such as Android, iOS, and Windows, is highly recommended. Including code for all languages and platforms may not always be feasible; hence, you should evaluate the most popular languages and focus on including tutorials and sample code for them.

Service-Level Agreements

A service-level agreement (SLA) defines the API's non-functional requirements. This can include the expected throughput, response time, rate limits for various tiers (if applicable), maintenance or downtime information, and so forth.

API Documentation Standards: OpenAPI, RAML, and API Blueprint

The daunting task of API documentation is keeping the documentation in sync with the actual implementation. If you take a bottom-up approach and create the API documentation manually after the implementation, you risk the documentation falling out of sync if there are enhancements to the API interface in the next version, especially if the process does not enforce regeneration or validation of the API document. Similarly, with a top-down approach, you may start with the API documentation and manually create the skeleton of the API interface according to the defined interface. But later, you still risk the API documentation getting out of sync with the actual implementation when enhancements are required. Hence, defining the API interface and keeping the documentation in sync is a big challenge. This challenge can only be addressed if there are tools that autogenerate API documentation from the API interface in a bottom-up approach or tools that generate the API skeleton and client code from the API interface document in a top-down approach. Standards and tools based on these approaches are needed to aid API documentation.

There are many competing tools for API documentation. Some of them are in a fairly mature state, while others are still evolving. The next few sections look at the OpenAPI, RAML, and API Blueprint frameworks to see how they are used to document an API interface. The tools that they provide are also discussed.

OpenAPI

OpenAPI specification (OAS) is one of the most broadly adopted standards for describing APIs. It provides a vendor-neutral and language-agnostic description format to document HTTP-like API interfaces. Thus, it can be used to document HTTP-based REST APIs and other protocols like CoAP (Constrained Application Protocol) or WebSocket. OpenAPI was originally based on Swagger 2.0 specifications that SmartBear donated.

OpenAPI allows humans and computers to discover and understand the capabilities of a service without requiring access to source code, additional documentation, or inspection of network traffic. It provides a common specification that can generate documentation, SDKs, client code, test cases, and more. It makes the APIs shareable, extensible, reusable, and consistent for internal and external stakeholders and reduces overall development efforts. Many API management tools today support the Open API specification, making creating and maintaining APIs easy.

The following three terminologies need to be clarified to understand OpenAPI.

- **OpenAPI** specification (OAS) is an industry standard that outlines how the Open API files should be structured.
- The **OpenAPI definition** defines the API in a machine-readable JSON or YAML format.
- **API documentation** is a visual and human-readable representation of the API structure generated using HTML, CSS, and JavaScript.

OpenAPI definition consists of three main parts.

- **Metainformation** provides high-level information about the API, such as version, title, license, contact, description, and service URL endpoint.
- **Paths** are items describing the methods and their parameters, request and response bodies, accepted content type, tags, security, and expected error information. The security provides the list of permissions for the endpoint.
- Reusable **components** are objects that describe various reusable components like schemas, data models, and objects that can be referenced to describe the parameters, request bodies, responses, examples, security schemes, and callbacks for the API.

Figure 4-6 shows the structure of OpenAPI specification.

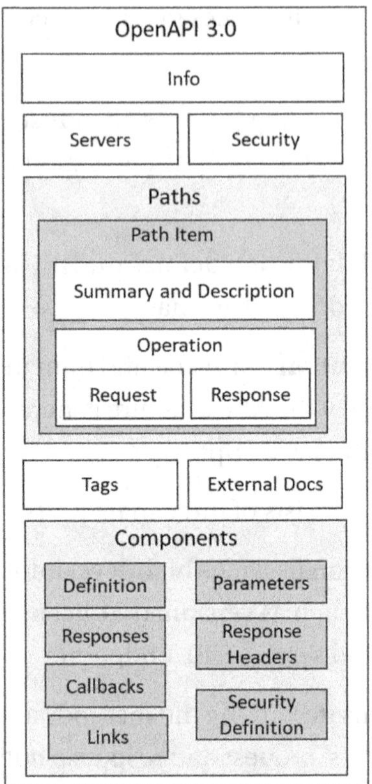

Figure 4-6. *OpenAPI specification*

More information on OpenAPI specifications is at `https://spec.openapis.org/oas/v3.1.0`.

OpenAPI Tools

There is a growing ecosystem of open source and commercial tools to help API developers develop, test, document, and generate support code around their API following OpenAPI standards. These tools can perform the following.

- Generate OpenAPI specification document from API implementation code
- Convert to and from OpenAPI standards to other API documentation formats
- Validate API requests and responses against the defined specification
- Create user-friendly API documentation from the API specification for non-technical people
- Integrate and provide support for the API gateway to host the API
- Generate mock responses as per the API definition in response to incoming HTTP requests
- Generate client codes in different programming languages from the API definition
- Editors generate OpenAPI specifications and documentation

RAML

RAML stands for *RESTful API Markup Language.* It is a YAML-based modeling language to describe RESTful APIs. It makes it easy to manage the entire lifecycle of an API: design, build, test, document, and share. RAML is both machine-readable and human-friendly. RAML is designed to support an API-first, top-down development approach. It provides the format for the contract between the API provider and the API consumer.

Why RAML?

RAML designs API interfaces that are developer- and user-friendly. Using RAML, API interfaces can be designed, tested, and shared with users to get feedback without writing a single line of code. APIs can be described in a human-readable text format. Tools like API Workbench and API Designer provide visual design. The RAML construct lets you reuse libraries, code, and design patterns in the API design, which saves a lot of work.

RAML code generation tools create server-side code from the spec for different languages, such as Node.js, Java, JAX-RS, .NET, Python, Mule, IoT, and others. A RAML specification can also generate test cases for the API using many open source and commercially available API testing tools. This takes advantage of the test-driven development approach and generates test cases that can be integrated with the continuous improvement process.

API documentation can be easily generated dynamically on the fly from RAML with tools such as API Console, RAML2HTML, API Notebook, and others. This keeps the API documentation in sync with the implementation. API definitions in RAML can integrate with other systems. Many open source and commercial tools available today can generate SDKs for different languages from RAML definitions.

Professional services such as APIMatic.io and REST United offer to generate up to two SDKs at no cost. Oracle and MuleSoft provide built-in functionality in their API management products to import the RAML definition, which automatically pulls in the API resources, methods, and other properties, thus avoiding any manual setup of API calls in these tools. With API Notebook, developers can use RAML definitions to create interactive API walk-throughs and sample use cases using simple JavaScript.

More information on API Notebook is at `https://api-notebook.anypoint.mulesoft.com`.

RAML Structure

This section looks at the high-level structure of a RAML-based API specification document. The detailed schema and syntax are in the RAML specifications document at `https://github.com/raml-org/raml-spec/blob/master/versions/raml-10/raml-10.md`.

A RAML API specification can be structured and organized into the following sections.

- **Security scheme information** describes the basic information about the API, such as the *title* to identify the API, its *version*, the `baseURI` to specify its network location for invocation, supported *protocols*, and *default media type* and *security* requirements. Any user documentation that can serve as a user guide or reference documentation can also be optionally included in this section.
- The **data type** describes any data passed as a parameter for the API. A parameter can be in the URI as query parameters, the header as header parameters, or the request/response body. The data can be described using built-in types or a new custom type definition created using a combination of the built-in data types. The data types can be defined using XML, JSON schemas, or RAML types. These can coexist as well. For more information on the data types definitions allowed in the RAML spec, please refer to `https://github.com/raml-org/raml-spec/blob/master/versions/raml-10/raml-10.md#raml-data-types`.

- **Resources** specify how to access the API's resources and subresources using URIs relative to the `baseURI`. The resource definition should start with a slash (/). A resource defined at the root level is called the *parent resource*. Each parent-level resource is identified using its own URI relative to the `baseURI`. Each parent resource may optionally have one or more child resources defined under it.

  This approach builds and defines a nested hierarchy of resources. The relative URI of a resource may consist of multiple URI path fragments separated by slashes; for example, `/cart/items`. This approach can be used only if an individual path item is not a resource. If the path items are separate resources, they should be defined as nested subresources. There is no limit to the level of resource nesting that is allowed. Template URIs containing URI parameters can be used when the resource identifier is a variable; for example, `/products/{productId}`.

  For more information on defining resources and nested resources using RAML, refer to `https://github.com/raml-org/raml-spec/blob/master/versions/raml-10/raml-10.md#resources-and-nested-resources`.

- **Method** describes the allowed HTTP verbs and the request parameters that can be used to manipulate a resource. The HTTP verbs that can be specified are GET, POST, PUT, PATCH, DELETE, HEAD, and OPTIONS. Each method can have an optional friendly name and description to describe its functionality. Any optional or mandatory HTTP headers required for a method should be specified under this section. The header parameters' structure and any constraints or patterns that the API consumer should know need to be specified here.

Similarly, any optional and mandatory query parameters to be passed as query strings should also be specified. The request body for POST and PUT methods can be optionally described in this section. For more information on using methods in a RAML definition, please refer to `https://github.com/raml-org/raml-spec/blob/master/versions/raml-10/raml-10.md#methods`.

- **Response** contains the schema and description of the response object received from the service for a method invocation. The response has two main sections: header and body. The header describes the possible HTTP status codes expected in the response header under various conditions. The body is optional and describes the media type and the structure of the message payload included in the response body. The structure can be defined using types defined in the data type section. For more information on the response definition, refer to `https://github.com/raml-org/raml-spec/blob/master/versions/raml-10/raml-10.md#responses`.
- **Resource types and traits** define reuse patterns and resources across the RAML definition. You may want to define the pattern for an HTTP header, a query parameter, or a message payload, then reuse it at different places within the RAML definition.

A *resource type* partially defines a resource that can specify security schemes, methods, and other properties. A resource that uses a resource type inherits its properties. A resource type can use another resource type.

Traits are similar to resource types. The difference is that a trait is a partial method definition. It can define method parameters, such as headers, query strings, and responses. Resources and resource types can also be used and inherited from one or more traits. For more information on resource types and traits, refer to `https://github.com/raml-org/raml-spec/blob/master/versions/raml-10/raml-10.md#resource-types-and-traits`.

- The **API security** scheme definition is specified in this section of the RAML definition. This section defines the OAuth, Basic, and Digest Access authentication mechanisms for API security. Any other forms of authentication can also be specified using `x-<other>` headers. Any headers or query parameters that pass through can also be specified in this section under the `passthrough` attribute.

  The `securedBy` attribute can specify any API method requiring a special security mechanism. This overrides whichever security scheme has been applied to the API. If a method does not require any security scheme, it can be specified by the `securedBy` attribute for that method with a `null` value. Multiple security schemes for a method can also be specified using the `securedBy` element with an array list of security schemes.

RAML Tools and Projects

The developer community supports RAML with a long list of tools and projects that address different API needs. These tools address different aspects of the API development lifecycle—from designing the API spec to sharing it with the broader community. New tools are also evolving to address newer requirements and languages. Some of the languages supported at the time of this writing are Java, JavaScript, .NET, Ruby, Node.js, Python, Go, and Haskell. This section briefly previews the most commonly used RAML tools.

- **API Workbench** is a tool by MuleSoft that provides a full-featured integrated development environment (IDE) that design, build, test, document, and share RESTful APIs. Using API Workbench, you can create RESTful APIs using a simple *design-first* approach based on RAML specifications. It supports both RAML 0.8 and RAML 1.0 versions of the specifications. This tool is based on the Atom code editor developed by GitHub. The following are some of the main features of API Workbench.

    - An IDE that supports autocomplete, advanced search, live debugging, and symbol-based navigation
    - Dynamic generation of API Mocking Service and API Console
    - Wizard-driven creation of API definitions based on RAML specifications
    - Automatic validation of RAML-based API definitions

  - Built-in support for integration with Git for source control and versioning
  - An integrated scripting engine and tooling for API testing and documentation

- **API Designer** is a tool from MuleSoft that allows users to see real-time post-processing of their API definition. It provides three panels with areas to organize RAML files and folders, displays the document's contents, and offers an interactive text editor. The text editor provides features such as autocomplete, export, and contextual tag lists. It also saves the API definition. For more information, please refer to `https://github.com/mulesoft/api-designer`.
- **Restlet Studio** provides a lightweight IDE that can help accelerate API design. Built using Angular.js, it provides a web-based UI for API design. The following are some of the main features of Restlet Studio.
  - A visual web-based editor to define and edit API definitions for endpoints, resources, methods, and so forth
  - Group resources and representations into sections with a scrollable navigation panel helps extend support for even the most complex API definition
  - A built-in language translator switches between OpenAPI and RAML definitions
  - Generates server skeleton code using a built-in code generator based on APISpark and OpenAPI
  - Generates client SDKs using a built-in code generator based on APISpark and OpenAPI

For more information on Restlet Studio, please refer to `http://restlet.com/products/restlet-studio/#`.

- **API Notebook** is another RAML tool by MuleSoft. It helps with live testing and exploring APIs. An API RAML definition can be imported into Notebook to create a client for the API, send requests, and view responses. Notebook's autocomplete feature explores the API. Once a RAML definition for the API has been imported, the method definitions appear in the tool-tip hints. The path segments of the API resource, separated by slashes (/), become nested JavaScript objects; for example, `/my/myresource` becomes `{clientName}.my.myresource`.
- **RAML for JAX-RS** provides tools that generate a Java + JAX-RS-based application from a RAML API definition. It also provides roundtrip support by doing the reverse to generate a RAML API definition from an existing Java + JAX-RS definition.
- **Abao** provides a REST API testing tool for APIs defined using RAML. It tests the RAML definition for the API against the back-end implementation. This tool can be integrated with continuous integration (CI) tools such as Jenkins to test and update API documentation. It uses the Mocha framework to test the validity of the API response. The following are some of its features.
    - Validates the API endpoint definition
    - Validates that each URL parameter defined in the RAML API spec is supported in the back-end service

    - Validates that each HTTP request and response header parameter defined in the RAML API spec is supported in the back-end service
    - Validates that the JSON schema for the request and response payload meets RAML specifications

- **RAML Tools for .NET** provides a Visual Studio extension for RAML-based APIs. It allows you to easily integrate and consume APIs defined using RAML and to create a new ASP .NET REST API implementation from a RAML definition using a design-first approach.

Many other tools are available as RAML projects that address the various needs of the developer community, building and consuming REST APIs from a RAML definition. Based on the functionality, these tools can be primarily categorized by design, prototype, build, frameworks, test, document, share, parser, and converters. Most design tools provide a visual interface or plugins that can be used with other visual editors to design the RAML definition for the API. The prototype tools can mock up responses for APIs defined using RAML. They can test the API interface and create stubs to replace the actual implementation for testing purposes. The build tools and frameworks generate the client SDK and server skeletons based on the RAML definition of various languages. This promotes the design-first approach for API development.

These tools test API documentation and implementation. They can generate test cases for APIs based on the RAML definition for the API. They validate the RAML definition against the actual implementation and thus keep the two in sync. The documentation tools create API documents in various formats; graphical API consoles, HTML, wikis, PDFs, and other formats can be shared with API consumers. The parser tools are libraries for different languages, which parse the RAML definition of the API. The converters convert the RAML to other API specification formats, such as OpenAPI.

API Blueprint

API Blueprint is a document-oriented language for describing REST API using Markdown syntax. This specification, brought in by Apiary.io, uses Markdown syntax to describe the complete specification of an API or its parts.

API Blueprint Document Structure

An API Blueprint document is structured into logical *sections*. For example, headers, URL parameters, and request/response can each be described in logically grouped sections. Each section has predefined keywords. Depending on the section, the keyword is written as a markdown header or list item entity. The following are the reserved keywords for defining the header and list entities in an API Blueprint document.

- Header keywords
  - Group
  - Data structure
  - HTTP methods
  - URI templates
  - Combination of HTTP methods and URI templates
- List keywords
  - Request
  - Response
  - Body
  - Schema
  - Model

- Header and headers
- Parameter and parameters
- Values
- Attribute and attributes
- Relation

At a high level, the API Blueprint description for a REST API is organized in the following structure.

- **Metadata** describes the API Blueprint specification version used for documenting the API interface. It also contains the API name and a brief description.
- **Resource and resource group** describe the resources and the group of related resources used by the API. For example, in an online shopping experience, a customer may have one or more orders. So, *orders* is defined as a resource group; within this group, a resource can return a collection of orders.
    - **Actions** describe the operations that can be performed on a resource. It is specified using one of the HTTP verbs within square brackets.
- **URI templates** specify the variable parameters in the URI; for example, an order may be identified using an order ID. So, to get the details of a specific order, you specify it using `/orders/{order_id}`.
    - **URI parameters** describe the variables being passed in a request URI or as a query parameter; for example, `/path/to/resources/{varone}?path=test{&vartwo,varthree}`.

For more information on each of these keywords, please refer to the API Blueprint Specification document on GitHub at `https://github.com/apiaryio/api-blueprint/blob/master/API%20Blueprint%20Specification.md#def-api-blueprint-language`.

API Blueprint Tools

A good number of tools support the API Blueprint spec. This section discusses some of the most commonly used API Blueprint tools.

- **Apiary.io** provides a comprehensive tool that supports the collaborative design, creation of API mockups, automated testing, autogeneration of interactive API documentation, API traffic inspection, and more.
- **Dredd** is an HTTP API testing tool. It is a command-line tool that can be used to test the API documentation written in API Blueprint against the back-end implementation. This tool can be integrated with CI tools to ensure up-to-date API documentation.
- **Drakov** provides a Node.js implementation of a mock server for APIs written using API Blueprint.

Many other open source tools support the API Blueprint format for SDK generations. They have various language formats, testing API interfaces, and plugins for API test clients; they can also convert API definitions from other formats to API Blueprint and vice versa. Since API Blueprint and its tools are open source, they can be freely integrated with products to extend support for API Blueprint.

Comparing OpenAPI, RAML, and API Blueprint

Tables 4-1, 4-2, and 4-3 compare OpenAPI, RAML, and API Blueprint.

Table 4-1. *Overview Comparison*

Criteria	OpenAPI	RAML	API Blueprint
Format	JSON, YAML	YAML	Markdown
Availability on Web	GitHub	GitHub	GitHub
Primary sponsor	Linux Foundation	MuleSoft	Apiary
Is there a workgroup?	Yes	Yes	No
When was it first committed?	January 2016	September 2013	April 2013
Design approach	Top-down and bottom-up	Top-down	Top-down
Current version	3.0.3	1.0	A4

Table 4-2. *Tool Support*

Criteria	OpenAPI	RAML	API Blueprint
Authoring tool	Swagger.io	API Designer	Apiary.io
Ad hoc testing	Swagger UI	API Console	Apiary.io
Documentation	Supported	Supported	Supported
Mocking	Extended support provided by third party	Extended support provided by third party	Extended support provided third party
Server code	Supported by third party	Supported by third party	Supported by third party
Client code	Supports multiple languages	Supports multiple languages	Supports a few languages
Generate from code	Supported by Java (third party)	Supported by third party	Supported by third party
Validation	Supported	Supported	Supported
Parsing	Java.js	Java.js	C++(Node.js, C#)

Table 4-3. REST Modeling Capabilities

Criteria	OpenAPI	RAML	API Blueprint
Resources	Supports resource definition	Supports resource definition	Supports resource definition
Nested resources	Supports nested resource definition	Supports nested resource definition	Supports nested resource definition
Representation metadata	Supports the JSON schema	Supports inline and external definitions in any format	Supports only inline definitions in any format
Composition/ inheritance	Inheritance supported by subtypes	Supports inheritance of traits and resource types	Supports resource model inheritance
API version metadata	Supported via `version` tag	Supported via `version` tag	No explicit tag to specify the API version
Authentication	Tags defined to support Basic, API Key, and OAuth2	Supports Basic, Digest, and OAuth2	Supported via custom header definitions
Methods/action	Supported	Supported	Supported
Query parameters	Supported	Supported	Supported
Path/URL parameters	Supported	Supported	Supported
Header parameters	Supported	Supported	Supported
Documentation	Supported	Supported	Supported

Tools for API Documentation

Today, there are several commercial and open source tools for API documentation. You do not have to write the documentation from scratch. These tools allow you to easily create the initial framework of the API document, which can be enhanced later with details. These tools also allow you to validate the generated documentation for syntactical errors. These tools also ensure that the documents have a consistent style and content. Some tools also provide features to organize and publish these documents systematically. Next, let's discuss some popular API documentation tools.

Swagger

Swagger is one of the most popular API documentation tools using OpenAPI specification. OpenAPI was part of Swagger until 2016, when the specification became brand-agnostic for documenting APIs. Swagger editor allows editing API specifications in YAML format inside the browser. It dynamically generates a nice real-time preview of the API document using HTML, CSS, and JavaScript. Swagger also provides a few other tools to parse OpenAPI specs and generate client libraries and server stubs from OpenAPI specs.

Some of the other tools for API documentation are Aglio, DapperDox, Slate, and Redoc.ly.

Postman

Postman is a popular API testing tool. Recently, many new features have been added that allow documenting APIs following Open API specifications. It automatically generates API documentation from a template containing information about the endpoint, methods, input and output parameters, headers information, query parameters, and more.

Its in-built editing tools also allow editing an existing API document using a visual editor. Postman highlights syntax errors and constraints for minimum and maximum values.

Best Practices for API Documentation

API document is necessary to promote its adoption and use by consumers. The following are some of the best practices for documenting an API.

- Use clear and simple language to document the use and functionality of the API. It is better to avoid any technical jargon that can be difficult for the app developers and API consumers to follow.
- Start the API documentation with an overview of the API capabilities and the business benefits it can provide.
- Provide a getting started guide with step-by-step instructions to use the API.
- Document the security requirements that should be met to successfully invoke the API. The document should explain the authentication methods required to access API information and how the developer can get API keys and access tokens to use the API.
- Include common error codes and messages, as well as troubleshooting guidelines for resolving common issues.
- Include code snippets in different languages and example payloads for different use cases.

- Provide an interactive documentation tool that can be used to test the API endpoint directly from the document.
- Provide information about the different API versions and how the versioning information can be provided in the request.
- Include any rate-limit policies, usage restrictions that the developers should know, and instructions to handle situations when limits are exceeded.
- Keep the document up-to-date with regular changes to the API.

CHAPTER 5

API Patterns

APIs should be designed for longevity. Any change to an API carries the risk of breaking the client's application code. Frequent changes to an API frustrate the developers and the consumers using it. Building APIs from robust and proven patterns fosters a happy developer community and saves the company a lot of money.

This chapter looks at some API design principles and patterns that have stood the test of time and make developers happy.

Best Practices for Building a Pragmatic RESTful API

APIs are the face of your enterprise. They provide users with access to enterprise data, services, and assets. Hence, while security should be ingrained in it, the API interface should be simple and elegant to attract developers. It should be intuitive and developer-friendly to make adoption easy and pleasant. Adherence to web standards is equally important. APIs should be designed with user experience in mind. Many of these principles were covered in earlier chapters. The following summarizes some of the approaches for designing a pragmatic RESTful API interface.

- **Design APIs with RESTful URLs:** Design an API based on the logical grouping of identified resources. The API URL should point to a collection of resources/subresources or an individual entity

B. De, *API Management*, https://doi.org/10.1007/979-8-8688-0054-2_5

within the collection. For example, `/customers` should refer to a collection of customers, while `/customers/{customerId}` should refer to an individual customer entity within the collection. The URL should be intuitive enough to easily identify and navigate the resources.

- **Use HTTP verbs for CRUD actions on resources:** Use the HTTP verbs to perform CRUD action on the resources. Use POST to create a new resource, GET to read, PUT to update, and DELETE to delete a resource. Additionally, you may consider providing support for the PATCH verb in the API resource for partial updates. OPTIONS verb can be used to determine the metainformation about the resource, such as the methods supported, HTTP headers allowed, and so forth.

- **Use operations in the URL when an HTTP verb cannot map to the action:** Often, an action on a resource cannot be directly mapped to an HTTP verb. For example, actions such as `register`, `activate`, and so forth, cannot be directly mapped to an HTTP verb. These operations may be applicable on a resource collection or a single resource entity, or to a group of resources of different types. In such cases, it makes sense to have this operation in the URL and treat as a subresource. For example, the resource URI `/customers/customer123/activate` can be used to activate the account of customer with ID `customer123`.

- **Use SSL/TLS for all communication with REST APIs:** RESTful APIs expose enterprise data and assets. These can be accessed from within the company or from outside the firewall over the Internet from anywhere. This poses a security threat to the data transferred over the network. Hence, to protect the data against any eavesdropping or any impersonation in case security credentials are compromised, it pays off to use SSL/TLS for all API communication.

Using SSL communication also simplifies authentication efforts. Mutual authentication with SSL/TLS can help the server to validate the identity of the client in addition to the client validating the server.

- **Do not redirect from non-SSL API endpoints to SSL endpoints:** This is a practice to always avoid when designing REST APIs. Malicious clients may gain access to actual secured and encrypted API resources through such redirections. It is recommended to respond with a proper error message if the non-SSL endpoint is not supported in the API.

- **Use API versions:** Versioning iterates and improves APIs by providing a smooth transition path. It supports multiple versions of the APIs simultaneously and provides time for clients to upgrade to new version and provider to retire the old version. There are multiple approaches to versioning the API.

  The most common of them is to include the version information in the URI base path. Version information can also be included in custom HTTP header. A hybrid approach of including the major version in the URI and minor version in the HTTP header can also be adopted. Information about API versioning approaches are covered in Chapter 6.

- **Design the API interface to support filtering on the result set:** The response to a GET request for an API resource may sometimes be quite large. Displaying this large response in the consumer app may be quite challenging considering the limited form factor and processing power on the device. Also transmitting a large payload over the network would also impact the bandwidth and the overall performance. Hence, the client app using the API would obtain a lean and filtered response for a GET request. This can be achieved only if the API supports filtering on the result set.

  Filtering criteria may be specified as unique query parameters for each field that supports filtering. For example, when querying for a customer's orders, you may want to limit it by the order date, such as orders placed in the previous month, six months, or year. This can be specified using a GET request with an `orderDate` such as `GET /customers/customer123/orders?orderDate>'YYYY-MM-DD'` query parameter.

- **Design the API to support pagination:** Pagination is yet another feature that is useful in handling large responses from an API. Even the filtered response from the back-end service for an API may contain hundreds of records. In such a scenario, it makes sense to display only ten of them on a page in the consumer app and provide a link to the next page with the next set of records. Supporting pagination for an API response can address this need to the app developer. This includes pagination parameters in the request as query parameters. `limit` and `offset` are the most common query parameters to specify the pagination requirements. For example, `orderDate` is like `GET /customers/customer123/orders?orderDate>'YYYY-MM-DD&limit=5&offset=0`. `limit` indicates the number of records to be included in a page, and `offset` denotes the page number.

Also, the API response should include the pagination metadata in the response. This can be included in human-readable format as envelope within the response or in a machine-readable format using the `Link` header. The following is an example of pagination metadata included as an envelope within the response.

```
"_metadata":
  {
      "offset": 2,
      "limit": 5,
      "page_count": 25,
      "total_count": 127,
      "Links": [
        {"self": "/orders?offset=2&limit=5"},
        {"first": /orders?offset=0&limit=5"},
        {"previous": "/orders?offset=1&limit=5"},
        {"next": "/orders?offset=3&limit=5"},
        {"last": "/orders?offset=25&limit=5"},
      ]
  },
  "orders": [
    {
      "id": 1,
```

```
            "item-name": "Widget #1"
        },
        . . . . .
        . . . . .
        ]
    }
```

Machine-readable metadata can be included by using the Link header, as follows.

```
Link: </orders?offset=2&limt=5>;rel=self,</orders?offset=0&l
imit=5>;rel=first,</orders?offset=4&limit=5>;rel=previous,</
orders?offset=3&limit=20>;rel=next,</orders?offset=25&limit=5
>;rel=last
```

The total count of records can be included in the response using custom headers such as `X-Total-Count`.

- **Return resource representation in response to creating and updating:** The response for POST, PUT, and PATCH operations results in creating and/or updating a resource. The API response payload for these methods should include metainformation such as `created_at` or `updated_at` along with the created or updated representation of the resource. Successful execution of a POST request should return a HTTP *201 Created* status code along with the `Location` header containing the URL of the newly created resource. Successful update requests should return with HTTP status code 200 OK.

- **Use HTTP headers to specify the media type for the message payload:** When sending a request or a response, include the `Content-Type` header to specify the content type for the message payload. This lets the message recipient easily identify the parser to be used for processing the message. For example, the `Content-Type` header with the *application/json* value indicates that the payload is in JSON format and the recipient should use a JSON parser to process the message. Similarly, use the `Accept` header in the request to indicate the format of the response expected by the consumer from the provider.
- **Use HTTP headers to support caching:** HTTP provides built-in features to support caching. HTTP provides several useful headers to efficiently communicate caching information. The `ETag` header contains a hashed value of the resource information. Instead of including the entire resource representation in the message payload in XML or JSON format, the `ETag` header with the hash value can be used to communicate information about the resource. Similarly, headers can be used to communicate resource modification date/time, expiry time of the cache, validation rules, and the cacheability of a resource. These headers should be used effectively for handling cache.
- **Secure APIs using authentication information in the HTTP header:** APIs exposing data and assets should always be secured. Authentication credentials should be included in the HTTP `Authorization` header. Since REST services are stateless, cookies should not be used. Session information if any should be passed in custom HTTP headers.

Basic authentication should be used when the API needs to identify the end user. OAuth-based authentication can be used when a third-party application needs to access the API on the behalf of another user. In case of authentication failure, the API should respond with *401 Unauthorized*. All communications containing sensitive information or any security credentials should be encrypted using TLS.

- **Handle errors using HTTP status codes and appropriate error messages:** In case of errors, APIs should respond with useful error messages in a consumable format. Appropriate HTTP error response codes in 4XX or 5XX series should be used. 4XX response codes should be used if the error occurred due to fault of the client. 5XX response codes should be used in case of server errors in processing the request. The error response payload should at a minimum communicate the following.

    - An **error message code** is a unique alphanumeric code to uniquely identify the error.
    - An **error message** is a summary of the error.
    - An **error description or reason** is a description of or reason for the error.

This is an example of an error response payload.

```
{
  "code" : Err_POL0001,
  "message" : "Address missing",
  "reason" : "No Address specified in the 'Address' field"
}
```

API Management Patterns

Enterprise services provide access to assets and legacy systems. SOAP and REST APIs are the two most common implementation technologies used for building services. An API management platform is used to transform and manage these services to make them more flexible, scalable, and secure. Various implementation patterns have emerged to address different challenges. This section looks at some of the most common API management patterns.

API Facade Pattern

The API facade pattern helps the API team create developer-friendly API designs and connect to complex enterprise legacy record systems.

Back-end and internal system of records are often quite complex. They could be built using variety of technologies and sometimes even legacy ones. These are difficult to change due to the strong dependencies built over time and the complexity involved. A lot of investment was made to make them robust and stable. Hence, it is difficult to replace them as well. Therefore flexibility and agility needed for the digital business becomes difficult to achieve. Creating an API for a single system of record may still be possible, but the real problem is in creating an API for a group of complementary systems that needs to be used to make an API really valuable to the developer. In this situation, API facade patterns come in handy for creating a simple API interface for a set of complex back-end systems that are hard to change for digital transformation. This pattern provides a layer between the back-end systems and the consumer apps. This layer not only build a simple API interface but can also implement other functionalities such as security, data transformation, version management, orchestration, error handling, routing and much more. Apps access the API exposed through this facade. The facade handles the complexities to interact with the back-end systems (see Figure 5-1).

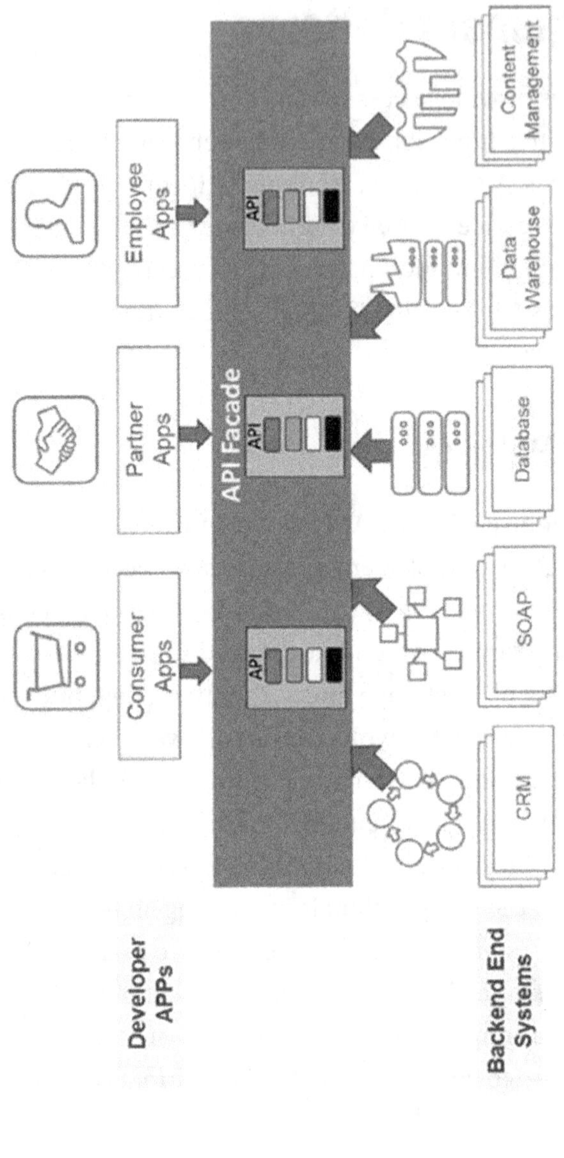

Figure 5-1. *API facade pattern*

The API facade can be used in a variety of ways, as described in the next few sections.

API Composition

Take for example that an app needs to interact with three different services for one of its transactions (see Figure 5-2). In this case, the client app has to be built so that it makes multiple calls directly to services, negotiates any security challenges, and does data format changes as required. With this approach, the client app is responsible for all the orchestration, data transformation and normalization, security, service connectivity, and retry mechanisms. This is indeed an overhead on the client app, considering the limited processing power available on the mobile devices. It is useful for the developer building the app, if all these tasks can be off-loaded somewhere.

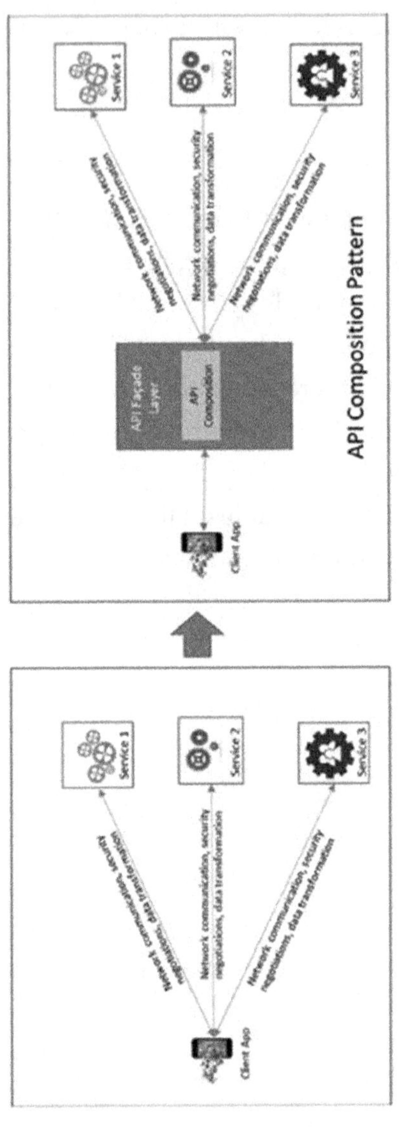

***Figure 5-2.** API composition pattern*

Implementing the API composition pattern in the API facade layer can be a solution to this problem. With API composition, the developers can concentrate on the UI and business functionality. It makes the communication less chatty with reduced network calls between the app and the back-end services. Security negotiations with the back-end service are handled by the API composition at the facade. The client app or device only needs to authenticate once at the API facade layer. API composition also shields the client from changes to the back-end systems. Different service provider can be plugged in without having to change the app. The new API composition can validate and throttle requests before it reaches the back-end. Any data format change or intermediate message processing can be done using this pattern. The API composition pattern can also improve the overall performance by bringing in some parallelism in making calls to the back-end system.

Using an *API gateway* to implement the API facade pattern for composition is a common practice. An API gateway is a server that acts as a single point of entry into the system. It encapsulates the internal system architecture and provides an API that is customized for the client. It handles the responsibilities of request routing, orchestration, protocol translation, and finally, composing an interface as required by the client. The client communicates with the API gateway, which then fans out the request to all the back-end APIs. It invokes multiple back-end microservices and aggregates their responses. It also does the translation between web protocols such as HTTP(s), WebSocket, and other web-unfriendly protocols used within the enterprises. The API gateway provides an interface that is customized for the client's needs by following the composition pattern. It reduces the client overhead for making multiple calls to different services and aggregating them, thus simplifying the client code.

Session Management

API services should be designed to be stateless. But sometimes state management becomes necessary for designing an app with better user experience. Shopping cart, hotel booking are some examples where session management is necessary. Sessions maintain the client context on the server. In the API world, managing session information in the client apps running on devices is difficult. Devices are already constrained for memory and processing capacity. Hence, session management is an additional overhead, which can slowdown the overall performance. Managing the state information in the back-end server is expensive too. An API facade can use HATEOS principles to facilitate state management. Using these principles, the resource state information can be returned in the response payload as a URI from the facade. This URI can be used by the client in subsequent interactions to communicate the state of the resource. For example, in the shopping cart API, the GET request to fetch product information by a user may look like the following.

```
GET https://www.foo.com/products/sku/2345?user=USR123&c
art=CT1234
```

The response for this request can be as follows.

```
{
"Product":{
    "item-name":"Canon EOS 5D Mark III",
     "description":"DSLR camera",
      "price": "2500 USD",
      "sku": "2345",
    "link":{
       "AddPrdURL":
```

```
        https://www.foo.com/cart/CT1234/product/sku/2345?user=
        USR123
      }
    }
}
```

Note that the response contains a URL that has the cart ID (CT1234) and the user id (USR123), which acts as the session information. The app can use this URL for the next call to add the product to the user's cart. The session information can also be communicated as custom HTTP response headers.

Two-Phase Transaction Management

In a two-phase transaction, the transaction coordinator *prepares* the participating resources for a transaction in the first step. If the first step is successful, the *commit* is issued to the participating resources in the second step. The two phases for a two-phase commit transaction is shown in Figure 5-3.

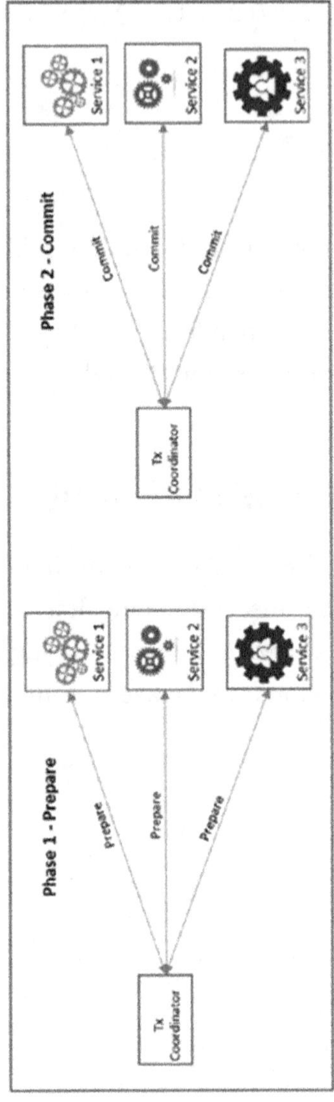

Figure 5-3. *Two-phase transaction management of APIs*

Exposing each transaction phase as an API and expecting the client app to coordinate the transaction, and roll over in case of failure, is an over kill. Managing all transaction from the client app is going to result in a chatty conversation. The complex processing logic in the app for transaction coordination and management definitely yields a poor app performance. The solution is to handle the conversation from an API facade. The logic to prepare, commit, and roll back two-phase transaction management is implemented in the facade. The facade exposes only one API that is invoked by the client. For example, a hotel booking service can expose only one endpoint to access it (`/hotelbooking`). This endpoint may in turn invoke two separate endpoints: one to reserve the hotel (`/reserve`) in the prepare phase and the second to make the payment (`/payment`) to confirm the reservation in the commit phase. This way the client need not directly access both `/reserve` and `/payment` services and nor does it have to manage the two-phase transaction. Figure 5-4 shows how the two-phase transaction is handled by APIs.

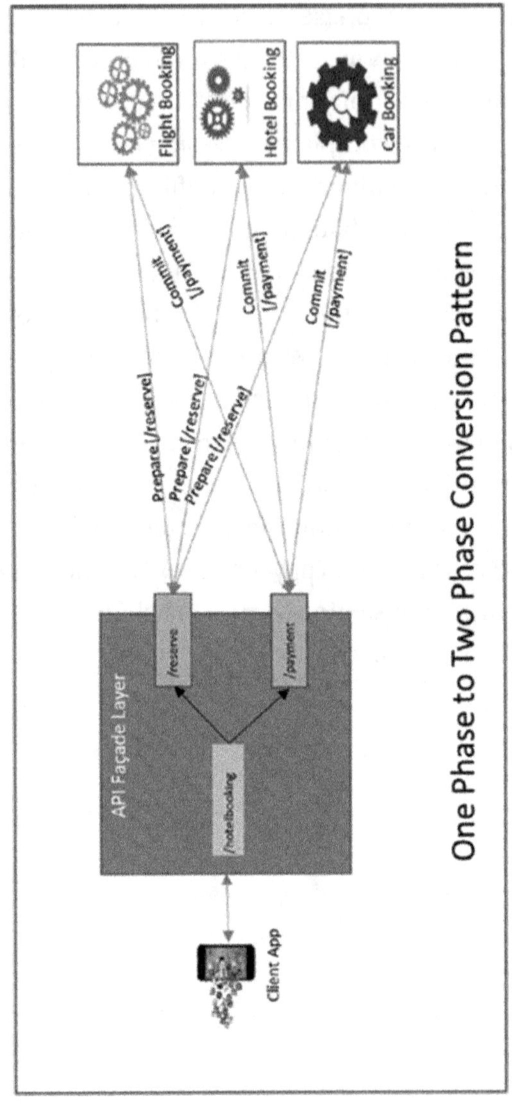

Figure 5-4. *Two-phase conversion pattern*

Synchronous to Asynchronous Mediation

In many scenarios, the application client needs to access a long-running back-end service that may not provide an immediate response. The mobile app cannot wait for the entire duration till the response is received. A typical example is sending a message. Suppose that you are building a mobile app that sends an SMS to a given number. After the message is sent, the mobile network takes time to deliver it to the recipient depending on various factors. Depending on the network traffic and other factors, the message delivery status may be available almost immediately or after some time. The back-end service is asynchronous. However, the mobile app expects a synchronous response. So how do you implement this? An API facade can provide a solution to this. Implementing a callback pattern on the API facade is the first step to this solution. The high-level steps for the solution are as follows.

1. The client app makes a call to the API facade.
2. The API facade makes a call to the back end with a callback URL pointing back to the facade layer.
3. The API facade sends a response back to the client with a URL to check the response status.
4. After some time, the target system sends the updates (e.g., delivery status) to the API facade at the callback URL. API facade layer forwards the notification to the notification URL of the mobile app.

Figure 5-5 shows the steps to implement a synchronous to asynchronous mediation using an API facade.

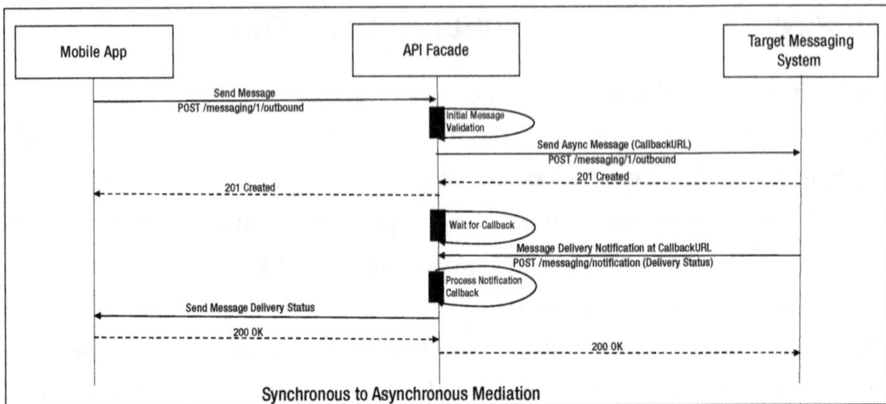

Figure 5-5. *Synchronous to asynchronous mediation pattern*

Routing

In a complex service composition scenario, the routing rules may not be fixed. The back end to which the request should be routed may have to be dynamically determined based on parameters in the incoming request. This is also known as content-based routing. The parameters for routing may be present in the request header or the message payload. In the API facade, these parameters are extracted and inspected to determine the back-end endpoint to which the request should be routed. A common example where this pattern can be applied is when routing a request to a back-end based on the originator of the request. Based on the customer category (Platinum/Gold/Silver) you may want to route the request to different back-end services that contains business logic for each category of customer (see Figure 5-6).

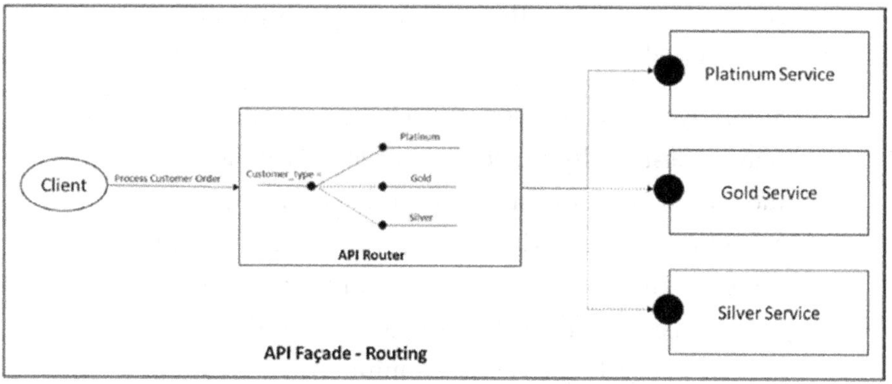

Figure 5-6. *API routing pattern*

API Throttling

When an enterprise opens their API to the external world, it is expected to see an increase in the API traffic. Developers use these APIs to build new innovative apps. As more apps are built and adopted by users, the overall traffic is bound to increase. Also since the APIs are now open to the public, there may be some unexpected and unwanted load coming from some malicious apps, which may try to bring down the system. The current back-end systems may not have been designed to scale up and withstand this increased load. To maintain the performance and overall stability, it is important to maintain the overall traffic within the capacity limits of the back-end system by throttling the API. The following are the common approaches to throttling.

- **SpikeArrest**: With SpikeArrest, you can detect sudden unexpected changes to the traffic pattern. Applying a SpikeArrest policy smooths out the traffic by uniformly distributing the traffic across each smaller interval. For example, if the set spike arrest limit is 60 per minute, then only one request is allowed every second. If in any second there is more than one request, they would all be throttled.

Similarly, if the spike arrest is 200 per second, then only one request is allowed per 5 milliseconds. If there is more than one request in any 5-millisecond interval, subsequent requests is throttles. The value of the spike arrest should be calculated based on the capacity of the back-end services. The limits should be configured for shorter intervals such as sec or minutes. This feature protects the back-end services against sudden traffic burst coming from some malicious users or apps.

- **Rate limit or quota:** With a rate limiting approach (also sometime referred to as quota), the requests are throttled based on the originating app or user, region of origination, time of the day and various other factors over a period of time. The request within the specified limit is routed successfully to the target system. Those beyond the limit are rejected. For example, if the quota is defined as 1,000 requests per day, all requests after the 1,000th request are rejected. It doesn't matter when these 1,000 requests are made. They could have been made in the first minute, or in the final minutes, or evenly paced.

  Additional requests are allowed only after the quota is reset at the end of the time interval. The rate limit values depend on the API product sold to the user. It controls the number of calls allowed for APIs in that product. For trail product, the limits might be less. For high-value products, the limits allowed could be more. Unlike spike arrest, rate limit allows calls to go through till the limit is reached. Hence, the rate limit values should be carefully derived by looking at the overall capacity of the back-end systems and the expected load. The rate limit values are normally specified for a longer duration such as minute, hour, day, or month.

- **Concurrent back-end connections:** Sometimes, legacy back-end systems might restrict the number of connections that can be made. By implementing throttling using concurrent connections, you can limit the number of simultaneous connections that can be made from the API to the back-end services at any given point in time. Based on the value specified, the API gateway container controls the number of connections made to the back-end and rejects requests once the connection limit is reached. The limits to be set should be determined based on the capacity of the back-end services.

Caching

The caching pattern can be used within an API gateway to cache back-end responses or any information required for processing the request. When a client makes the same request, the cached response is returned to the client instead of forwarding the request to the back-end. This improves the overall API performance and the system's stability by reducing the load on the back-end servers. Each cached response is normally stored against a unique key. The key is derived based on the parameters in the request. Hence, if the app or client makes requests using the same URI, the cached data is sent in the response, if not expired. If the cache is expired, the request is forwarded to the back-end system to fetch the latest data, which can then be cached in the API gateway to serve subsequent requests.

Caching the response data is useful when the data is updated only periodically. The cache expiry time should be set based on the update interval of the back-end data. Static data such as list of stores or hotels is a good example of where caching can be beneficial as these dint change frequently. Dynamically changing data should not be cached. Also if the data changes very frequently, the caching strategy should be examined carefully, else it can result in incorrect response to the client. The caching strategy should consider the cache expiry time, cache key, the cache skip conditions, size of the cache object as some of the top factors.

Logging and Monitoring

Logging is one of the best ways to identify and track problems. It is no different in the world of APIs. In fact, given the distributed nature of APIs, the importance of logging and monitoring increases significantly. To identify problems during the processing of API requests, critical information should be logged. The information for logging should be collected at all stages of message processing and logged at the end of message processing or in the event of an error. Logging can be done to syslog or to a local file system. The ability to log to a local file system is generally available on a private cloud setup of API management platforms. While using a public cloud instance of the API management platform, it is recommended to log information to a syslog server. If syslog server is not available, public log management services such as Splunk, Loggly, Sumo Logic, and so forth, may be used.

Once you know how to log, it is important to determine what information should be logged. The information logged should provide sufficient data to detect, find, and analyze the issue. Since APIs are used for distributed communication, log information should locate the source of the issue. It should also provide information about the date/time of the issue, a description of the issue with error codes and messages, and a correlation ID to relate it to events in other applications of the system.

It is a good practice to log certain metainformation from the request and response, even in success scenarios (see Figure 5-7). It can be used for auditing purposes. All logging should be done using asynchronous mechanisms to avoid impact on the actual API performance. Using a separate thread to send the log information to a messaging queue is a common approach most API management vendors use to send logs to their destinations.

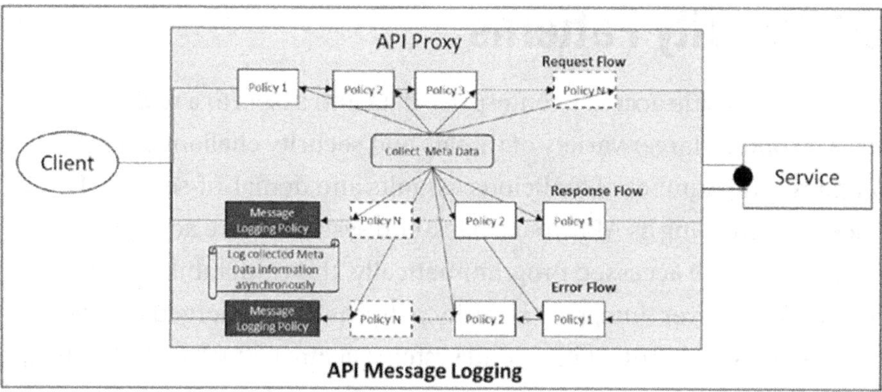

Figure 5-7. *API message logging pattern*

API Analytics

Implementing APIs for digital transformation is not enough. You need visibility into your API program to measure its success and make strategic investments. API analytics provide insight into the API program through information about the API traffic pattern and performance metrics. An API analytics dashboard can tell you which APIs are used most frequently and how traffic varies over time. You can also get behavioral information about the target services in terms of response time, error rates, payload size, and so forth. API analytics can also gather information about developer adoption of an API and the geographic distribution of API traffic.

Additionally, you can collect custom data from the message payloads and derive useful analytics data for making informed business decisions. Analytics data is normally stored in databases and later processed, aggregated, and analyzed. Hence, like the logging information, analytics data should also be collected at different points in the message flow and processed asynchronously to move it to the back-end database for dashboard reporting.

API Security Patterns

When APIs provide access to enterprise data and assets to a wide audience, they also open a larger variety of threats and security challenges for the company. The number of malicious assaults and denial-of-service (DoS) attacks is increasing as APIs make back-end systems more accessible. Since APIs can be accessed programmatically, the vulnerability is even greater. Hence, over time, new security patterns have emerged to secure access to APIs and protect back-end systems against attacks. The challenge is providing easy access to legitimate and authorized users while making it difficult for unauthorized users to access APIs. Hence, getting API security right can be a challenge. This section looks at the different approaches that have emerged as patterns for securing APIs against attacks from potential hackers.

Common Forms of Attack

Hackers can attack to get access to the system, steal valuable information, or even bring down the system, which impacts your business. The following are the most common forms of attack on APIs.

- **DoS attacks**: Malicious users flood your system with high-volume API traffic that the back-end systems cannot handle, bringing it to a halt.
- **Scripting attacks**: In this kind of attack, attackers inject malicious code into the system to get access

and possibly tamper back-end data and assets. The malicious code can be an SQL, XPath, or XQuery statement or some script that tries to exploit design flows in the system access to back-end data.

- **Eavesdropping**: In this attack, the hacker gets access to an API request or response while the data is in transit over a non-secure API communication channel. He can then manipulate the message and send it to the ultimate recipient.
- **Session attack**: In this kind of attack, the hackers gain access to the session ID used by a user or app. This information is then used for personifying and accessing the user's account and resources. In this common attack, an app makes an API call and passes the credentials or session information in the header, which can provide access to the underlying assets. The risk is worse in scenarios that use a multiparty authentication scheme, such as OAuth, to grant permissions to a third party to access their private data.
- **Cross-site scripting (XSS)**: This is a special scripting attack that takes advantage of known vulnerabilities in a website or web application. An attacker injects a malicious link or code executed on the victim's web browser. This attack bypasses the same-origin policy that requires everything on a web page to come from the same source. When a same-origin policy is not enforced, the attacker can inject a script or modify the web page to achieve their purpose. An XSS attack delivers tainted content to the API from a trusted source with permission to access the system. Hence, the API must protect itself by validating the `Origin`

header in the request payload to check for the origin before allowing access to back-end resources.

API Risk Mitigation Best Practices

Approaches and patterns have emerged to protect APIs from various security threats and provide comprehensive security. The approaches for securing APIs should control access to APIs and monitor and limit API usage. Controlling access to an API should authenticate and authorize users or apps making API calls. It should also scan incoming messages for well-formedness and potential threats. A monitoring approach should detect sudden changes in the API traffic pattern and block the user from making calls. A comprehensive API security approach should look at all the links in the API value chain, starting from the users and apps that consume the API, to the API team that builds the API, all the way to the API provider that exposes the data and services in the back-end systems. Since APIs provide omnichannel access, the API security approaches should also be omnichannel security. The security architecture should be flexible and responsive enough to prevent, detect, and react to all forms of API threats in near real time.

Next, let's discuss some of the best practice approaches for building security into an API management solution.

Authentication and Authorization

Identifying and authenticating API consumers is critical in mitigating security threats. Apps consume APIs, and consumers use the app. Hence, it is essential to differentiate between the app and the consumer/user and control the operations that they can perform. Every app is associated with a unique API key. Hence, API key validation on an API management layer can identify the app and thus control access to the APIs. Once an app has been identified and validated, the user should be verified to validate the end user's permissions to access an API resource. This can be done through OAuth scope validation in the API management layer or by integrating with another identity and access management system, such as LDAP, Tivoli Access Manager, Microsoft Active Directory, and so forth. This kind of integration performs single sign-on and provides a seamless experience to the user. While authenticating the user, the API provider should also consider the context in which the app or the API is being used. Validating context information, such as geolocation, device capability, and time, as part of the security framework can build strong security for APIs.

API keys identify the app. The app is responsible for storing them securely and protecting them from misuse. The app should encrypt and store the key in a secure vault to prevent misuse. HMAC-based encryption can be used for encrypting API keys. Also, keys should be transmitted in encrypted form over the network using SSL for any authentication between the app and the API gateway. The API key is the identifier of an app and not the end user. Hence, it should not be used as a substitute for end-user authentication or authorization.

OAuth should be used to authorize a third-party application for access to an end-user resource on their behalf. OAuth assists with granting authorization without the need to share user credentials. OAuth 2.0 uses SSL for all of its communications. Hence, all user and app information in the OAuth dance with the OAuth provider is secured in transit. Many prominent API management platforms, such as Apigee, Mashery, and Layer 7, remove the complexity of implementing OAuth and integrating with external identity and access management systems. This should be leveraged instead of natively implementing it.

Protect Against Attacks

Since APIs expose a lot of valuable business data, they are prone to different kinds of attacks. API management platforms come with built-in features to detect and eliminate such attacks. These platforms provide configurable policies or assertions, which can detect attacks using malicious contents or malformed XML or JSON when activated or attached to the request pipeline. Some API platforms can also detect virus signatures. Schema validation or threat detection policies attached to the request-processing pipeline can mitigate the risk of SQL injections, malicious code injection, and business logic or parameter attacks. CORS header validation protects against XSS attacks. IP whitelisting is another approach to reduce risk from untrusted sources.

Preventing APIs against DoS attacks is another important security consideration. Most API management platforms protect against DoS attacks using SpikeArrest and Quota policies. The SpikeArrest policy identifies an unexpected surge in the API traffic and rejects all requests exceeding the configured limit. This maintains a uniform distribution of requests flowing to the back-end systems per their capacity. On the other hand, the Quota policy restricts the number of API calls that a client app is allowed over a time interval. Alerts should be sent if APIs are overloaded, or any suspicious pattern of API calls is detected. Using rate limits and quota policies along with a licensing model that establishes a contractual obligation between the API provider and the consumer app and enforces payments for violations of contracts can minimize the risk of DoS attacks.

Today, various AI-powered network components can detect DDoS attacks using bots. They provide services to detect network abuse and intrusion. They can be custom-tailored to suit any customer need, architecture, and threat profile to provide advanced DDoS protections.

The following are some of the best practices to prevent DDoS attacks on your APIs at the network and infrastructure level.

- Use load balancers to distribute incoming traffic across multiple back-end servers.
- Use a content delivery network (CDN) to distribute and cache content closer to the user. Many CDNs have built-in DDoS protection mechanisms preventing

unusually high traffic volume from reaching the origin servers.

- Deploy anti-DDoS hardware devices to detect and mitigate attacks at the network level.
- Use cloud-based solutions. Today, most cloud providers offer robust DDoS protection services. Solutions like Cloud Armor from Google AWS Shield provide managed DDoS protection services to safeguard applications on the cloud. Hence, critical API backends can be moved to the cloud to protect them from DDoS attacks.

Encrypt Message Exchanges

Often, message payloads sent in API calls contain sensitive information that can be the target for man-in-the-middle attacks. An API management platform is an API gateway between the client app and the API service provider. All communication between the client app and the API service provider through the intermediate API gateway should be secured using SSL/TLS encryption by default (see Figure 5-8). A two-way SSL between the client app and the API gateway assists with client authentication. SSL should also be enforced for all communications between the API gateway and the back-end service. A pervasive security approach for encrypting data using SSL prevents man-in-the-middle attacks.

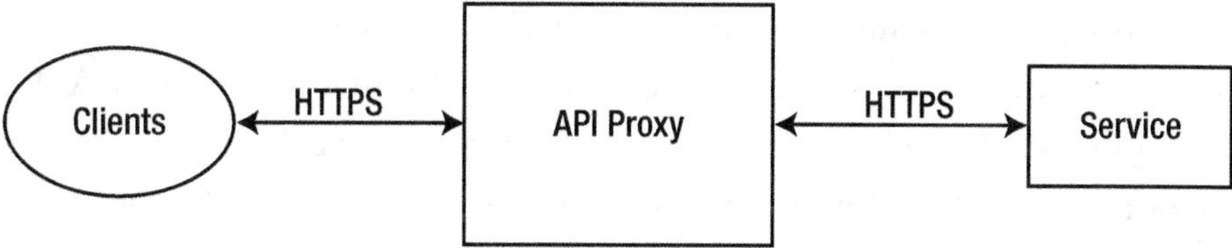

Figure 5-8. *API transport security using HTTPS*

Monitor, Audit, and Log API Traffic

The API management solution should monitor, log, and analyze API traffic. It understands API usage patterns. An API provider is interested in knowing which is their most popular API operation, who is the most popular user of the API, what is the rate of growth of API consumers, and what is the traffic pattern over a period of time. An insight into all this information assists with planning the API extensions to strengthen API security.

Logging metainformation from an API traffic flow is also useful in the root cause analysis of any problem. In the event of any security breach, it provides information about the time of the incident, the message payload, and the attack mechanism. If appropriate information is logged, it can also identify the source of the attack. Hence, monitoring APIs and capturing the right information from the API traffic logs is essential in securing APIs.

Logging and Auditing is also one of the major regulatory compliance requirements. Various national and industry-specific laws require minimum logging. Regulatory compliance requirements in the financial industry mandate that you log certain API traffic information and make it available as part of the audit and compliance process. For example, you might be required to prove that you mask sensitive data or can detect unauthorized users in the logs captured from API request and response processing.

Build API Security into the SDLC Process

API security is impossible without a comprehensive set of security policies and processes ingrained within the development life cycle of API development. API architects should plan to address security at the API program's start. They should provide guidelines for authentication and authorization to make APIs secure. Policies to protect APIs against attacks and vulnerabilities should be defined as part of the security architecture and design. These security policies should be implemented and thoroughly tested during the development and testing phases. Penetration testing of APIs should be a mandatory step in the testing phase. After deployment, APIs should be continuously monitored for potential threats and performance issues that could indicate any security incident.

Use a PCI-Compliant Infrastructure

PCI compliance specifications define a set of guidelines for handling credit cards and other sensitive information during a transaction or at rest. The consortium of industries began in 2006 and includes payment card processing companies like Visa, Mastercard, JCB, and Discover. The PCI-DSS compliance requirements apply to all organizations that store, process, or transmit credit card or payment information. This specification intends to protect cardholder data and give confidence to consumers that their sensitive information will not be misused. The following are some of the important guidelines for PCI compliance.

- Build and maintain a secure firewall. Do not use any default passwords.
- Protect stored data and encrypt sensitive data in transit.
- Use strong access control measures so that applications and systems are secured and protected against unauthorized access.
- Antivirus and vulnerability management programs should be kept updated.
- Monitor network access and test systems regularly.
- Maintain an information security policy.

No product will make you PCI-compliant. Products and processes can help you implement and enable PCI compliance requirements. If an API handles sensitive payment information, it must adhere to the PCI guidelines. Also, the API gateway infrastructure on which such APIs are deployed should be PCI compliant.

API Deployment Patterns

APIs need to be deployed on a platform that is scalable and flexible. The platform should simplify API development and deployment. It should also enable the business to manage the entire API ecosystem. The platform should drive the customer reach of the APIs and support business growth. To meet these demands, most API platforms provide two deployment models: cloud and on-premise. Choosing the right deployment model depends on the business needs. Let's look at the characteristics of each deployment model.

Cloud Deployment

The cloud deployment of API gateways is hosted and managed by API platform providers on a public cloud, such as AWS or Azure or GCP. For example, the Apigee cloud instance is hosted on Google Cloud. Cloud deployment provides customers with seamless product upgrades and improves the pace of innovation. The cloud deployment option leverages the economics of scale. However, it also puts the data and services outside the traditional enterprise firewall, which can be a security and regulatory concern.

The main advantages of a public cloud platform are as follows.

- **Higher reliability and availability**: Cloud platforms provide clustered environments distributed across multiple data centers and regions. This mitigates the risk of data center and network outages and increases the reliability and availability of the platform. The API platform vendor handles traffic fluctuations and adjusts capacity to meet the guaranteed SLA.

- **Faster time to market**: The cloud instances of the API platforms can be spun off almost immediately by the API vendors. This saves time and hassle of hardware procurement, setup, and configuration. The cloud instances are up and running very quickly, thus reducing the overall time to market for the API program.
- **Reduced capital and operational expenditure**: Cloud deployments are generally available in a subscription model. You pay by usage, like the number of API calls. This avoids upfront capital expenditures and reduces ongoing in-house operational costs.
- **Reduced management overhead**: Letting the API vendor focus on the data center infrastructure helps enterprises focus on building their API services. The API platform provider manages the overhead of running and managing the data center. They address all availability and performance management of the underlying infrastructure. Software updates and fixes are rolled out seamlessly by the vendors. The API provider can focus on creating the API and its back end.
- **Increased scalability and agility**: The licensing for the cloud platforms is generally by API traffic volume. If the traffic increases, API providers only pay an additional licensing fee for the increased traffic. They do not need to bother about capacity planning, hardware procurement, installation, configuration, and training needs for the operations personnel. The platform vendor makes the required changes to provision the

additional capacity requested. This makes cloud environments ideal for horizontal scaling to meet the increased demand.

- **Regulatory compliance**: Often, regulatory compliance requirements come in the way of adoption for cloud-hosted solutions. However, most leading API management vendors have achieved industry compliance for their cloud-hosted platforms and products. PCI DSS for the payment industry and HIPAA for the health industry are the most common industry compliance requirements. Since the platform complies with industry standards, it helps clients easily meet the PCI security and log management requirements on the cloud and other industry compliances.

These are the main disadvantages of cloud deployment.

- **Network latency**: The distributed nature of the cloud infrastructure and additional network hops on the cloud introduce additional network latency. An API Delivery Network (API-DN) can route the traffic intelligently and decrease the latency disadvantages. API-DN routes the request to the closest data center, thus reducing some of the network latencies.
- **Control over data:** On a cloud-hosted platform, all API traffic data is available in the cloud. This reduced the control and security the client can have for their data passing through a cloud-hosted API solution.
- **Reduced flexibility for platform configurations:** With the complete installation and setup being managed by the platform provider, customers have very limited capability to customize the setup and configuration to

suit their needs. They must either go with the default configuration provided by the vendor or pay additional license fees for the desired flexibility.

On-Premise Deployment

In an on-premise deployment model, the API provider purchases the software and is responsible for setting up and running the entire platform in its data centers. The API provider takes up all the management overhead of installing, running, and maintaining the API platform. They are responsible for the hardware procurement, data center setup, and network configuration. The responsibility to monitor the API platform performance, deal with outages, update and manage software versions, and capacity scaling lies with the API provider. Managing the entire API platform also needs additional training about the platform. Though initial challenges exist in setting up the on-premise infrastructure, the following reasons can be the main drivers for on-premise deployment.

- **Enhanced security**: With an on-premise deployment model, the API service provider fully controls the data security. They can manage where the underlying data stores would be present, how infrastructure and data are secured, and who can access it. It also meets the increased security audit needs of the enterprise.
- **Reduced network latency**: Since the API gateway is installed within the enterprise's network, it cuts down on multiple network hops. API providers may also plan to install the API gateways within the same network as the back-end services. This reduces the network latency and increases the overall performance of the APIs.

- **Better management and control**: On-premise versioning provides better management and control over performance and scaling. You can decide on the number of instances of the product components to be installed to support increased load. You have control over changes to the environment configuration, such as software and hardware upgrades.
- **Reuses existing infrastructure**: With an on-premise setup, customers can reuse their existing hardware to install the API management platform. They can also integrate it with their existing security, logging, and monitoring infrastructure.

Hybrid Deployment

In a hybrid deployment, the runtime components of the API management platform that route the API traffic are deployed and maintained by the customer within their network—either on the cloud or on-premise data center. The management components of the platform are deployed and managed by the platform provider. This deployment model provides the following advantages.

- **Greater flexibility to set up platform components**: The hybrid deployment model allows the API provider to set up new environments in a region of their choice.
- **Improved latency**: Since the customer can deploy the runtime components in a region or data center of their choice, it can be set up closer to the back-end services. This reduces network hops and latency and improves overall performance.
- **Enhanced data security and regulatory compliance**: With the runtime components being deployed within

the customer's network, it gives more control to decide where and how the metadata about the APIs would be stored. Even when API payload information must be logged for any reason, such information would not go outside the customer's network periphery. Regulatory requirements for data residency within geographic limits can thus be met. Customers get more flexibility to decide on the data retention period from the API logs, which can be archived for longer.

However, this deployment model comes with the following disadvantages.

- **Longer infrastructure setup and configuration time**: Since the customer is responsible for the setup of the runtime components, they must plan for the required infrastructure procurements, network configuration, and the actual installation of the API Management platform components. This can take some initial lead time and increase the setup and configuration time to roll out the platform.
- **Higher infrastructure and maintenance costs**: The customer must procure and set up the infrastructure required for setting up the runtime components. This is an additional cost on top of the license cost that the customer must bear. They must take care of regular maintenance and version/patch upgrades whenever the provider releases them. This requires the availability of in-house skilled resources and planning to carry out the necessary activities at regular intervals.
- **Infrastructure monitoring**: With hybrid configuration, the customer needs to integrate the runtime

components with their existing monitoring infra and take necessary actions, which also increases the maintenance overhead.

API Adoption Patterns

APIs are used by businesses to move ahead with their digital transformation initiatives and increase revenue and customer reach. RESTful APIs are used to expose data and services and deliver an engaging experience to customers. Businesses have also used APIs for internal application integration and partner integration. It makes data more readily available for consumption. As APIs have evolved and been used by more consumers, a pattern has emerged in their adoption. The following are the four most common API adoption patterns.

- APIs for internal application integration
- APIs for business partner integration
- APIs for external digital consumers
- APIs for mobile and Internet of Things (IoT)

Let's look at the business drivers for these different adoption patterns and the considerations for architecting and sharing the APIs for consumption.

APIs for Internal Application Integration

Enterprises use SOA for building services to achieve loose coupling and reusability. These services are used for internal application integration. SOAP and other protocols are used for integration. SOA provided the right level of security and governance but faced the challenge of making the services easily discoverable and consumable. The complexities associated with UDDI and service registries to publish and discover service were one of the main ones. APIs built on top of SOA address the consumption side of it. It makes services easy to publish and discover through the API portal. The REST API's developer-friendly and intuitive interface makes it easy for developers to consume and build apps using them. APIs have been used for integration within and across lines of business.

With huge investments already in SOA services and many business processes built around them, companies are less likely to throw it all out to embrace REST APIs. Hence, building an API on a clean slate is a rare opportunity. APIs must be built on top of the SOA services that expose the back-end services to make them more consumer-friendly. APIs address the consumption side of the equation—making it easy for developers to discover and consume services. API management platforms provide the functionality to create developer-friendly REST APIs from SOAP services that are easy to consume. An internal API portal publishes an API catalog, making the APIs searchable and visible to internal consumers. It brings in an open and collaborative practice for developers while controlling the visibility of APIs and combining it with the right level of security and governance required for internal consumption.

APIs for Business Partner Integration

Enterprises have been consuming third-party APIs to simplify and expand business partnerships. They grow the business rapidly when APIs are used for B2B partner integration. APIs provide faster integration and an improved partner/customer experience. The technicalities of creating APIs for partner integration are not much different. However, they are more rigorous and have a commercial aspect. Instead of being open to all, they are available to a select list of business partners. The legal business contracts for using the APIs bind the API consumers and providers. These business contracts govern the service levels and other aspects of API delivery and consumption. Both API consumers and API providers are responsible for the success of an API program.

APIs for External Digital Consumers

Enterprises have adopted APIs to accelerate digital transformation, increase customer reach and loyalty, and discover new revenue streams. Companies can now expose their business assets and services to a larger community of developers with an easy-to-use and intuitive API interface. External developers and partners adopt these APIs to build innovative apps. These apps can bring in a completely new business model for the enterprise. Hence, companies must create external-facing APIs to expose their data and services.

APIs exposed to external digital consumers need an interactive platform that proactively supports the developer community. An API portal provides such a platform. It publishes information about the APIs that developers can use for building apps. Interactive API documentation, blogs, and forums help the developer determine the suitability of an API. It also fosters collaboration with a bigger community of developers. An API portal quickly onboards external developers through a smooth developer onboarding process. Developers register their apps to get app keys and secrets on the portal, which are required for secured access to the APIs.

Externalization of APIs and collaboration with other developers build an ecosystem of innovation. It helps developers share ideas and read about the experiences of others. It generates new and innovative ideas that otherwise would not have been possible. Many companies have seen a northbound trend in their API traffic due to the new experiences brought in by apps created by external developers using their APIs.

APIs for Mobile

Mobile apps have changed the way that humans interact with enterprises. Even though computing power is shifting from server rooms to mobile devices, mobile apps are still limited in resources and restricted by bandwidth. Hence, building a mobile app mandated a simpler interface that can be consumed easily. Also, the interface should be such that it can be easily shared with developers to consume them in the apps. RESTful APIs have all these characteristics, making them popular for mobile consumption. The API provider should consider the API's design, security, and operational aspects to make them suitable for mobile consumption. Additionally, caching should be considered an alternative for improving performance and reducing chattiness. Instead of sending bulk payloads, paginations, filtering, and other mechanisms should be supported to reduce processing overhead on the mobile app. Standard web API security protocols such as OAuth and OpenID Connect should be supported to secure APIs and make them suitable for mobile consumption.

APIs for IoT

The *Internet of Things* (IoT) refers to the network of devices, sensors, and actuators that communicate with each other over the Internet using API technologies to build a new customer experience. It refers to wearable devices—like the iWatch, connected cars, and connected sensors, such as Nest thermostats and intelligent light bulbs. It is estimated that by 2030, there will be 50 billion connected devices. APIs form the communication foundation for these connected devices. But the challenge is with the diverse and newer communication protocols, such as MQTT, AMQT, XMPP, and many others, that need to be supported by the API platform. A future generation of infrastructure powered by autoscaling capabilities may also be needed to support the scale of IoT communication traffic.

CHAPTER 6

API Version Management

Change is inevitable, and this is no different with APIs. If APIs are successful, they evolve over time. New requirements may drive you to make changes to your APIs. Advancements in technology are also a contributor to changes to APIs. Handling these changes to minimize client impact is the art of versioning.

Once you publish a REST API, developers start using it in their client app as defined in the contract. Developers write software that relies on the API contract. Whenever there is a change to the API, there is the potential to break the client software that relies on the contract. Hence, API changes need to be controlled and predictable, which brings in the need for API version management. This chapter looks at how API versioning differs from normal software versions, the need to version APIs, and the different approaches to API versioning.

B. De, *API Management*, https://doi.org/10.1007/979-8-8688-0054-2_6

API Versioning vs. Software Versioning

Every software release is versioned. The common format for versioning software is as follows.

```
<MajorVersion>.<MinorVersion>.<PatchVersion><OptionalPackage
Identifier>
```

```
For example, v2.4.16-RC4.
```

The checksum of the software package is normally used to identify a particular version. If the checksum changes, the version is considered different. However, this approach does not apply to REST API versioning; if a new version is introduced for every minor change to the API, it would cause a maintenance nightmare. Apps dependent on the API might stop working, creating a frustrated developer community. Also, maintaining too many API versions for the client would be a nightmare.

The REST API version should correspond to the service version, not the software or package version implementing the service. Every new version of the service implementation need not warrant a change in the service version; hence, the REST API exposes the service. A new API version should be created only when there is a change in the service interface or the contract that the client is using.

The Need to Version APIs

An API defines a contract for communication between the client and a server hosting a resource to operate on them. The client may want to create, read, update, or delete a resource as defined in the contract. A change in the resource may or may not require a change in the contract. Some changes, such as minor bug fixes, may not require any alteration to the contract. Others, such as a change in the structure of the resource or the way of communication, may require a change in the contract. Changes may or may not be backward-compatible. If the change is backward-compatible, handling it within the same API version may be possible. Changes that are not backward-compatible require a new API version to be introduced. This lets the consumer know they may need to change their app code. Versioning APIs maintains compatibility, enabling debugging and dependency control.

API Versioning Principles

The following are some of the main principles of API versioning.

- An API version should not break any existing clients.
- Keep the frequency of major API versions to a minimum.
- Make backward-compatible changes and avoid making new API versions.
- API versioning should not be directly tied to software versioning.

The API Version Should Not Break Any Existing Clients

As APIs are adopted by app developers, introducing new versions of the API brings with it the risk of breaking the client's apps. The API versioning strategy should be such that it does not break any existing client apps; otherwise, it will easily frustrate the developer community and slow down the API adoption.

Keep the Frequency of Major API Versions to a Minimum

Every time a new API version is released, it kick-starts a fresh cycle for app developers. They need to understand the new API, analyze the impact on their apps, debug issues, and so on. This is a huge burden on both sides in terms of time and money. Even the API provider must maintain multiple versions of the API for a sufficient time to enable a smooth transition. Supporting multiple versions requires significant investment by the API provider and the consumers.

Make Backward-Compatible Changes and Avoid Making New API Versions

The simplest way to avoid making new API versions is to make the changes backward-compatible. Changes such as adding new API resource methods or supporting a new data format do not impact the client. Some changes to the input data elements may be backward-compatible; for example, adding an optional element in the input request in the body or introducing support for an additional query parameter does not mandate any change to the client code; these are backward-compatible. These kinds of changes do not necessarily require changes to the client app. Hence, it is not necessary to introduce a new version of API backward-compatible changes. However, adding a new mandatory parameter in the request or changing the name of a field in the response requires a new API version to be created because these require changes to the client application code.

API Versioning Should Not Be Directly Tied to Software Versioning

As discussed at the start of the chapter, software evolves very rapidly. Every major release, enhancements, and bug fixes result in a new software version. If you start tying the API version to its software implementation, it results in an unprecedented number of API versions. This would frustrate the consumers dealing with the API and result in maintenance nightmares for API providers. Hence, the API version should never be tied to the software version of the back-end data/service. A new API version should only be created if a change in the API contract impacts the consumer.

Approaches to API Version Management

There are multiple approaches to introduce versioning in your API. The next few sections discuss the most common ways to version an API.

Versions Using URLs

An API is normally identified by its URL. In API versioning, it makes sense to introduce the version information in the URL as follows.

```
http://www.foo.com/v1/customers
```

In this URL, `v1` defines the major version identifier. When this identifier changes, it is assumed that all resources under it change—in this case, the `customers` resource. If a new version of the customer is introduced in the next version, it should use a new version identifier, like `/v2/customers`. The new version can be accessed as follows.

```
http://www.foo.com/v2/customers
```

This approach to API versioning is followed by the likes of Google, Yahoo!, and many others. Using a dot notation for API versioning to indicate the minor revision (e.g., v1.1 is also a common practice). However, that does not add much value compared to just using the major version and incrementing the version number to the next integer. Some popular API providers, like Twilio, use the date as a version identifier for their APIs. For example, if the API was released in 2015, the provider may use the following URL format.

```
http://www.foo.com/2015/customers
```

The version that came up the next year used this URL format.

```
http://www.foo.com/2016/customers
```

This could be extended to include the month as follows.

```
http://www.foo.com/2016/02/customers
```

or

```
http://www.foo.com/2016-02/customers
```

This approach might be needed only if multiple versions of API releases exist in a year. However, monthly or frequent releases are against API versioning best practices.

The advantage of this approach is that it is easy for users to understand which version of the API they are using.

Versions Using an HTTP Header

Another approach to API versioning is to use an HTTP header. With this approach, the client uses an HTTP header to specify the API version it wants to invoke. The advantage of this approach is that it keeps the API version out of the URI that is used to refer to a resource. The other benefit of this approach is that you can easily ignore or silently upgrade if the user does not specify any version or a deprecated API version.

The use of an HTTP `Accept` header is one of the preferred choices. The GitHub API follows this approach and expects it to be passed in the request as follows.

```
Accept: application/vnd.github[.version].param[+json]
```

Using a custom HTTP header like '`X-API-Version`' in the request is yet another approach to API versioning. However, this has its own disadvantages. What if the client does not add this header to the request? What should the default behavior be? Should the server respond with an error message or handle it using the latest API version? If handling using the latest API version is the default approach, how do you then handle breaking changes when introducing a new API version?

Versions Using Query Parameters

This is yet another common approach to versioning API. In this approach, the client specifies the version number as a query parameter in the request.

```
http://www.foo.com/customers?version=v2
```

The server may choose to honor the query parameter or even ignore it. One advantage of this option is that the `version` parameter can be optional or required, depending on how you want the API to be used. In this case, the `version` is optional. A default behavior may be assumed to be the latest version when it is left off. Being in the URL, this is very easy to see and understand.

This approach works well when the resource representation is versioned. In such cases, it is necessary to also put in transformation logic to transform the resource representation based on the version specified.

Versions Using a Hostname

Another approach to API versioning using a URL is to use a different hostname. For example, Facebook's first version of an API is available at `api.facebook.com`, whereas their new graph API is available at `graph.facebook.com`. This approach is only used when there is an extensive revamp of the API.

The downside of this approach is that it not only requires a change in the URL used by the client to access a resource, but it may also require changes in the security settings on the client side due to the change in the hostname. Also, this may require setting up a completely new infrastructure to support the new version, adding to the cost. The only advantage is that you can completely revamp the URI structure and route client requests to a different server without changing the older version. The old instance processes client requests for older API versions.

Handling Requests for Deprecated Versions

As new API versions are introduced, the API provider should notify the expected behavior when a client makes calls to older and deprecated API versions. During the transitions phase, the provider may handle requests to older versions by responding with a redirection URL pointing to the new API version. Alternatively, the API provider may respond with an HTTP 404 error code indicating the requested resource version was not found. If a client calls a deprecated API version, it should fail with the 404 HTTP status code.

API Version Lifecycle Management

Introducing non-breaking changes to APIs is fairly simple and can be pushed out without much fanfare. However, as a best practice, such changes should be published through a blog post, updated in API documentation, or logged in the API release notes' change log. However, making changes requires more planning, extensive testing, customer hand-holding, and communication. Since there may be a lot of consumers for the API, it is important to notify them of any changes to the APIs. There are multiple ways to do that. The following are some of the most common approaches.

- Announce new upcoming versions and versioning schedules, if any, in the API developer portal.
- Send emails to registered developers about upcoming new API versions.
- Introduce "warning" headers in alerts on older versions being deprecated.
- Define a migration period and cut-off date for support to older API versions.

Releasing a new API version as a beta release to a restricted group of developers is a good approach to introducing new API versions. Provide enough time for the developers to test and provide feedback on the new API version. Only after a successful beta version launch should it be taken to production and opened for general availability. Even after successfully releasing the new API version, never immediately deprecate or remove support for older versions. Once in production, old and new versions of an API should run simultaneously to give enough time for developers to migrate their code to the new version. Set a date for deprecation of the older API version so that developers have a clear target to migrate their apps to the new API version. When new versions are introduced, there should be clear communication and coordination between the API provider and the consumer community. This reduces the risk of breaking trust with any version upgrades.

CHAPTER 7

API Security

APIs provide a very good opportunity to build engaging and innovative customer experiences. They help businesses build new channels of integration and partnership. As companies look to expose their assets and data as REST APIs in an effort to provide new customer experiences and expand their business, security becomes a main concern. To a chief security officer at an enterprise, it is of paramount importance to secure the APIs and protect underlying assets from misuse, attacks, or any kind of threat.

The security threats to APIs can be of various types. The security model to protect against these threats depends on the type of asset or service exposed and the associated risk. For example, APIs dealing with sensitive financial data over public networks require stronger security measures than APIs dealing with publicly available data over a restricted network. There is no one-size-fits-all approach that can be applied to protect APIs against various threats.

This chapter looks at some of the important security threats to consider when building a security solution. It also looks at the various approaches and the security models for protecting APIs against these threats.

The Need for API Security

APIs allow consumers to interact with and access an enterprise's data and services. It is no good to have assets locked down within the enterprise. Exposing assets helps enterprises grow business and revenue. Creating

B. De, *API Management*, https://doi.org/10.1007/979-8-8688-0054-2_7

APIs that enable customers to use their assets builds enriching customer experiences and increases customer engagement and loyalty. However, since assets have a business value, they are prone to theft and attacks to gain unauthorized access. APIs that act as the front door to these assets should therefore be secured. An API without security is like keeping the door to your vault open. Since APIs are used by in-house developers, trusted partners, and third-party developers, they should be protected intelligently. Considering that APIs may sit at the edge of the enterprise and can be accessed by a wide variety of customers through different channels, such as mobiles, smartphones, tablets, web apps, connected cars, kiosks, IoT devices, and more, they should be secured thoroughly to prevent any kind of misuse of the underlying assets.

Today, APIs introduce a new form of security threat by hackers. In the past, hackers sat behind a console and tried out attacks to find vulnerabilities. Due to the programmable nature of APIs, hackers can now use them to automate their attacks and try out different things to find system vulnerabilities. Hence, the security model in the APIs should be able to identify such attacks and reject requests in order to protect the back-end assets.

APIs today form a critical part of any digital strategy. Lack of API security can bring your digital transformation journey to a grinding halt. Hence, having a well-defined strategy for API security is of principal importance.

API Security Threats

APIs provide channel of access to enterprise assets. Hence, they introduce many more types of security threats that were previously non-existent or were not considered a genuine threat. The different API security threats can be broadly classified into the following categories.

- Authentication
- Authorization
- Message or content-level attacks
- Man-in-the-middle attacks
- DDoS attacks (distributed denial-of-service)

APIs allow a new range of third parties to access enterprise assets. Without proper security policies in place, anyone can access these assets—even before a formal relationship has been established with third parties. Apps built by third parties can compromise enterprise security. Hence, it is important to have a proper registration and onboarding process for third-party organizations and app developers. Apps built by third parties should be registered with the API provider before they can use the APIs. Only authenticated systems, apps, and developers should be allowed access to the APIs in order to eliminate any risk of security compromise.

Third-party apps often access information on behalf of the end users. This information may be sensitive and private and can be accessed only after proper authorization has been obtained from the end user. Hence, APIs should be secured to check for the right level of authorization to grant in the request. Access to the resource should be granted only after authorization checks succeed.

Attackers can place malicious content, such as malware, in API requests to attack the system. They can also inject scripts in the request that are executed in the back-end systems. The impact can be devastating. It can corrupt systems and provide an outsider with unauthorized access to sensitive and business critical data. This can put a company's reputation at stake. APIs should be protected to detect any such malware or scripts, or malformed payloads in the request.

In a man-in-the-middle attack, hackers get access to credentials and tokens that can be used to get access to APIs. These credentials and tokens may be harvested and used nefariously. All data should therefore be encrypted in transit and protected from unauthorized access while at rest.

Attackers can launch DDoS attacks from one or more IP addresses via APIs to bring down the system. Since APIs provide a programmatic access to underlying resources, launching a DDoS attack is very easy. An API security model should be able to identify a DDoS attack and take the right action to protect back-end systems.

The next few sections look at how to design a security framework to protect APIs and their underlying resources against various forms of attack.

API Authentication and Authorization

Authentication determines the identity of the end user or the party requesting access to a protected resource. It validates who you are.

Authorization determines the access level and permissions of the end user to perform a certain operation. It determines the actions that the client is allowed to perform on the protected resource.

The following are some of the most common forms of authentication and authorization used for API security.

- API keys
- Username and password
- X.509 client certificates and mutual authentication
- SAML
- OAuth
- OpenID Connect

API Keys

An API key identifies the application using an API. It provides a simple mechanism to authenticate the apps. API keys allow an API to determine which applications are using it. API keys are generally long series of random characters typically passed as an HTTP query parameter or header. This makes it easy to use an API key in an API request for application authentication. API keys are also known by other names, such as app ID, client ID, app key, or consumer key.

When a developer registers his app with an API provider, a unique API key is provided to the developer. The developer needs to secretly store this API key and use it in the application requests when making an API call from the application. The key identifies the application making the request and helps the provider monitor which application is making the request. The developer also gets insights into how his application is used by end users.

An API key is normally a long alphanumeric string that is opaque and without any signature or encryption. This makes API keys less secure for authentication purposes. The use of API keys is best for auditing and identification. An API key validation policy in the request flow of the API can validate the API key and capture important metadata information, such as developer, organization, and so forth, related to the application. This may be good for APIs that only need to know who is using it. API keys can also be used to enforce API call quotas for an application (see Figure 7-1).

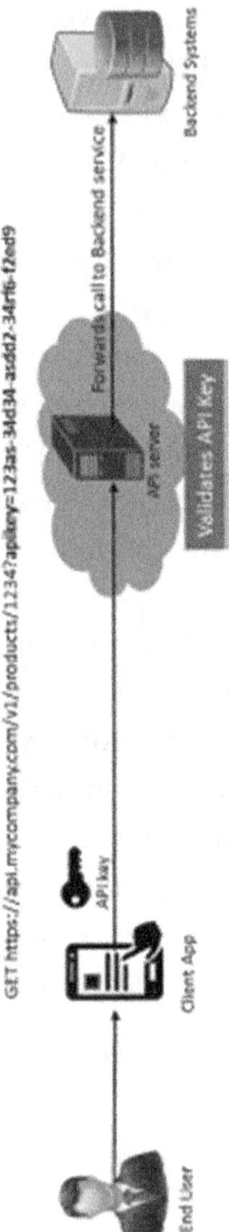

***Figure 7-1.** API key usage to secure back-end services*

Thus, API keys can filter or turn off access to rogue applications that might flood the system with API calls. Providers can revoke an API key to block traffic coming from that application. Where enhanced security is required, API keys can be used to generate tokens using OAuth and OpenID flows.

Username and Password

A username and password is the most common form of authentication and is useful when dealing with sensitive data in an API call. In this form of authentication, the client presents the server with a unique name (username) and a secret code (password). The server validates the username and password against its credential store and provides access to the client only on successful validation.

For a REST API call, the client can pass the credentials (username and password) in an HTTP header using the Basic authentication scheme. As per this scheme, the client sends the server authentication credentials using an `Authorization` header, which is constructed as follows.

1. The username and password are combined with a single colon (:).
2. The resulting string is then Base64 encoded.
3. The authorization method and a space (`Basic `) are then entered before the encoded string.

The username *John* and password *John@123*, results in a header that looks like the following.

```
Authorization: Basic Sm9objpKb2huQDEyMw==
```

HTTP Basic authentication is the most common form of authentication; it is supported by nearly all clients and servers. It is easy to implement without the need for any special processing. The client needs to ensure that the password is protected and kept secret. If the client needs to store the password, it must be encrypted in some way to protect it against any attackers reading it from the store. SSL should be used for all client-server communications to protect credentials in transit from eavesdroppers.

API key validation with Basic authentication can be combined for better API security. For example, the app identity may be sent as API key and the end user credentials may be passed in as Basic authentication header. The API server may first validate the app identity from the API key and then validate the credential of the end user accessing the client using the Basic authentication headers.

X.509 Client Certificates and Mutual Authentication

An X.509 certificate contains a public key that validates an end entity, such as a web server or an application. It is a good alternative to a username/password for authentication purposes in application-to-application communication. The X.509 certificate contains the identity of the subject. The subject information is described as a distinguished name (DN), common name (CN), along with other optional attributes, such as country (C), state (ST), location or address (L), organizational unit (OU), and organization name (O). All of this certificate information is digitally signed by a trusted certificate authority (CA). This certifies the public key of the subject and ensures that the certificate is not tampered with. The certificate's private key is always kept secret with the user and is never divulged to the signing authority or anyone else.

After the subject receives a signed certificate from the certificate authority, it can be used as identification. It allows secure access to protected APIs. For a mutual authentication using two-way SSL, the API resource server needs to import the client certificate in its trust store.

The SSL handshake starts with the API resource server sending its X.509 certificate to the client. After the client app has validated the server certificate, it sends its public key to the API resource server. The server validates the client certificate against the list of certificates present in its trust store. A two-way SSL is established after the mutual authentication by the server and the client is successful. Only then can the app can make an API call. Figure 7-2 shows a high-level view of the message exchanges to establish a two-way SSL and make an API call.

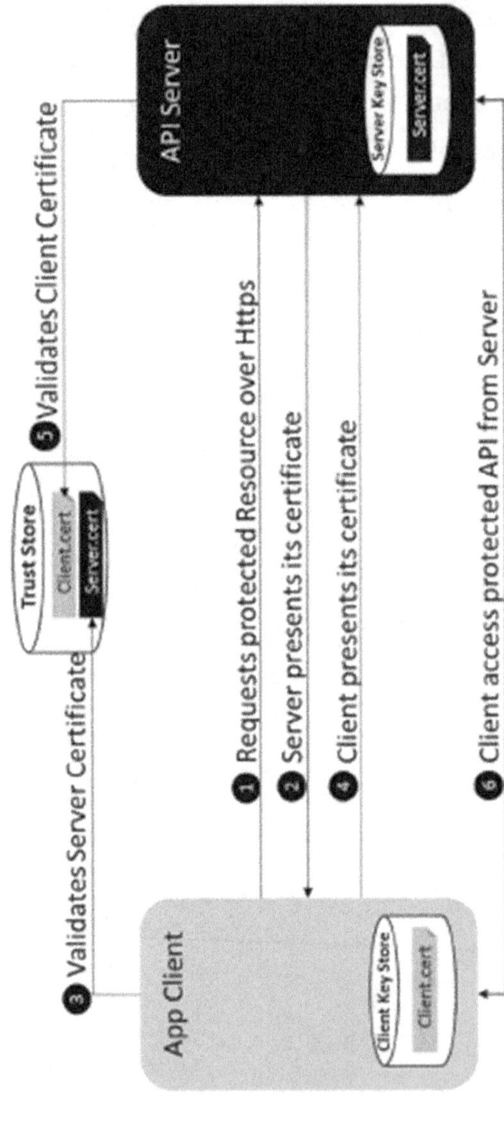

Figure 7-2. *Two-way SSL for mutual authentication*

OAuth

OAuth 2.0 is a protocol that allows clients to grant access to server resources without sharing credentials. As per the IETF specifications, the OAuth 2.0 authorization framework enables a third-party application to obtain limited access to an HTTP service, either on behalf of a resource owner by orchestrating an approval interaction between the resource owner and the HTTP service, or by allowing the third-party application to obtain access on its own behalf. For example, a shopping app can use access to its customer data in Facebook. When a customer accesses the shopping app, he is redirected to log in via Facebook. The customer is redirected to the shopping app after he has successfully logged in. The shopping app can now access customer data and can even post status updates on Facebook on behalf of the customer (if authorized to do so).

So what problem is OAuth trying to solve? Let's look at the scenario where a user wants to post some reviews about a product from the shopping app (say, Amazon) to Facebook but doesn't want to type their Facebook password on Amazon. This is possible if the Amazon app is able to store the user's Facebook password somewhere and use that to post on their Facebook page. But why should the user trust Amazon with their Facebook password? Also, what happens when the user changes their Facebook password, which is now stored in multiple locations with different apps? The user now has to manually go and update their Facebook password in all the locations that it is stored, which definitely is not a good user experience.

Instead of storing the Facebook password on every application that wants to access the Facebook account, what if you create a token that is authorized to perform limited actions, such as post on Facebook on their behalf. This token is generated after the end user has authorized Amazon to access their Facebook account.

The token has a defined validity and is understood and recognized by Facebook. So when Amazon presents the token to Facebook within the validity period of the token, it is allowed to access and post reviews on the user's Facebook page. In this way, users do not need to share their Facebook password with every other application that needs to access their Facebook account to post any updates. The access is automatically revoked when the validity of the token expires. The token can be revoked even earlier than its expiry time, if required.

Using OAuth tokens for API security makes APIs more resilient to security breaches, since they don't rely on passwords. In the previous example, if the user finds out that their Facebook password has been compromised, they only need to change it in one place, without impacting other applications that need to access their Facebook account. Those applications continue to access the Facebook account using the access token until it has expired or has been revoked.

OAuth Basic Concepts

To understand OAuth better, let's look at some basic concepts in the next few sections.

Actors in OAuth

OAuth protocol defines a sequence of message exchanges that need to happen between the various parties to grant the client access to a server resource. The various actors involved are resource owner, client, resource server, and authorization server.

- A **resource owner** is the end user who authorizes an application to access various resources in their account. For example, the user of a Facebook account can be the resource owner. The photos and activities like the posts and likes in the Facebook account are the data owned by the resource owner. The list of resources that an application can access or the operation that an application can do, is determined by the "scope" of the authorization granted.

- A **client** is the application that is trying to get access to a resource owner's account.
- A **resource server** hosts the protected resources of the user. In the API world, it is the server where the API resources are hosted. For example, Facebook is the resource server hosting the APIs to view or edit photos and user activities. Access to the API resources is allowed only after the client has been authorized by the resource owner or the user.
- An **authorization server** validates the identity of the user and then issues the access token to the client, which can be used to get access to resources.

Figure 7-3 shows the various actors involved in an OAuth flow.

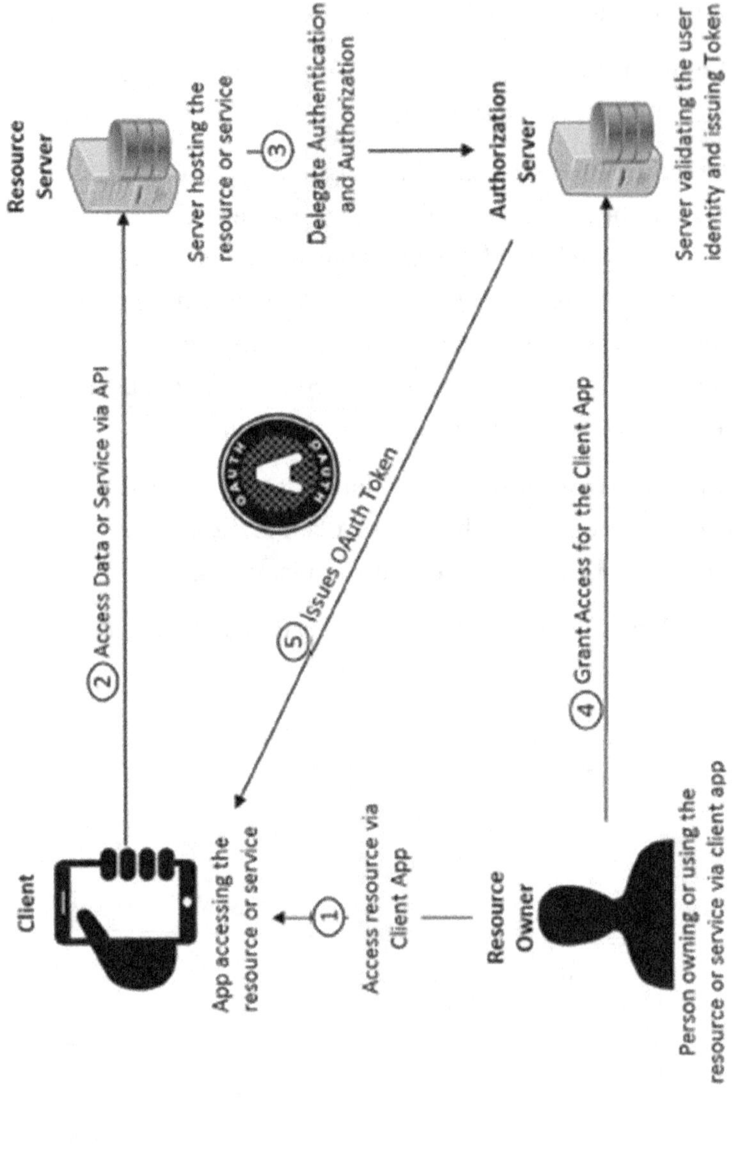

Figure 7-3. *The various actors involved in an OAuth flow*

In most cases, the server on which the API is hosted acts as the resource and authorization server. An API gateway can play this combined role, as shown in Figure 7-4.

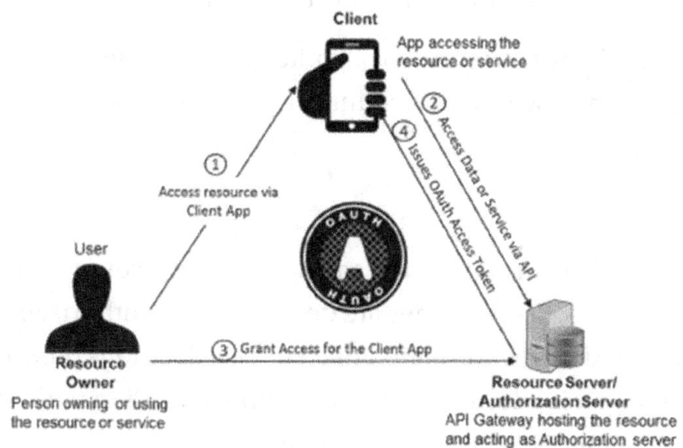

Figure 7-4. *Role of API gateway in OAuth*

Tokens

Tokens are issued to allow access to specific resources for a specified period of time and may be revoked by the user that granted permission or by the server that issued the token. There are two different kinds of tokens used in the OAuth flow: *access tokens* and *refresh tokens*.

- **Access tokens** allow access to a protected resource for a specific application to perform only certain actions for a limited period of time. They are a long string of characters that serve as a credential. They are generally passed as bearer tokens in an authorization header. An access token can also have restrictions or scope associated with it that specify the API resources that can be accessed using the token. An access token generally has an expiry duration and can be refreshed using refresh tokens for certain grant types. In situations where an access token is compromised, it can be revoked to prevent any further use of that token.

- **Refresh tokens** represent a limited right to reauthorize the granted access by obtaining new access tokens.

Scope

Scope identifies what an application can do with the resources that it is requesting access to. Scope names are defined by the authorization server and are associated with information that enables decisions on whether a given API request is allowed or not. When an application requests an access token, the scope names are optional.

Grant Type

An *OAuth grant type* can be thought of as the interactions that an app goes through to get an access token. OAuth 2.0 defines the following four grant types.

- Authorization code
- Client credentials
- Resource owner password credentials
- Implicit

Each of these grant types have their own pros and cons. The grant type used for generating a token depends on the business use case. One of the important considerations for choosing a grant type is the trust in the app accessing the resource.

Let's now look at each of the grant types in detail and learn about the flows involved for generating an access token for them.

Authorization Code

An *authorization code* is one of the most commonly used grant types. It is considered the most secure because it involves authorization from the end user, who actually owns the resource. The experience of using an authorization code grant type is similar to signing in to an app using a Facebook or Google account. This is sometimes referred to as "three-legged OAuth" since it involved three parties.

- the end user
- the client app
- the authorization server

The following is the high-level process involved with the authorization code grant type.

1. Generate an authorization code.
    a. The end user logs in and grants consent to the application to access resources.
    b. The authorization server generates an authorization code that contains the scope information for which authorization was given.
2. Exchange authorization code for access token. The client application exchanges the authorization code for an access token from the authorization server. A refresh token is also generated and given to the client.
3. Use the access token. The client app uses the generated access to make API calls.

Figure 7-5 shows a detailed sequence of flow for generating an access token using an authorization code grant type.

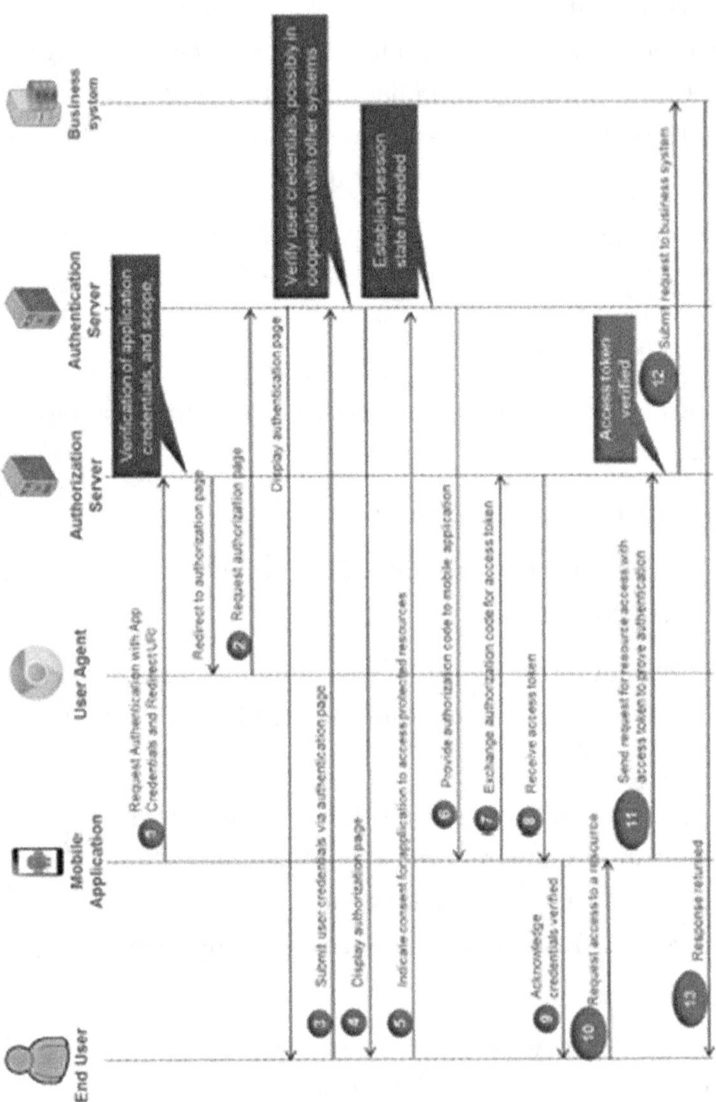

Figure 7-5. *Authorization code grant flow for OAuth 2*

Client Credentials

The client credentials grant type is suitable for machine-to-machine interaction and does not require any user permissions to access data. The following describes the high-level flow sequence (shown in Figure 7-6).

1. Generate access token.
    a. The client sends a message with its identity and the scope of access required to the authorization server.
    b. The authorization server validates the client's identity and issues an access token.
2. Use the access token. The client app uses the generated access token to make API calls.

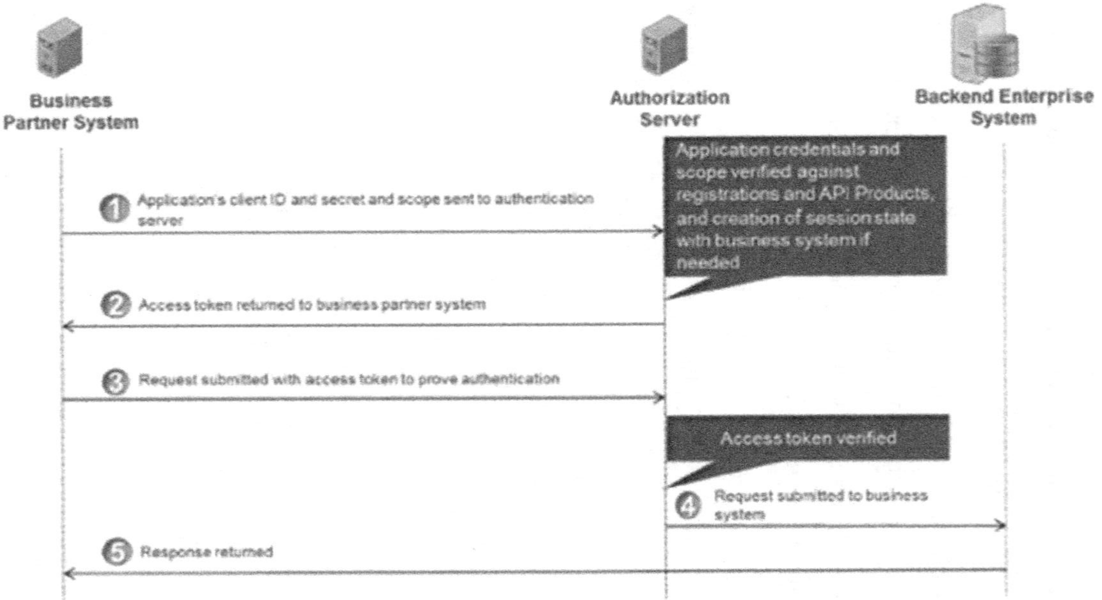

Figure 7-6. *Client credential flow*

Resource Owner Password Credentials

The resource owner password credentials grant is used when the end user's credentials must be authenticated before access can be granted. The following describes the high-level flow sequence (see Figure 7-7).

1. Generate access token.
    c. The client sends a request with its identity, scope, and the user's username and password.
    d. The authorization server validates the client's identity and user credentials.
    e. The authorization server issues an access token.
2. Use the access token. The client app uses the generated access token to make API calls.

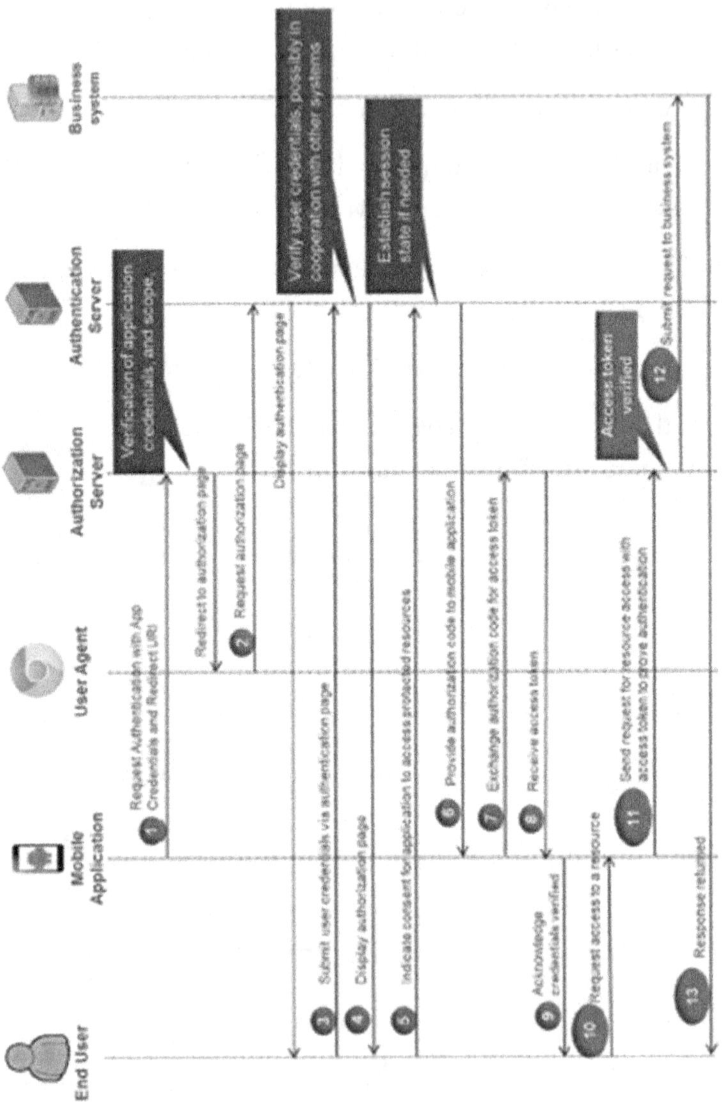

Figure 7-7. Resource owner password credential flow

Implicit

Implicit grant type is used by mobile apps and JavaScript applications running in the web browser. In this flow, the access token URL is given to the user agent to be forwarded to the client app via a redirect URL. Since the access token is encoded into the redirect URI, it may be exposed to the user and other applications running on the same device. The identity of the client is also not validated by the authorization server in this flow. Unlike the authorization code flow, where the client makes separate calls for authorization and for the access token, in the implicit flow, the client gets the access token as a result of the authorization request without any client authentication. The resource server only verifies the redirect URI that was originally registered. This makes the implicit flow easy but less secure. No refresh token is generated with implicit flow. Figure 7-8 shows the sequence of flow for the implicit grant type.

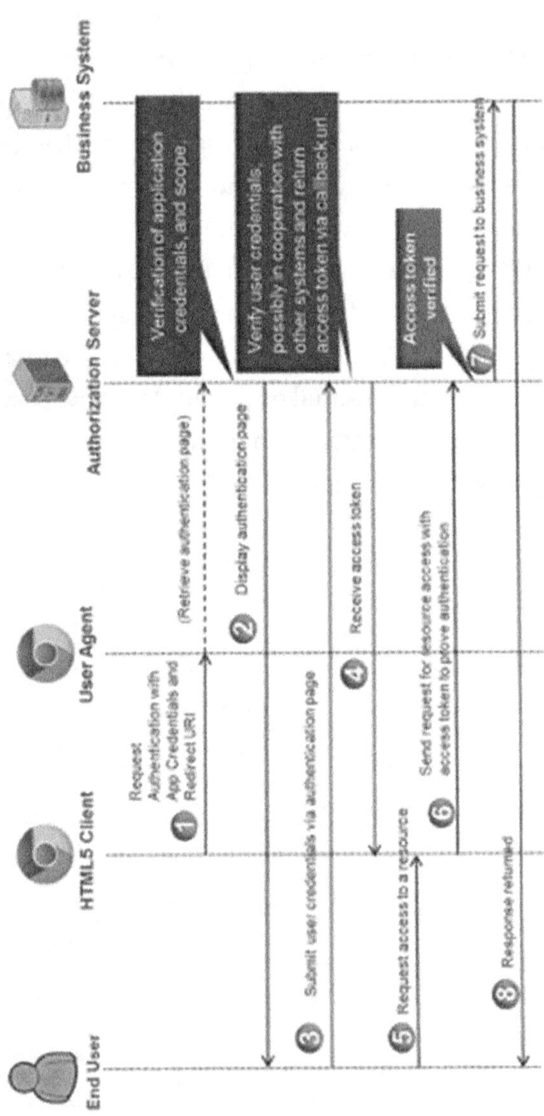

Figure 7-8. *Implicit flow*

OpenID Connect

OpenID Connect 1.0 is an authentication protocol that builds on top of OAuth 2.0 specs to add an identity layer. It extends the authorization framework provided by OAuth 2.0 to implement authentication. OpenID connect introduces an ID token in addition to the access and refresh tokens provided by OAuth 2.0. The ID token contains the identity information of the end user in JWT format. OpenID Connect defines *identity* as a set of claims or attributes related to an entity, which can be a person, a service, or a machine.

Actors in OpenID Connect

The following are the various actors involved in an OpenID Connect authentication flow.

- **OpenID Connect provider (OP)**: An OAuth 2.0 authorization server that provides authentication as a service. It authenticates the end user entity and provides the claims or attributes of the entity to the client.
- **Relying party (RP)**: An OAuth 2.0 client that requires end user authentication or claims from the OpenID Connect provider.
- **End user**: The entity that requests identity or claims information from the OpenID provider. The entity can be a human participant, a machine, or a service and is the owner of the resource that the client is trying to access.

Figure 7-9 is a high-level illustration of how different actors in an OpenID Connect protocol interact with each other.

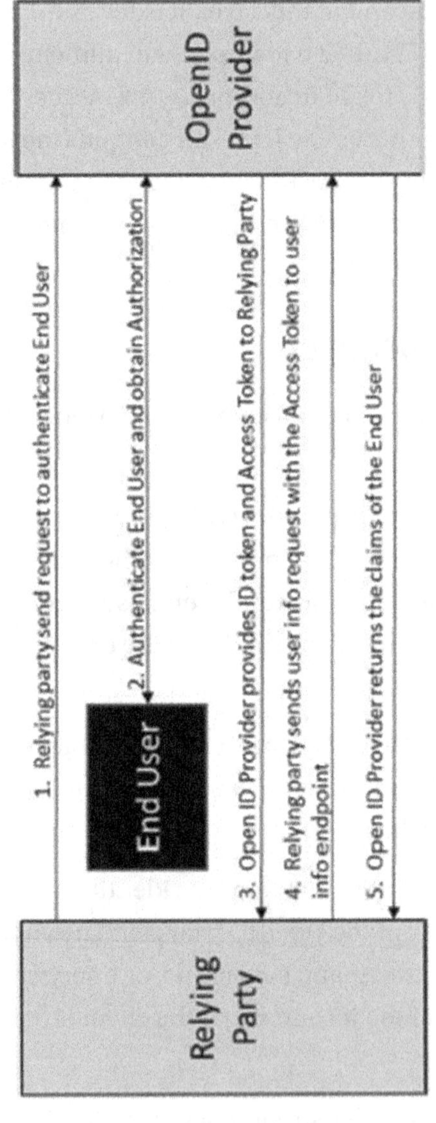

Figure 7-9. *Interaction between parties in OpenID Connect flow*

By using OpenID Connect, clients can request and receive identity and authenticated session-related information about the end user from a central identity provider and validate it. OpenID Connect can be used by clients of all types—including web-based, JavaScript, and native/mobile clients—to create a distributed and federated model for SSO.

ID Tokens

ID tokens are the main enhancements introduced by OpenID Connect on top of OAuth 2.0. An ID token is like an identity card that contains claims information about the authenticated end user. The ID token is represented as a JSON web token that is signed by the OpenID provider. The ID token contains the following claims information related to the end user in JSON format.

- **Subject identifier** (`sub`) is locally unique and asserts the identity of the end user.
- **Issuer identifier** (`iss`) identifies the issuing authority of the token. It is a case-sensitive URL using the `https` scheme. It contains the scheme, host, and optionally the port and path components.
- **Audience information** (`aud`) is what the ID token is intended for. It identifies the relying party and other audiences that can use this token. The OAuth 2.0 `client_id` of the relying party must be present in the audience information.
- An **alphanumeric string** (`nonce`) associates a client session with the ID token to prevent replay attacks. The nonce value is normally passed unmodified from the client authentication request to the ID token. If this value is present in a client authentication request, it must be included in the ID token response by the

authorization server acting as the OpenID provider. If the nonce is present in the response, the relying party must validate that the value received in the response is equal to the value passed in the original request.

- The **time** (`auth_time`) when the end user authentication occurred.
- The **authentication context** class reference (`acr`).
- The **time** that the ID token was issued (`iat`).
- The **expiry date** of the ID token (`exp`).
- Optionally, it may contain other details about the entity, such as name and email address.

The following is a sample JSON format of the set of claims in an ID token.

```
{
  "iss": "https://example.server.com",
  "sub": "2340051",
  "aud": "s6Bhdr4k9qt3",
  "nonce": "n-078_WzB3Mj",
  "exp": 1317881970,
  "iat": 1316780970,
  "auth_time": 1311280969,
  "acr": "c2id.loa.hisec"
}
```

The ID token is a JWT token created from the JSON format of the claims. JWT generally has three parts: a header, a payload, and a signature.

- The **header** specifies the algorithm used for signing and the token type in JSON format, as follows.

```
header = '{"alg":"HS256","typ":"JWT"}'
```

- The **payload** contains the claims in JSON format.
- The **signature** is calculated by Base64 encoding the header and the payload, concatenating them with a period separator, and then applying the signature algorithm on the concatenated string.

```
key = 'mysecretkey'
unsignedToken = encodeBase64(header) + '.' + encodeBase64(payload)
signature = HMAC-SHA256(key, unsignedToken)
```

- The **ID token** is created by concatenating the Base64-encoded value of the header, payload, and the signature with a period as the separator between them. This is done so that the token can be easily passed around.

```
token = encodeBase64(header) + '.' + encodeBase64(payload) + '.' + encodeBase64(signature)
```

eyJhbGciOiJIUzI1NiIsInR5cCI6IkpXVCJ9.eyJsb2dnZWRJbkFzIjoiYWRtaW4iLCJpYXQiOjE0MjI3Nzk2Mzh9.gzSraSYS8EXBxLN_oWnFSRgCzcmJmMjLiuyu5CSpyHI

OpenID Authentication Flows

OpenID performs authentication to log in an end user or to determine whether the end user is already logged in. The result of the authentication is securely retuned by the authorization server to the client in an ID token so that the client can rely on it. For this reason, the client is also referred to as the *relying party*. OpenID Connect defines the following three paths or flows for authentication to obtain the ID token.

- Authorization code flow
- Implicit flow
- Hybrid flow

Authorization Code Flow

In this flow's first step, an authorization code is returned directly to the client after authenticating the end user and receiving consent. In the second step, the client exchanges the authorization code to get an ID token and an access token. Since OpenID Connect is built on top of OAuth 2.0, the message exchange sequence is almost the same for both. The main difference is that the end user is authenticated against an OpenID provider and an ID token is generated and returned to the client in addition to the access token. The following are the high-level steps for the authorization code flow.

1. The client sends an authentication request to the authorization server containing the client_id, secret, redirect URI, and scope.
2. The authorization server authenticates the end user accessing the client against the identity provider.
3. The authorization server obtains consent and authorization from the end user for the client to access resources owned by the end user.
4. The authorization server sends the end user back to the client with an authorization code via HTTP 302 redirect.
5. The client sends a request using the authorization code to the token endpoint.
6. The client receives a response that contains an ID token and an access token in the response body.
7. The client validates the ID token and passes the access token to retrieve the end user's subject identifier.

An authorization server must implement the following endpoints to support the OpenID connect authorization code flow.

- Authorization endpoint (`/authorize`)
- Token endpoint (`/token`)
- User information endpoint (`/userinfo`)

An *authorization endpoint* is used to authenticate the end user and provide an authorization code to the client. The user agent is sent to the authorization endpoint hosted by the authorization server for authentication and authorization. The authorization request contains the following information.

- `scope`: Mandatory information sent in the request. For OpenID connect flows, this must have the `openid` value. It can also have other values for which the client requests access on the end user's behalf.
- `response_type`: This value determines the authorization processing flow to be used. For an authorization code flow, it must have the value of `code`.
- `client_id`: The identifier of the client making the request. The client gets this at the time of registration.
- `redirect_uri`: The redirection URL to which the response is sent. For security reasons, it must match the value of the redirect URI provided by the client at the time of registration to the OpenID provider.
- `state`: An opaque value to maintain the state between the request and the callback. It is typically used to mitigate cross-site resource forgery (CSRF) attacks.

Other request parameters defined by OAuth 2.0 specifications may also be used.

The authorization endpoint must validate all the information sent in the authentication request according to OAuth 2.0 specifications. If the request is valid, the authorization server attempts to authenticate the end user or determines whether the end user is authenticated. The method used for authentication is beyond the scope of the OpenID specification.

The authorization server may display an authentication user interface to the end user, depending upon the values in the request parameters and the authentication method. The authorization server must authenticate the end user if not already authenticated or if the authenticate request contains the `prompt` parameter with the `login` value.

After the end user has been authenticated, the authorization server must obtain consent from the end user before releasing any information to the relying party. The end user consent can be obtained through an interactive dialog with the end user. After the authorization server has successfully authenticated the end user and received the consent, it responds with a successful authentication response containing the *authorization code* and the *state* information. This information is returned as a query parameter added to the `redirect_uri` specified in the authentication request. The following is a sample response from the authorization server.

```
HTTP/1.1 302 Found
Location: https://client.example.com/cb?
code=Tplxl0BeZMMYbYS7WxSbIA &state=af2ifjhldbj
```

After successful user authentication, the client uses a *token endpoint* to obtain the following.

- ID token
- Access token
- Refresh token

The client or the relying party makes a token request by presenting the authorization code received from the authorization endpoint. The token request can be made using an HTTP POST call over TLS (Transport Layer Security) 1.2, as follows.

```
POST /token HTTP/1.1
Host: myserver.example.com
Content-Type: application/x-www-form-urlencoded
Authorization: Basic bzZCaGRSa4F0MzpnWMFmQmF0M2JZ

grant_type=authorization_code&code=Tplx1OBeZMMYbYS7WxSbIA
&redirect_uri=https%3A%2F%2Fclient.example.com%2Fcb
```

The token endpoint must validate the token request as follows.

1. Authenticate the client and validate its client credentials.
2. Validate that the authorization code was issued to the authenticated client.
3. Verify the validity of the authorization code and ensure that it has not already been used.
4. Validate that the `redirect_uri` presented in the token request is the same as in the authorization request.

After successful validation of the token request received from the client, the authorization server returns a successful token response containing the following.

ID token

Access token

Refresh token

The following is a sample token response containing the three tokens.

```
HTTP/1.1 200 OK
Content-Type: application/json
Cache-Control: no-store
Pragma: no-cache

{
  "access_token": "SlAV32hkKG",
  "token_type": "Bearer",
  "refresh_token": "8xLOxBtZp8",
  "expires_in": 3600,
"id_token":"eyJhbGciOiJSUzI1NiIsImtpZCI6IjFlOWdkazcifQ.ewogImlzcyI6ICJodHRwOi8vc2VydmVyL
mV4YW1wbGUuY29tIiwKICJzdWIiOiAiMjQ4Mjg5NzYxMDAxIiwKICJhdWQiOiAiczZCaGRSa3F0MyIsC
iAibm9uY2UiOiAibi0wUzZfV3pBMk1qIiwKICJleHAiOiAxMzExMjgxOTcwLAogImlhdCI6IDEzMTEyODA5N
zAKfQ.ggW8hZ1EuVLuxNuuIJKX_V8a_OMXzR0EHR9R6jgdqrOOF4daGU96Sr_P6qJp6IcmD3HP99Obi1PRs-c
wh3LO-p146waJ8IhehcwL7F09JdijmBqkvPeB2T9CJNqeGpe-gccMg4vfKjkM8FcGvnzZUN4_KSP0aAp1tOJ1z
ZwgjxqGByKHiOtX7TpdQyHE5lcMiKPXfEIQILVq0pc_E2DzL7emopWoaoZTF_m0_N0YzFC6g6EJbOEoRoSK5
hoDalrcvRYLSrQAZZKflyuVCyixEoV9GfNQC3_osjzw2PAithfubEEBLuVVk4XUVrWOLrLl0nx7RkKU8NXNHq-r
vKMzqg"
}
```

The client receiving the token response must validate the received ID token as follows.

- If the ID token is encrypted, the client must first decrypt it using the keys and the algorithms that the client specified during the time of registration with the OpenID provider.
- The client must—at a minimum—validate the following information in the ID token.
    - The OpenID provider's issuer identity must match the value in the `iss` claim attribute.
    - The audience (`aud`) claim attribute must contain the `client_id` value that was issued to the client by the OpenID provider at the time of registration.
    - The algorithm value (`alg`) must be negotiated at registration time.
    - The ID token's expiry (`exp`) claim must be greater than the current time.

    - The ID token's issued at (`iat`) claim is not too far from the current time. The client can decide on the value of this duration.
    - If sent in the authentication request, the *nonce* value must match the value received in the ID token.

- The client should also provide other information, such as `acr` claim and `auth_time` claim.

The *userinfo endpoint* (`/userinfo`) is an OAuth 2.0-protected resource that returns claims about an authenticated end user. The client makes a request to this endpoint using the access token received from the token endpoint to get claims and attribute information about the end user. The end user claims are returned as a name:value pair in a JSON object. All communication to the userinfo endpoint must use TLS. This endpoint must support both HTTP GET and POST methods. The endpoint must be able to accept and process a request containing an accepted token in bearer format sent in the authorization header. The following is a sample userinfo request.

```
GET /userinfo
HTTP/1.1 Host: myserver.example.com
Authorization: Bearer SlBV35hkKH
```

On successful processing of the request, the endpoint returns the end user claims in a JSON format, as follows.

```
HTTP/1.1 200 OK
Content-Type: application/json
{
  "sub": "548286761004",
  "name": "Fred Sweet",
  "given_name": "Fred",
  "family_name": "Sweet",
  "preferred_username": "fred.sweet",
  "email": "fredsweet@myserver.com",
  "picture":"http://myserver.com/fredsweet/fred.jpg"
}
```

Implicit Flow

Implicit flow is mostly used for browser (JavaScript)-based apps. In this flow, the client obtains the ID token and, optionally, the access token from the authorization endpoint. The authorization endpoint does not perform explicit client authentication but uses the redirect URI as an alternative way to verify the client's identity. After the client receives the tokens, it may expose them to the end user and applications using the same user agent. Hence, this flow is only used for untrusted clients to obtain identity tokens. Unlike the authorization code flow, no refresh token is generated in this flow.

The implicit flow consists of the following steps.

1. The client prepares and sends an authentication request to the authorization server.
2. The authorization server authenticates the end user.
3. The authorization server obtains the end user's consent.
4. If requested, the authorization server sends the end user back to the client with the ID token and optional access token.
5. The client validates the token and retrieves the end user's subject identifier.

When the relying party wishes to validate the client, it prepares the authentication request and sends it to the authorization endpoint. The client can send this request using the HTTP GET or the POST methods. For an implicit flow, the value of the `response_type` parameter in the request must consist of `id_token` and `token` as a space-delimited list, as shown in the following example.

```
https://myserver.example.com/authorize?
response_type=id_token%20token
&client_id=c6BhdTkqt3
&redirect_uri=https%3A%2F%2Fclient.example.org%2Fcb
&scope=openid%20profile &state=bflifjsldkj
&nonce=n-0S7_WzA3Mk
```

After authenticating the end user and obtaining consent, the authorization server responds with the `id_Token` and optionally `access_token`, as follows.

```
HTTP/1.1 302 Found
Location: https://client.myexample.com/cb#
    access_token=TlAV35hkKH
    &token_type=bearer
    &id_token=exJ0 ... NiJ8.eyJ2d ... I6IjJifX0.EfWt4Ru ... Zxso
    &expires_in=3600 &state=af0ifjsldkj
```

Hybrid Flow

The *hybrid flow* is a combination of the authorization code flow and the implicit flow, hence the name. This flow allows the client to immediately use the ID token to access the client's identity and retrieve an authorization code that can request a refresh token. The refresh token can gain long-term access to back-end resources.

The hybrid flow consists of the following high-level steps.

1. The client prepares and sends an authentication request to the authorization server.
2. The authorization server authenticates the end user.
3. The authorization server obtains end-user consent.
4. The authorization server returns the end user to the client with the authorization code. Depending on the `response_type` parameter, one or more parameters may also be returned.
5. The client requests a response using the authorization code at the token endpoint and receives a response containing the ID token and the access token in the response body.
6. The client validates the ID token and retrieves the end user's subject identifier.

In the hybrid flow, the client makes the authentication request to the authorization server. The `response_type` parameter in the request can have the following values.

- `code id_token`
- `code token`
- `code id_token token`

The following is an example request using the hybrid flow that the user agent would send to the authorization server in response to the client's corresponding HTTP 302 redirect response.

```
GET /authorize?
    response_type=code%20id_token
    &client_id=f6BhdKkqg
    &redirect_uri=https%3A%2F%2Fclient.example.org%2Fcb
    &scope=openid%20profile%20email
    &nonce=n-2S6_XzA2My &state=afligjslfku HTTP/1.1
Host: myserver.example.com
```

On receipt of the authentication request, the authorization server does the following validations before responding with a code and the ID token.

1. It validates the `scope` parameter present in the request.

2. It validates the `client_id` provided in the request and that the `redirect_uri` is the same as provided by the client at the time of registration.

3. It validates that all the mandatory parameters are in the request per the specifications.

4. It authenticates the end user or determines whether it is already authenticated.

5. It obtains the end user's consent for the client to access the protected resources.

After successfully processing the authentication request, the authorization endpoint returns the authorization code. Depending on the value in the `response_type` parameter, the authorization endpoint returns the `id_token` and, optionally, the `access_token` in a response format, as shown in the following example.

```
HTTP/1.1 302 Found
Location: https://client.myexample.org/cb#
code=Tplxl0AeZQQYbCS6WxSrIL &id_token=eyK0 ... NiK9.eyW1c
... I0IjIifL5.GeWt1Qu ... ZQsj &state=af9ifjs0dkj
```

Benefits of Integration with an Open Identity Provider

Applications often need to validate the identity of an end user. The following are possible ways to achieve this.

- A local database for user accounts and credentials for each app
- A central identity provider used by all end users to register apps and validate their information

With a local database for each app, end users must register for each new app they want to use. Many people find the registration process tedious and not a good customer experience. Maintaining separate user databases for an enterprise providing multiple apps brings in additional administrative and operational overhead. Hence, having a central identity provider provides a better option from user experience, maintenance, and administrative standpoints. Organizations such as Google and Facebook, which have large registered user bases, provide identity provider services that can be used with OpenID Connect. Organizations can streamline and simplify customer onboarding and login processes by integrating with identity provider services.

Protecting Against Cyber Threats

In the era of social, cloud, and mobile technologies, where enterprises expose their sensitive data and information via APIs in a zero-trust environment, protecting them against malicious attacks is paramount. Adding authentication and authorization to protect APIs is not enough. The API security framework must be able to detect any kind of cyber threat and take necessary actions to protect the back-end resources. To protect its APIs from different types of threats, an organization must build an API proxy in front of the APIs with an API management platform and implement security policies in these proxies to protect against such threats. Some of the most common types of threats are as follows.

- Injection threats
- Insecure direct object reference
- Sensitive data exposure
- Cross-site scripting (XSS)
- Cross-site resource forgery
- Bot attacks

The next few sections detail each threat and discuss options for protecting against them.

Injection Threats

Injection threats are common attacks in which attackers try to inject malicious code that, if executed on the server, can divulge sensitive information. Malicious code can be in any of the following forms.

- XML and JSON bombs
- Script injection attacks

XML and JSON Bombs

Attacks using XML and JSON bombs try to use structures that overload the parsers and thereby crash the service. Parsing corrupt or extremely complex XML/JSON payloads with a long list of elements, attributes, long tag names, values, or multiple levels of nesting can easily use up system resources—such as memory and CPU—and thus induce an application-level DoS attack. Such attacks can be mitigated by using XML and JSON threat protection policies.

XML threat protection policies can be used to check the message payload for the following and reject the message if any allowed limits are exceeded.

- The length of the names of elements, attributes, and namespace prefixes
- The length of the values of elements, attributes, and namespace prefixes
- The node depth of an element
- The number of attributes in an element
- The number of namespaces defined for an element
- The number of child elements for an element

JSON threat protection policies can be used to check the message payload for the following and reject the message if any of the allowed limits are exceeded.

- The length of a property's name within a JSON object
- The length of a property's string values within a JSON object
- The container depth of the JSON object
- The number of entries allowed in the JSON object of an element
- The number of array element entries allowed within a JSON object

Script Injection Attacks

Script injection attacks can be in various forms.

SQL Statement Injection

SQL statement injection is a technique in which a hacker presents a malicious SQL query to an application's input parameter. This can be dangerous if the application takes this input in the request to directly query into the database. For example, an API (`/employees?EmpName=<Employee Name>`) that provides the details of an employee from the employee database. This API is implemented to execute the following SQL statement in the database.

```
"select * from Employees where employeename =" + queryparam.
EmpName + ";"
```

In this situation, the effect can be catastrophic if an attacker invokes the API with the following parameters.

```
/employees?EmpName=Lary;drop table Employees;
```

Hackers can use SQL statements like the following to bypass authentication.

```
select userid FROM customerdata WHERE username = ' ' OR 1 = 1

-- customer_passwd = 'abcd';
```

Hence, any API that accepts input that can be inserted into an SQL database must be protected against SQL injection attacks. Regular expressions matching certain SQL keywords can detect malicious SQL content in the API request.

Script Injections

Script injections can be in various forms: JavaScript injection, XPath injection, or Java exception injection.

JavaScript is a powerful technology that modifies and sends data. Such scripts can reveal sensitive data if injected through an API. For example, hackers can get an unsuspecting user to execute a script in an

API request to get access to their authorization token or cookies. The token or the cookie can then be used to log in to the system and steal sensitive information. This is known as a *cross-site scripting* (XSS) attack.

Hackers also use XPath injections to gain unauthorized access to sensitive stored in an XML format.

Input data in API request parameters should be validated and sanitized to harden the APIs and protect against script injection attacks. Regular expressions can detect the presence of malicious JavaScript and XPath in the payload of an API request. However, no regular expression can stop all content-based attacks. Hence, multiple mechanisms should be combined to enable defense-in-depth.

Insecure Direct Object Reference

In an Insecure Direct Object Reference attack, the hacker modifies an existing API request to get access to information. The hacker may try to modify parameters in the request to get a higher level of access. For example, the following API provides access to user account information identified by the account number specified in the following URI.

```
GET http://api.myownbank.com/user/account/1234
```

A hacker can attempt to change the account number to get access to a different account. Alternatively, they may try to get admin access to an account using the following URL.

```
GET http://api.myownbank.com/admin/account/1234
```

This kind of attack can be prevented by using OAuth2/OpenID Connect with the right scopes set for the API.

Sensitive Data Exposure

APIs expose internal services and enterprise data. Some of this data may be customer-sensitive and highly confidential. Such sensitive data should always be kept private, encrypted, and masked. Regulatory compliance standards, such as PCI, HIPPA, and so forth, require that all sensitive data—such as credit card information and customers' private data—should always be encrypted. When sensitive data is sent in an API response, it should be encrypted and tokenized to prevent inadvertent exposure. Again, there may be scenarios where only certain API users may be authorized to view certain information sent in an API response. Some response data may be filtered or masked if another user calls the same API. Sensitive data logged in the debug trace should also be obfuscated.

Encryption of data in transit can be achieved by using SSL. Using SSL to encrypt sensitive data is the least any API should do. Another alternative is to selectively encrypt part of the API message that contains the sensitive information. This requires the API provider and the client to take on the additional overhead of managing the private/public key. Hence, deploying APIs that require selective encryption of sensitive data can be complex.

Cross-Site Scripting (XSS)

Cross-site scripting (XSS) is among the top 10 open web application security threats. It is a script injection attack that exploits a vulnerability in a website the victim visits. The attacker injects malicious code, generally JavaScript, into otherwise benign and trusted websites. When a user visits the website, the malicious JavaScript is delivered to the victim's browser, which appears to be a legitimate part of the website. The user information or data is compromised when these scripts are executed on the non-suspecting user's browser.

Figure 7-10 shows an example of how an XSS attack is done.

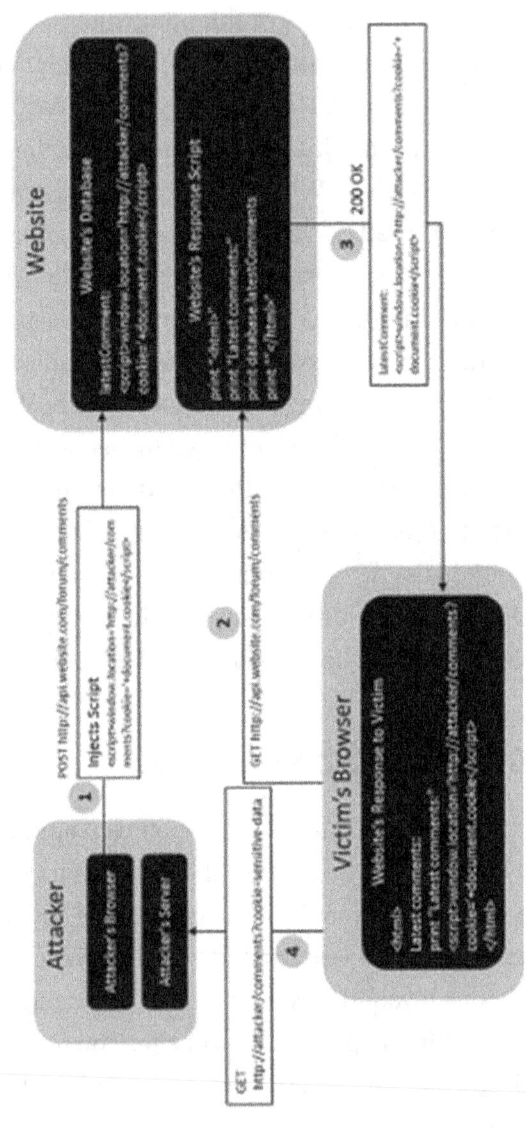

Figure 7-10. XSS attack approach

The following describes the process of an XSS attack.

1. The attacker injects malicious JavaScript into a website's database using a POST request to submit a form.
2. An unsuspecting victim requests a page from the website using a GET request.
3. The website responds to the GET request with a malicious script from its database.
4. The victim's browser executes the malicious script in the response, sending sensitive data to the attacker's server.

Hence, to protect against XSS attacks, all user input for an API request must be encoded and validated. Encoding helps to escape the user input so that the browser interprets it only as data and not as code. Validations must include schema and data type validations and check for the presence of any malicious scripts. Adding a Content-Security-Policy header in the HTTP response constrains the browser from viewing a webpage by only using resources (script/stylesheet, etc.) loaded from a trusted site. With a properly defined Content-Security-Policy header, even if the attacker succeeds in injecting the malicious code, it is not executed on the browser since the attacker's site is not among the list of trusted sites.

Cross-Site Resource Forgery (CSRF or XSRF)

Cross-site resource forgery is a type of attack where a user is tricked into executing unwanted actions on a web application in which they are already logged in. The attacker can target the web application via the victim's authenticated browser. Using social engineering like email or chats, the victim is tricked into clicking a link that sends a forged request to a server where they are already authenticated. Since the user is authenticated, it is difficult for a web application to distinguish between a legitimate request and a forged one. This type of attack is different from XSS. In XSS, the attacker exploits the user's trust in a website; in CSRF, the attacker exploits the website's trust. Figure 7-11 shows an example of how an attacker can launch and execute a CSRF attack.

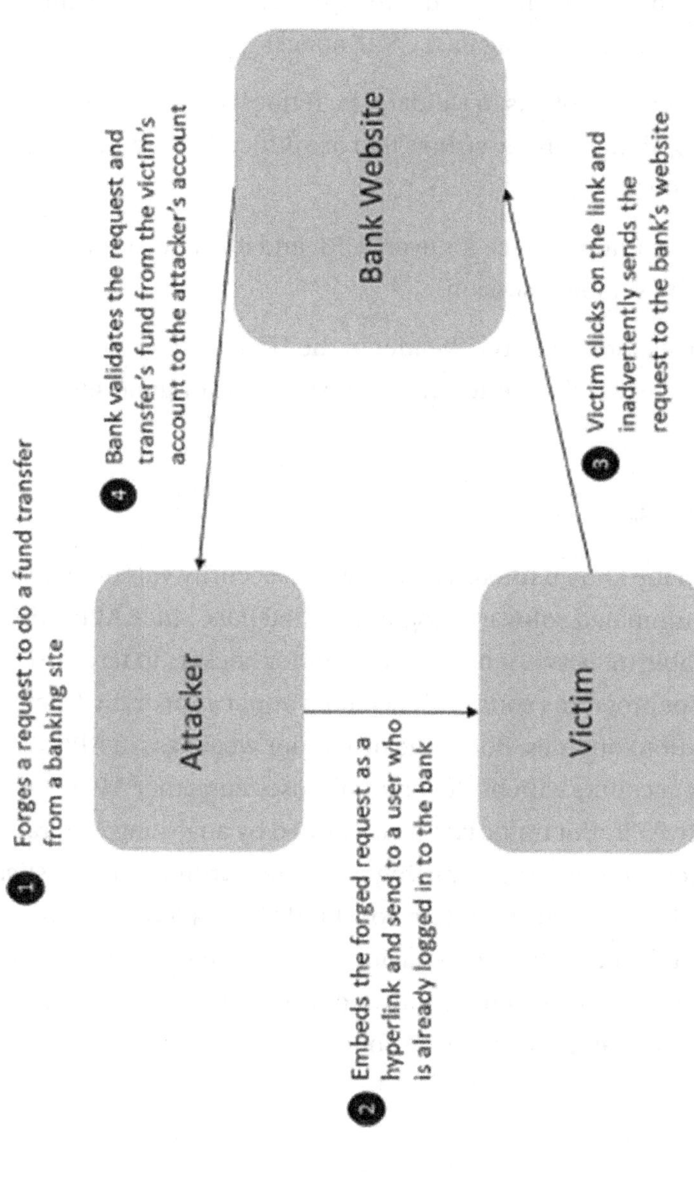

Figure 7-11. *CSRF attack approach*

An attacker uses CSRF to execute unauthorized fund transfers, change passwords or customer data, and many other things that can be detrimental to both the business and the user. The following techniques can be used to protect APIs against CSRF attacks.

- Use OAuth tokens to validate the requests. Tokens are long alphanumeric strings that are difficult for attackers to guess.
- Use a unique nonce for every URL and form in addition to the standard session.
- Check for a "referrer" header in the HTTP request to ensure that the request has come from the original site.

Bot Attacks

In addition to the known threats, a new type of security vulnerability arises from using automated software programs called *bots*. Since APIs provide a programmable interface, it becomes easier for hackers to target APIs using bots. Bot programs constantly scan the application infrastructure for security vulnerabilities. Bot traffic probes for weakness in APIs, abuses guest accounts with brute force, and uses customer API keys to access private APIs. Bot traffic can be identified by analyzing API traffic and access behavior patterns. By using machine learning and statistical models, an adaptive security system constantly learns "good behaviors," which helps it distinguish "bad behaviors" and enforce dynamic policies that block bots from accessing a protected resource. Bot traffic can be identified as anomalous activities, as follows.

- Logical walk-throughs of the application resource paths by bots
- Requests originating from a bot network, low-reputation IP address, ISP, or compromised proxies and devices (Malware installed in rooted devices and PCs may be used to generate bot traffic.)
- Unexpected high traffic volumes from certain IP addresses or endpoints
- High traffic volumes to URIs (resources) that end users do not generally access
- High rates of form submissions with slight variations in the input parameters (This is a common technique bots use when applying brute force to get access.)
- High error rates on access to resources, especially those available to privileged users or applications

API security strategies must consider how bot activities can be easily identified by analyzing API access anomalies. Research has shown that more than 50% of Internet traffic involves bot activities. Retailers and e-commerce service providers that provide dynamic pricing, loyalty programs, financial services, and so forth are on the radar of bot attacks. Bots are known to target APIs with any valuable or sensitive data. Bot traffic can have a major load impact on API infrastructure, cause performance concerns, and hurt a company's brand and bottom line due to content theft. Advanced API analytics functionality with machine learning capabilities that can identify malicious bot activities should be considered for building a robust and adaptive API security system.

Considerations for Designing an API Security Framework

There are many aspects to consider in building the right API security framework. Some of the most important considerations include (but are not limited to) the following.

- **The nature of the asset or the service being exposed as APIs**: What is the impact/loss if data gets into the hands of someone who is not supposed to see it or if a service goes down?
- **The regulatory compliance requirements for securing an API**: Which regulatory standards should be followed for securing an API?
- **The authentication requirements for using the API**: Is it OK to authenticate only the client? Or is it necessary to authenticate even the end users before they can use the APIs?
- **The authorization is needed before a client app can access an API resource**: Should the end user authorize access to an API before the client app can access it?
- **Threats from API consumers**: How can consumers and attackers misuse the API and use loopholes to gain unauthorized access?

API Security Threat Model

To develop the right security strategy for APIs, the security architect must create a threat model for API exposure and consumption. The following are some security threats that need to be considered in API security.

- Unauthorized applications and users may imitate that of another app or user
- Denial of service due to rogue apps or inadvertent errors
- Replay attacks
- Man-in-the-middle attacks
- Data tampering
- Malicious data injection attacks
- Theft of credentials, API keys, and tokens
- Network eavesdropping

Best Practices for API Security Implementation

An API-centric security architecture that enables defense-in-depth security practices must be adopted to protect data and services from API security threats. This approach builds a security capability that includes role-based access control, fine-grained policies for authentication and authorization, and threat protection against malicious payload content and DoS attacks. The following are some API security recommendations for building a robust API security architecture.

- All API communication involving sensitive data must be secured and encrypted using TLS.
- Build a mechanism to detect malicious content injections and defend against such attacks. This protection is ideally built at the beginning of the API request flow at the edge of the network.
- All incoming and outgoing data must be validated and sanitized. Input data type and format validation must be done at a minimum for all APIs with input request parameters. This prevents any malicious content from entering the system.
- APIs accepting input parameters via HTTP POST or PUT methods must validate the payload. Such validations detect large payloads or malformed content that can overload computing resources. Replay attacks and message tampering can also be detected early through these validations. Input parameters passed as query parameters in GET methods should also be validated to check for malicious content.
- Use a combination of approaches to identify the source of the request. IP address validation may not be sufficient to identify the originator of a request since IP addresses can be easily spoofed.
- Protection via API key validation can be used only for non-sensitive and read-only data. API key validation identifies the applications and developers making API calls. If the data exposed is non-sensitive and read-only, such as Google Maps APIs, tracking consumer identities through API key validation might be sufficient.

- Each API key should have limited permissions as required for its intended usage. Granting excessive privileges to API keys can increase the risk of its misuse.
- Implement API quotas and monitor application usage based on API keys to prevent abuse and DoS attacks.
- API keys must be long, complex, and generated using a secure random generator. They should be stored securely and encrypted in secure key stores/key vaults. Regularly rotating the API keys is recommended, and they should never be hardcoded in the application logic or configuration files.
- Application usage of API keys should be monitored and audited to prevent misuse. The audit logs for API keys should be reviewed regularly to detect and respond to potential security issues.
- Use IP whitelisting to restrict API access to trusted sources only.
- Use OAuth2 for public or private APIs that are intended for use by native and mobile apps. With OAuth2, users are not required to share their password with the app and device used. When a user authenticates in an OAuth flow, she enters her credentials in a web browser screen rather than the application itself. Hence, the application never gets to see the user's password. This becomes a crucial factor when untrusted developers build these apps. Since OAuth uses tokens for authorization, API providers can revoke these tokens in any compromise without the need for users to change their passwords.

- The client_ID and client_secrets needed for OAuth token generation must be stored securely outside the client application code using secure storage mechanisms.
- Use OAuth scope to grant limited and required access to clients.
- OAuth access tokens should be short-lived to prevent misuse. Fresh token flows should be implemented where tokens may have to be used for a long duration. In case an access token has been compromised, it should be revoked by the resource owner to prevent any misuse.
- Use OpenID Connect for APIs that need end-user identity and authentication. The ID token provided in the OpenID Connect flow can be used by the client or relying party to validate the end user. The API provider can also use it to validate the end user trying to get access to a protected API resource.
- Use two-way SSL or TLS with mutual authentication for APIs used by a limited number of internal or partner systems authenticating the client. If the API is open to all, maintaining client certificates for many clients to implement two-way SSL may become a real challenge. The Basic authentication scheme can also be a suitable alternative for authenticating partners.
- Consider using *multi-factor authentication* (MFA) for APIs providing access to sensitive and critical operations.

- All sensitive information must be encrypted in transit using SSL.
- Integrate an API management platform with enterprise's *security information and event management* (SIEM) tools to detect, analyze, and respond to security threats.

  Overall, ensure that APIs are protected against OWASP API security top ten attacks using a combination of one or more techniques described earlier. Figure 7-12 shows an approach to implementing end-to-end security for APIs using an API gateway.

Figure 7-12 illustrates the recommended order in which API security policies must be implemented in an API gateway.

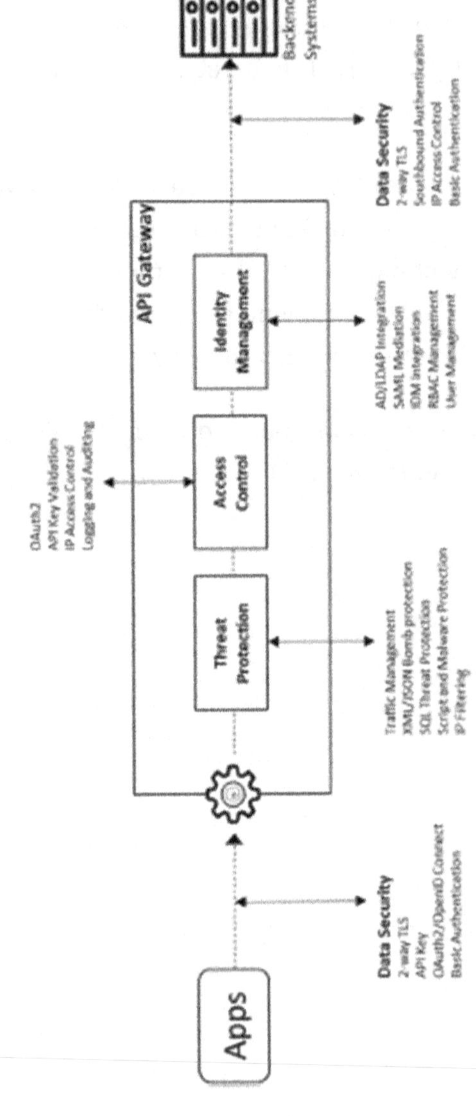

Figure 7-12. *Approach for building end-to-end API security*

CHAPTER 8

API Monetization

APIs securely expose digital assets and services of real value to end users and partners. Since they provide value to end users, it makes more sense to monetize the services and the APIs and build a business model for them. API monetization refers to the process by which organizations generate revenue or derive financial gains by allowing access to their products and services via APIs. It is all about creating the right business plan for your API to generate additional income. Having the right monetization model for APIs helps businesses reap the benefits of their investment in APIs.

This chapter looks at the various API monetization models and how an API management platform can monetize APIs and open the doors to new revenue opportunities. This chapter also touches upon the strategy and best practices for API monetization.

Why Monetize APIs?

One of the main business goals for any organization to build APIs is to increase their business revenue. So, what better way can there be than to monetize their APIs? According to Google's *The State of API Economy 2021 Report*, the usage of APIs exploded across many industries during the pandemic. API usage grew by 400% in healthcare and 125% in the financial services industry between 2020 and 2021. Increased API usage can drive more revenue if they are monetized. API monetization can help organizations in the following ways.

B. De, *API Management*, https://doi.org/10.1007/979-8-8688-0054-2_8

- **Generate revenue:** Organizations can create new streams of income by charging users for API access. The users would be willing to pay for API usage to get access to the data, services, and facilities provided by the APIs.
- **Diversify the business model:** With API monetization, organizations can get an additional revenue stream other than their traditional products and services. This revenue stream can be useful in situations when traditional products and services are impacted during uncertain economic times.
- **Sell unused resources:** Many resources currently under-utilized or unused within the organization may be significant to others outside the organization. Exposing those resources using APIs with the right monetization model can attract new customers and generate additional revenue.
- **Improve brand value:** Instead of providing a service free of cost, monetizing it with the right model increases its importance and value to its customers. When customers pay for any service, they expect the service to adhere to certain SLAs. The provider must also meet those SLAs when any consumer is paying for its usage. The customers also value those APIs more since they meet certain standards and are not free. Monetizing APIs thus improves the brand value of the product and service provided by the API.

Which Digital Assets Can Be Monetized?

APIs share your data and services with front-end applications in an easy and scalable manner. With APIs, you can track usage and billing information in real time. But what kind of data or services can be monetized via APIs? The following are some examples.

- Digital content such as maps, images, and analytical data are assets that developers are willing to pay to get access to.
- Digital services include address verification, credit checks, messaging, and location services.
- Payment gateway providers charge a certain percentage fee for every payment transaction processed through their gateway.
- APIs facilitate the sale of physical or electronic products on an e-commerce platform.

How to Increase Revenue Using APIs

Now let's look at how APIs can be used to increase revenue.

Increase Customer Channels

APIs expose enterprise services to third-party consumers. Developers build apps that consume these services via the APIs. These apps solve different business problems for different use cases. These apps open new avenues of customer interaction. Traffic through the APIs increases as more third-party applications are built and consumed. Other applications can also use APIs for faster integration with your services. With this integration, additional traffic gets routed to services. Thus, with a variety of apps and newer integrations using APIs, the inbound traffic to your services continues to grow as end consumers use them.

To summarize, APIs can increase the inbound traffic as follows.

- By providing extensions to build apps for end users
- By building a platform for integration on which numerous apps can be created and marketed

Using APIs to build a platform for integration takes advantage of the cross-marketing potential of the app economy. For example, APIs provided by Uber can be used by travel aggregators within their applications to book cabs and provide customers with a completely integrated travel experience. This helps the aggregator provide a better customer experience and increases traffic and revenue for Uber.

The goal of an API provider should be to create a growing ecosystem of third-party developers who can build innovative apps using APIs that provide a richer customer experience. This multiplies the chances of acquiring new consumers and increasing revenue. It also reduces business risks due to referral traffic from other third-party apps using your APIs.

Increase Customer Retention

Customer retention is the next important factor in generating more revenue and profit. After a certain point, business coming from repeat customers is more than that from new customers. Hence, customer retention becomes a key to the success of your business. The more people use apps that rely on your API, the higher the market share for that API. After a critical mass of users using an app is reached, it becomes difficult for the third-party app developer to migrate them to another API provider. When end users become accustomed to your apps and APIs, it is even harder for competitors to beat you. Thus, it becomes harder for users to switch to the competition, which increases your retention rate.

As an API provider, you must build a platform that grows the customer base and increases retention. To increase customer retention, build highly scalable APIs, which are highly quality and easy to use. APIs that provide personalized experiences with tailored content and recommendations based on customer behavior are more likely to have sticky and repeat customers. APIs that provide e-commerce services with loyalty programs to incentivize end customers and app developers for repeat transactions can increase retention. Gamification of API usage can keep users engaged and motivated to return. Swift responses and resolution of issues can improve customer satisfaction and retention. Implementing APIs that enhance the customer experience, add convenience, and offer value can increase customer satisfaction and loyalty, ultimately leading to higher retention rates.

Upsell Premium and Value-Added Services

Value-added and interesting API features can be made available at a premium to those who have purchased access. For example, a communication app may provide two-party voice services for free, but a multi-party voice conferencing service is available at a cost. Alternatively, customers may be charged after they have exceeded a particular limit. For example, the Google Maps APIs are available for free and with paid options. By default, Google Places API users get free access to 1,000 requests per day. Enhanced access requires credit card validation. This model attracts users to use the API, and they pay for increased usage only if they see value in it.

Well-established businesses with a good consumer base should use this model. Alternatively, the service provided by the API should be of high business value to the consumer.

Increase Affiliate Channels

As an API provider, sometimes turning third-party developers building apps using company APIs into an affiliate makes sense. With an affiliate program, the third-party app developer is motivated to build apps for your APIs and drive more traffic. This promotes your APIs and drives additional revenue for the company. If any of the apps from the affiliate partners become successful, it can drive tremendous revenue to the API program.

A reverse model can also be adopted, in which the API provider becomes the affiliate for the app. As an API provider, you may want to showcase how various apps have integrated your APIs. From the showcase page, you may drive traffic to your partners and gain a finder's fee for yourself. In this way, third parties assist you with app development and joint marketing and even pay you to drive customers to them.

Increase Distribution Channels

Often, a company's business depends on the number of people that get access to its contents and services. The more people interact or use the content, the more revenue is generated. In this situation, increasing the number of distribution channels for its content makes sense. New distribution channels via APIs can be used to share the content. Smaller companies may use APIs provided by large API providers to access data and resources they share in a revenue-sharing model. For example, small travel companies may use APIs provided by Expedia and Booking.com to provide hotel information on their websites. Expedia and Booking.com use APIs as a distribution channel to share hotel information in a revenue-sharing model with others looking to use it. This content distribution model helps the API provider increase their revenue by integrating their APIs into a third-party platform that needs to use their services. Smaller companies can quickly start their business by integrating these APIs into their platforms. In contrast, large companies providing these APIs gain from the additional business brought in by integrating these newer distribution channels.

API Monetization Models

An organization's data and services can be exposed and shared with partners via APIs. APIs extend the reach of an organization's core assets and bring in new revenue channels. The monetization model can be simple or complex, depending on the value and use of the assets. However, they can be broadly classified into the following four categories.

- A **free model** is used when the organization has a set of lower-value assets to advertise through different channels and devices. This model can be used even when the asset has a high demand, but the organization does not yet have the budget to develop and market all use cases for asset use. Examples include APIs that provide information about a store branch, location, or product catalog information.
- A **fee-based model** is used when the organization has assets that are of high value to the consumer. The consumer of this API is ready to pay for the value derived from it. The value to the consumer can be based on per use or the kind of data provided. Examples include APIs for payment processing, credit checks, or that provide valuable analytics data.

- In a **revenue-sharing model**, the organization shares revenue from using its service or product with the app developer consuming the APIs. This incentivizes the developer to build apps for the API provider that can expand its customer reach. An advertising API is a good example. Developers can embed advertisements within their apps by using the advertising APIs.

  The revenue earned by the organization through advertisements served on these apps can be shared with the developer. Revenue sharing can also be through an affiliate program. Affiliates get paid a share of the revenue as long as the customers brought in through their network programs remain customers of the API provider. For example, the Rdio affiliate program paid a cut of the subscription fee to affiliates as long as the subscriber recruited by an affiliate remained a Rdio subscriber. The revenue sharing for an affiliate program can also be based on the type of service the subscribers sign up for.

- In an **indirect model**, the API provider and the consumer mutually benefit. For example, using Facebook and Twitter APIs provides an easy way to sign up users, which continuously expands their consumer base. With an indirect monetization model, the API is free for the consumer. However, it influences and increases the sale of the underlying product of the organization. These APIs can be used to grow the ecosystem that would use the main product, enable product differentiation to make them more attractive to consumers, and thus grow revenue through the sale of the main product.

The first three monetization models can be further categorized, as described in the next few sections.

The Free Model

Free APIs are available for consumption at no charge to the consumer or the end user. Making APIs available for free drives adoption and popularity. As the adoption increases, the provider organization's brand value increases. This can also help the API provider expand into newer channels to increase customer reach. Facebook APIs are an example of free APIs. The company's Like and Share APIs embed the Like and Share buttons into any website or app, which facilitated Facebook expanding its reach and enrich its social reach and position. Facebook is a leader in the social recommendation space. As of 2015, Facebook had about 2.7 billion likes per day and around 8.8 million websites using its Like button.

The *freemium* model is a variation of the free model. The variations are based on duration, quantity, or a combination thereof. In a freemium model, the API consumer can freely access the API for a certain duration, usage quantity, or a combination of both. Another approach to the freemium model is based on the API's features. With a photo API, the free model may provide photos with watermarks or in a lower resolution. However, a paid model may provide higher-resolution images without any watermark.

- **Duration-based free model**: The consumer is not charged for API usage for a certain duration. For example, the consumer may sign up for free access to the APIs for the first month and then be charged from the second month onward.

- **Quantity-based free model**: The API provider provides free access to the API for a certain number of calls. For example, Pearson provides 5,000 API calls for free for its FT Press API. This means that the developer does not get charged for the first 5,000 calls, which gives them the flexibility to try out the APIs before they decide to buy. The Google Maps API provides geocoding services for free for up to 2,500 requests per day. So, if a consumer app makes up to 2,500 requests per day, it continues using the API for free but must pay if the daily traffic exceeds this limit.
- **Hybrid free model**: The API provider combines duration and quantity with free access. The consumer is charged as soon as either of these thresholds is reached. For example, an API call can be free for the first 5,000 calls or 30 days. In this case, the API consumer is charged as soon as 5,000 calls are made or after 30 days have passed, whichever occurs first.

The Fee-Based Model (a.k.a. Developer Pays Model)

An organization often exposes many assets of high value to its consumers. An organization assigns a price point to its digital assets that consumers are willing to pay to access. For example, Amazon Web Services (AWS) provides various services via APIs, including storage, databases, computing power, deployment, and management options. Consumers are willing to pay to use these services rather than hosting them in their own data centers. A fee-based model is perfect for monetizing these assets via API. With a pay-as-you-go model, Amazon generated $750 million in revenue in 2011. NASA saved $1 million after it moved its IT assets to

AWS. A fee-based model can monetize APIs that provide access to such assets. Analytical data or payment processing services are examples. The fee-based model can also have different variations, as follows.

- **One-time fee**: In this model, the provider charges the consumer a one-time subscription fee. The consumer then gets unlimited access to the APIs that she paid for.
- **Subscription fee**: In this model, the consumer is charged at a regular interval—weekly, monthly, or any other period that the API provider chooses—for using APIs. A subscription fee for a group of APIs is a typical example of this model. The volume of API calls allowed in a time period may be fixed or volume-banded, in which the subscriber pays for the excess use of APIs beyond the set limit.
- **Pay-per-API transaction**: This model has no minimum fee, and the consumer pays for the number of API transactions made. AWS uses this model to monetize its APIs; developers pay only for what they need to use.
- **Pay by transaction volume**: This monetization model is based on the volume of API calls or data accessed or returned in the response. This leads to a tiered approach for monetization, in which the rate applied depends on the usage tier. Google charges its AdWords API consumers a fee for every 1,000 API calls.
- **Tiered pricing model**: With a tiered pricing approach, the consumer is charged different rates for different bands of API calls. For example, 0 to 1,000 API calls in a month may cost $0.02 per API call, whereas 1,001 to 5,000 API calls may cost $0.01 per transaction, and an even lower rate for more than 5,000 calls within the

same time period. Typically, higher-usage band rates are less per call than lower bands. Charging lower rates for high-volume usage promotes developers/partners to use higher volumes. The API provider may also set other custom attributes for payment, such as the number of records accessed or returned in the response or the number of bytes/megabytes stored.

The Revenue-Sharing Model

In a revenue-sharing model, the API provider exposes its digital assets to partners who sell them on their websites and via apps. The provider shares a percentage of the revenue earned through the sale of these assets with the third party. Companies like Walgreens, Expedia, and Sears have successfully used this model to sell their products through third-party apps and websites hosted by their affiliate partners. This model helps the API provider extend reach by expanding business through various digital channels, increasing sales through affiliates, and reducing overhead costs by reducing physical branches. There are various types of revenue-sharing models, as follows.

- **Cost per action (CPA)**: The API provider pays only when a specific action happens, such as a product being purchased or a video being watched.
- **Revenue sharing**: The API provider shares a part of the revenue earned through API traffic routed from third-party apps. The revenue sharing can be as follows.
    - **Fixed revenue share**: The API provider shares a fixed percentage of the sales revenue earned.

  - **Flexible revenue share**: The API provider shares a variable percentage of the sales revenue earned through API sales. The percentage varies based on the volume of sales made over time.
  - **One-time revenue**: In this model, the affiliate partner receives a one-time referral payment for every subscribing customer through its website or app.

- **Recurring revenue**: In this model, the affiliate partner receives a recurring referral payment for every customer routed to the API provider through a website or app until the subscriber remains a customer of the API provider. For example, Rdio paid their affiliates each time a new subscriber signed up.

The API provider must generate periodic billing documents in a revenue-sharing model and apply a commonly used tax model to the generated statement.

Monetization Concepts

To set up monetization of your APIs, you need to be aware of the various concepts for API monetization. This section explains the basic concepts of API monetization.

API Product

APIs should be sold as a product for which developers or consumers will use and pay. An API product is a collection of APIs. Related API resources can be bundled into an API product and published to the developer community. Developers sign up to use APIs in an API product of their choice.

An API provider can create products by combining APIs for different use cases. So, instead of providing all APIs as a list of resources, related APIs that solve a specific business need can be combined into separate API products. For example, in the telco industry, APIs for sending SMS and MMS and retrieving their statuses can be clubbed into a single *Messaging API* product. In contrast, billing-related API resources can be combined into a *Billing API* product.

API products can also control access to a specific bundle of API resources. Internal API resources can be bundled into one API product, while external APIs can also be bundled into another product. API product attributes can also limit the number of API calls allowed for a consumer within a given time interval. So, multiple API products can be created to club the same resources, with different limits set for each. For example, a Silver API product might allow a consumer to make 1,000 API requests per day, while a Gold API product could allow unlimited API requests in a day. Another way to configure API products is to club APIs that provide read-only access to resources into a free API product. APIs that provide read/write access to resources are in a paid API product.

Developers can register their apps and select one or more API products to associate with their apps. The API key associated with an app accesses all the API resources available within the associated API product.

API Package

An API package is a collection of API products an API provider wants to monetize. An API provider may create one or more API packages with different combinations of API products. An API package is presented to the developer, who selects the rate plan they want to sign up for. One or more rate plans for monetization may be associated with an API package.

Rate Plan

A *rate plan* specifies the monetization approach of your APIs. It specifies how to charge developers for API usage or share revenue. The rate plan can be a prepaid or a postpaid plan with a charging model that is a fixed fee, a variable fee, or a freemium model, or may even be customized for the developer. The rate plan depends on the model followed for monetizing the APIs. At the time of registration, developers select an active rate plan associated with the API package. If an API package does not have an associated rate plan, developers can use the APIs within that package without any fee.

The rate plan can have an associated scope, which controls the availability of the plan to all developers, a select group of developers, or a developer category. This controls the rate plans, which a developer logged into a developer portal can view and select while registering an app.

A rate plan normally defines the following.

- The name and a brief description of the rate plan
- The developers (or the developer category) who can view the plan
- The currency for payment of the rate plan
- Frequency of payment for the rate plan, such as weekly, monthly, quarterly, or yearly
- Payment due dates
- Any recurring or setup fee information

Figure 8-1 shows the relationship between the API product, API package, and rate plan.

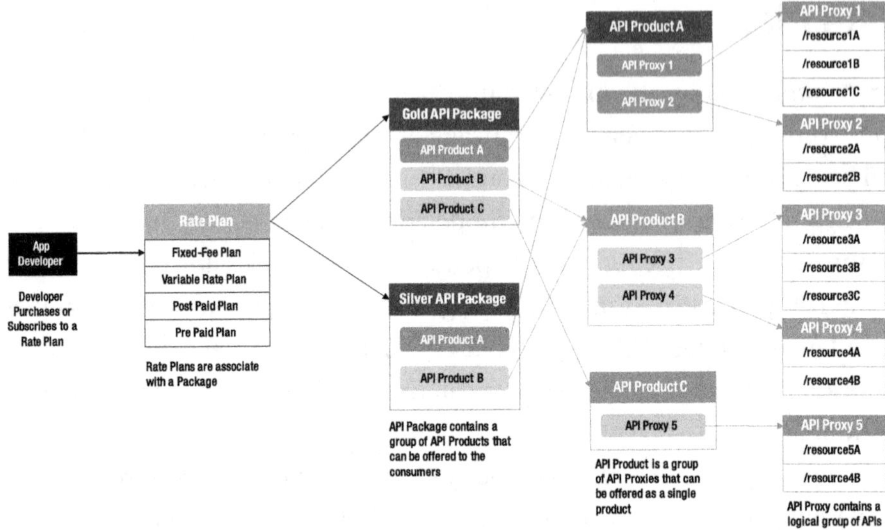

***Figure 8-1.** Relationship between components for API monetization*

Billing Documents

Billing is another important aspect of API monetization. Once APIs have been monetized, generating consumer bills at regular intervals is necessary. Some API management platforms provide an integrated billing solution that automatically generates billing documents such as invoices and revenue share statements at pre-scheduled intervals. These documents may be viewed in a draft state before publishing to their intended recipients. An API provider may want to first make adjustments to the billing documents to increase or decrease the revenue share or fees for a variety of reasons. API monetization also requires that the API provider manage credits, prepaid balances, and refunds. Credits can be provided by reducing the invoice charge or the developer's API traffic usage count. API monetization should also allow the API provider to refund a developer's purchase transactions.

Monetization Reports

Monetization without adequate reporting facilities creates havoc. API monetization should also be supported with reports that help API providers reconcile the data if required. These reports determine which applications, developers, API product bundles, or API products had transaction activity for a given date range. The following are some of the reports that should be generated.

- A **billing report** provides details of the developer activities that are charged. The report could cover a single billing month or a configurable period.
- A **prepaid balance report** provides a view of the balance refills that a prepaid developer has done in a month to be able to reconcile the payments received from the payment processor.
- A **revenue report** provides a view of the activities that result in revenue through API usage. It is useful to analyze the performance and popularity of the API package across developers.

API Monetization Best Practices

API monetization is a combination of art and science, and no direct guidelines can apply to all enterprises. The following are some of the best practices to effectively monetize APIs.

- You must understand the value it provides in the ecosystem to monetize APIs. Take an "outside-in" view of the APIs to determine their value to target customers.

- Use direct monetization models for APIs that provide direct access to important data or valuable digital assets that consumers are ready to pay for.
- Do not monetize APIs that provide indirect values. Instead, give away the API to drive adoption.
- Set up a developer portal to publish API documentation, sample code, and testing tools to make APIs developer-friendly.
- Market your APIs with an API evangelist to advocate their value and collaborate with the app developer community. Market APIs through conferences and events.
- Use a centralized API management platform to monitor consumer API traffic and set up monetization models for the APIs. Never embed monetization logic inside the service code.
- Package your APIs into a product and associate the right monetization model with a rate plan that is simple and transparent.
- Conduct market research and competitor analysis to determine the right price and attractive point for the APIs. Factors like the value API provides, ease of integration, and the ROI for the users should be considered to determine the price point.
- Set up monitoring for API performance and usage. Fine-tune and make necessary adjustments to the monetization model and pricing based on feedback from the API consumers.
- Provide analytics and reporting tools to let users track their API usage and understand costs.

There is no one-size-fits-all approach to monetization. It is an iterative approach to determine the right monetization model for the APIs. The monetization strategy should be tailored to the specific industry, target audience, and the unique value that the API brings to the market. The strategy should be assessed periodically and adapted as needed to reap the benefits of API through its monetization.

CHAPTER 9

API Testing Strategy

API testing is different from other GUI-based application testing. It tests the programmatic interface that allows access to the data or business logic. Instead of testing the application's look and feel, API testing tests the business logic of the remote software component and its communication mechanism. Hence, API testing is performed using special-purpose software that sends requests to the API and reads the response received.

This chapter looks at the importance of API testing, challenges, various testing considerations, and approaches for testing an API.

The Importance of API Testing

An API exposes business data and services through a defined standard-based interface. Developers use the interface to build applications that are dependent on the API. These applications use the API per the defined contract. The application invokes the API with a wide range and combination of data input. The API response depends on the input data and parameter combination. The API traffic pattern also varies by app usage. The API should be able to gracefully handle the traffic at different loads. With all these permutations and combinations, the importance of API testing greatly increases. The API should be tested against all expected data inputs to validate that it behaves as defined in the contract. There should also be testing for different load scenarios. API security testing is yet another important aspect.

B. De, *API Management*, https://doi.org/10.1007/979-8-8688-0054-2_9

Challenges in API Testing

Testing an API needs special software that sends messages to an API endpoint defined in the interface, gets the output, and logs and analyzes the response. The test software should programmatically generate messages with different combinations of input parameters to test the API interface and the underlying business logic. Since APIs do not have a visual graphical user interface, testing them needs deeper technical expertise about the API technologies. API testers must understand the desired API functionality from its defined specification document and design the test cases. Multiple endpoints, input parameters, and response data structures increase the complexity of API testing as testing must cover multiple combinations with different parameters. This is time-consuming and mandates API testing to be automated, which is the real challenge.

APIs developed for a business may require the execution of multiple APIs in a particular sequence. It could be a fixed or dynamic sequence based on the result of the previous API. The test execution may also require passing in dynamic values for different input parameters in varied combinations. Some of these parameters' values may need to be derived from an earlier API execution in the test scenario. These requirements necessitate the need for an automated API testing approach. It requires tools and frameworks that automate the test scenarios and reduce the execution time for running API tests with different permutations and input parameter combinations.

Often, APIs are exposed via an API management platform configured to implement different policies on top of the API business logic. These policies may implement security, traffic throttling, data transformation, routing, or orchestration. API testing strategy must consider testing these policies in the API gateway.

Testing API traffic management is tricky. APIs might be protected by policies that throttle traffic based on the nature of the consuming app, the time of day, or other parameters, such as location, originating IP, and so forth. The traffic management policies allow a certain number of requests within a given time interval. The interval can be calendar time or a rotating time. Accurately testing API traffic management rules may require precisely coordinating test executions, which can be challenging. Traffic management policies may also control the number of simultaneous connections to back-end services. Ensuring that excess connections are not made to the back-end services and that calls are rejected with proper error messages when the threshold limit is reached are also challenges in API testing.

Test data management is another challenge in API testing. Testing a set of APIs may involve managing a wide range of data sets to cover different permutations and combinations of API input parameters. Managing these data sets in multiple test environments could easily become a challenge. It needs a proper test data management approach to effectively manage the test data. If not managed properly, the test results are erroneous and misleading. For example, if an API key or OAuth access token generated in a SIT environment is used to test APIs in a UAT environment, it would result in errors.

The other big challenge with API testing is culture. Since automation is necessary for API testing, testers need to code to test the APIs. Some of the traditional UI testing is manual. And getting testers with experience in coding may not always be easy. Additionally, testers may need to know the latest API testing frameworks, such as Chai and Mocha, which adds to the challenges.

API Testing Considerations

APIs provide an interface for communicating with back-end business data and assets. The actual business logic is normally out of the scope of the API implementation. Only some exceptional cases—such as peripheral business logic like data validation—may be implemented in the API layer. Hence, API testing should focus on testing the following aspects of the API.

- API interface specifications
- API documentation
- API security

API Interface Specification Testing

An API interface defines the way to communicate with the API. It defines the input parameters required by the API and the expected response from the API. The input parameters may be passed as query parameters, in the body as form parameters, or as payload in JSON or XML formats or HTTP headers. API testing should validate the API response when the parameters are passed as documented in the specification. If the API specification describes the parameters to be passed in a query parameter, testing should verify the success and error scenarios for the right and wrong combination of parameters and parameter values. For example, consider testing an API that fetches the product details using an API interface (such as at `https://api.foo.com/v1/products`). This API may accept multiple optional query parameters as inputs—including category, name, and SKU, which may be passed as follows.

`https://api.foo.com/v1/products?<queryParamName>=<queryParamValue>`

Or, for example, `https://api.foo.com/v1/products?category=Electronics`

The approach to test this API should include the following.

- What is the default API behavior when no query parameters are passed?
- What is the API behavior when the right query parameter with the right value is passed?

- What is the API behavior when the parameter name passed is incorrect?
- What is the API behavior when the parameter does not have any value?
- What is the API behavior when the parameter value is incorrect?
- When multiple query parameters are passed in the right combination, what is the API behavior?
- When multiple query parameters are passed in incorrect combinations, what is the API behavior?
- What is the default data format for the API response when no information about the requested data format is passed?
- What is the data format for the API response for both success and error conditions?
- What is the HTTP response status code for different success and error conditions?
- What is the API response for unexpected HTTP methods, headers, and URLs?

API Documentation Testing

The API test team must validate that the API interface documentation is correct and up-to-date. When new versions of APIs are released, the API documentation should be updated to reflect the changes; otherwise, this can cause frustration among the developer community consuming the APIs, hindering effective adoption. Hence, with every release of a new version of an API, its corresponding documentation should be tested to ensure that it reflects the latest updates. The API test team should also ensure that the documentation provides enough information to interact with the API. If the API documentation is interactive, it should also be tested to validate proper responses for every API operation.

API Security Testing

APIs provide an access point for business services and data to consumers—internal and external. Depending on the criticality of the data, the API is a point of attack. Hackers may want unauthorized access to system resources for undue benefits. Hackers are always in search of security holes through exposed APIs. There could also be DoS attacks that put an API in an unavailable or unstable state. Hacked APIs can damage the brand value of an enterprise. Hence, testing API security is very important. This section looks at the various aspects of API security testing.

Authentication and Authorization

Testing an API's access mechanisms and access control policies is paramount. If an API exposes a protected resource, the security testing must ensure that only authenticated clients can access the APIs. Testing the security policies can include testing API access protected via API Key or Mutual Authentication using PKI or OAuth/OpenID token. Testing OAuth scope validation to ensure that APIs can be accessed using tokens having the right OAuth scope should form part of the API testing strategy. It is important to validate that the right HTTP error codes are returned in case of authentication or authorization failure while accessing an API.

API Fuzzing

API fuzzing is an attack in which the attacker tries to get information about the API and the system resources by sending random input parameters. The attacker sends all possible permutations and combinations of input parameters and analyzes the response to gain insight into the system resources. The attacker may try to analyze the error messages for various data combinations to understand system behavior. Hence, APIs should be tested with all permutations and combinations of input parameters, and the responses should be analyzed to ensure that the information provided in the responses is appropriate. Error responses provided under different combinations of invalid input data should only provide optimum information as required for the API. It should not reveal information about the internal data structure or database query, file system information, or any other information that can potentially be used to get unauthorized access to the system. For example, for an invalid input to fetch data for an entity, the response should not have any information about the SQL queries that failed to execute in the back end. The error response should indicate only the invalid parameters.

Malformed Payload Injection

APIs need to be protected against malformed or unexpected message injection attacks. Very large JSON or XML payloads, JSON payloads with long attribute names or values, and payloads with highly nested structures are used to attack the underlying systems. Processing complex payload structures can take up a lot of system resources and CPU cycles. A high volume of such requests may bring down the underlying systems, thus impacting the overall system availability. Hence, API testing should test the API's ability to withstand such vulnerabilities. An API testing strategy should include test cases that test API behavior when a request payload is an unexpectedly large or has an unexpectedly complex and heavily nested structure.

Malicious Content Injection

Injecting SQL scripts, JavaScript, and shell script through input parameters or payloads is also a common form of attack. If executed on the server or by a third party, these scripts may provide vital information to unauthorized users. The scripts might also be damaging enough to modify or delete data—impacting the business severely. Hence, API testing should test the API behavior when such scripts are injected into the API requests. The API should reject such messages with appropriate error messages. Testing the presence of malicious script should include testing the API behavior when different types of script like SQL, JavaScript, shell script, regular expression, XPath, XQuery, Python, or Groovy script are injected through the API payload.

Testing API Gateway Configuration

In many scenarios, a business service is exposed through an API gateway. The API gateway enforces policies in the request and response flow of the API, which may perform one or more of these depending on the requirements: security, throttling, data validation, transformation, routing, error handling, caching, and mashup. Most of these are implemented using policy blocks or filters within the flow. Unit testing of the API proxy must test the execution of these policy blocks and the conditions applied, if any. Verification methods look at the input and output of each of these policy blocks in the debug trace. If a policy block is to set a local variable or an HTTP header, you can validate whether it is being done properly by looking at the trace output. Similarly, if a policy is supposed to transform the message payload, the output of the policy execution should be the successfully transformed payload. It is also important to look at the average execution time of each of these policy blocks, either in debug logs or in the debug trace of the message flow execution. This can help identify potential performance bottlenecks at an early stage of the testing and reduce efforts to troubleshoot API latency issues at a later stage of performance testing.

API Performance Testing

APIs are no longer seen only as mechanisms for integration but have become mainstream for delivering data and services to end users through various digital channels. This increases the demand for APIs to perform well under loads. The overall performance of a client app is dependent on the performance of the underlying APIs powering the app. Hence, the importance of performance and load testing for APIs increases greatly. This section looks at the strategy for load testing an API.

Preparing for the Load Test

It is important to plan well and have a well-defined load testing strategy. Planning for API load testing starts with identifying the list of APIs to be tested. Load testing is most effective when the workload for the API is as close to the expected traffic. It is not useful to know that an API can handle, for example, 500 transactions per second without knowing whether the real traffic is higher than or lower than that. The first step in preparation for a load test is to gather information on the performance requirements that the APIs are expected to handle. This includes the following information.

- The average throughput in terms of the number of requests per second for each API deployed on the platform
- The peak throughput projects the maximum number of requests that each API is expected to handle at any given point in time (normally during peak loads)
- Throughput distribution across all the APIs deployed on the platform
- The traffic distribution patterns of client apps using the API to predict accurate API usage

- The number of concurrent users expected for each client app using the API, which predicts the total number of concurrent connections that the API platform is expected to handle under load

Having decided on the performance requirements for API testing, there may be different approaches to actual test execution. Actual test execution can start with the generation of repetitive loads for each of the API endpoints. This establishes the upper bounds of the performance that may be achieved in the test platform. If it is low, you should consider options to tune and optimize the API and platform parameters for better throughput. Adding hardware or instances in the cluster configuration can be the second option to look at if the results from the repetitive load test are not satisfactory.

Once the platform has stabilized and the upper bounds of load testing have been determined from repetitive load tests, it is time to simulate a realistic traffic pattern. A real traffic scenario might be ideal but not practical for various reasons. The simulated traffic should consider the following.

- Traffic distribution across various deployed APIs. For example, 45% of calls are to product catalog APIs, 35% to customer information APIs, and 20% to payment APIs.
- Traffic growth pattern during the day. For example, gradual increase or sudden spikes or a constant load throughout.
- API traffic for both success and failure responses.
- Geographically distributed API traffic to test for any network traffic congestion at high loads.

Data from production traffic logs of already deployed services can provide information to simulate realistic traffic scenarios for load testing.

API performance testing should consist of the following, to find the different performance parameters of the APIs and the API platform.

- **Baseline testing** determines how the system performs under normal expected load. The results from this test should be used to analyze the average and peak API response time and error rates. The CPU and memory utilization of the platform should also be investigated to eliminate any resource bottlenecks.
- **Load testing** studies an API's performance under growing API traffic volumes. Performance metrics, such as response time and throughput of the APIs, should be looked at to review the performance under load. The goal is not to find the breaking point but to understand the expected system behavior and capability to handle peak loads. Server performance metrics, such as CPU utilization, heap memory utilization, and network port utilization, should be analyzed to understand the state of the platform and its ability to handle high load.
- **Stress testing** finds the breaking point of the platform. It is used to determine the maximum throughput that the system can handle. In this form of testing, the API traffic load is gradually increased until a breaking point is reached when the performance degrade or errors from API calls increase.
- **Soak testing** determines whether there are any system instabilities in long-duration testing. The baseline test may be executed over several days or weeks to learn about any unwanted behaviors that may occur

when the system is used for a long time. The aim is to discover any issues with releasing system resources and make them available for the next execution cycle. If system resources are not getting released periodically, the system is likely to crash under sustained high loads. Normal baseline testing or load testing may not be able to unearth such problems, and then the importance of soak testing increases.

The load test strategy should consider the environments for doing the load test. A pre-production setup that is a replica of the production setup would be ideal for the load test. However, that may not always be available for practical reasons. Hence, a dedicated load test environment that is a scaled-down version of the production environment may be used for load and performance testing. Considerations should be made to scale down expected throughput by the same factor while performing the load test.

Setting up the Load Test

Having identified the environment for the load test and approach, it is time to identify the right tools to execute it. When choosing a tool, consider the team's familiarity with the tool interface, the testing requirements' complexity, and the load scale to be generated. There are many tools available to perform API load testing. The following are some of the most common API load-testing tools.

- **JMeter** is an open source Java-based tool with a powerful GUI used to easily simulate non-trivial HTTP requests to test REST APIs. It allows you to model complex workflows using conditions. A test plan in JMeter allows you to define the thread group used to simulate end-user behavior in terms of the number of concurrent users, the ramp-up time, and the REST API request sent by them.

The HTTP request can be parameterized. Parameterizing the test requests reuses it with different parameter values and dynamically passes the execution results from one test to another. Assertions can be added to validate the test results automatically. Listeners provide widgets that are used to view the test results.

JMeter is one of the best open source tools for functional testing to model complex user flows using conditions. The availability of many community plugins extends the built-in behavior. Its non-GUI-based option runs JMeter for test execution in an environment that does not support rich GUIs, such as Linux-based environments.

- **LoadUI** is a commercial API load-testing tool from SmartBear. LoadUI has an advanced feature that allows you to do distributed load testing by distributing the load tests to any desired number of LoadUI agents. It also allows running multiple test cases simultaneously and long-running tests that may run for days or weeks.
- **Wrk** provides a command-line interface to test REST APIs. Being multithreaded, it can take advantage of the underlying multicore processor; hence, it is used to simulate very high loads. The default reporting format for Wrk is limited to text only, which sometimes makes it difficult to interpret test results easily. However, its ease of use to simulate high loads makes it one of the best tools when the goal is to find the load that an API can handle.

- **Vegeta** is an open source HTTP load testing tool for performance testing of REST APIs. It is useful when the testing aims to learn how long the service can sustain a constant load of *x* requests per second. This is important when you have data about the peak load expected for an API, and you want to find out how long the service can sustain that peak load before you start seeing a drop in performance.
- **BlazeMeter** and **Loader.io** are two tools that run the load test for APIs in a cloud platform. They provide load-testing infrastructures as a service in the cloud. The cloud-based approach reduces efforts to set up the environment for load testing. BlazeMeter provides the option to upload a JMeter test plan and run it from its cloud infrastructure.
- **Locust** is another open source tool for API load testing. The user behavior can be specified in plain Python code to generate the needed load. It can generate load from multiple distributed machines to simulate millions of simultaneous users.

API Performance Test Metrics

API performance testing should look at the following metrics to measure the performance of the individual API and the platform.

- **API response time** measures the overall end-to-end response time of the API. Determines the time an end user is expected to get a response from the API. Minimum, average, and peak API response times should be measured as part of API performance testing.

- **API target response time** determines the time the API back-end systems take to respond. If an API is exposed through an API gateway, it measures the response time of the target back end for the gateway API proxy.
- **API latency** measures the latency introduced by any intermediary, such as an API gateway used in the API architecture.
- **Throughput** measures the number of requests processed in a second. Normally, this is measured in transactions per second (TPS).
- **Success and error rates** are important metrics for API performance testing. They measure the number of requests successfully processed under load.
- **CPU utilization** measures the capacity of the system under load. A low CPU utilization means that the system can handle a higher load. Higher CPU utilization is indicative of a system under stress.
- **Heap memory utilization** indicates how system memory is utilized to process requests under load. The system RAM may need to be increased if heap memory utilization stays at its peak throughout the performance test. Low available memory may impact the overall performance of the APIs.

Selecting the Right API Testing Tool

Having looked at the various aspects of API testing, it becomes important to look at the features that should be in an API testing tool to make it a success. The following lists can help with selecting the right API testing tools. They cover the features an API testing tool should have and other nice-to-have features.

Must-Have Features

This section discusses must-have API testing tool features.

- API test tools should support automated API testing to cover a wide range of scenarios, including the following.
    - Tests success conditions with different data combinations
    - Tests error conditions and corner cases
- The automation of functional test cases should support the following and must be repeatable for multiple deployments and environments. The tool must have the following capabilities for API functional testing.
    - Supports the creation of HTTP requests with different combinations of verbs, headers, query parameters, and payloads
    - Supports payload generation in multiple data formats (JSON, XML, SOAP) and even binary format
    - Supports the automated creation of API request templates by importing WADL, RAML, Swagger, API Blueprint, and so forth

- Supports automatic data validation based on a defined schema for request/response messages
- Supports parameterized test creation
- Provides the ability to define test flow logic
- Supports test visualization to understand the failure points of API executions.

- It should have the following **test asset management capabilities**.
    - Groups and tags test cases
    - Searches test cases and make changes to a group of test cases through find and replace
    - Easily creates new tests or update existing test assets based on changing API demands
    - Manages test data for different environments

- It should have the following **security testing capabilities**.
    - API authentication and authorization using protocols such as OAuth, OpenID, SAML, Basic authentication, and SAML
    - Message encryption and decryption
    - Penetration attacks, such as SQL/ script injection, malformed payload, virus attacks, parameter fuzzing, and so forth

- It should have the following **performance testing capabilities**.

- Calculates API response times, throughput, and error rates
- Simulates regular performance loads
- Simulates unpredictable and volatile performance loads with valid payloads
- Simulates spikes and sudden bursts of traffic in consuming apps

Nice-to-Have Features

The following are some of the nice-to-have features in an API testing tool.

- Records and replays API traffic
- Integrates with requirements management and issue tracking systems, such as JIRA and QC
- Integrates with CI tools such as Jenkins, Cloud Bees, Cruise Control, and so forth
- Uses federated and cloud testing to execute test cases in a distributed scenario
- Runs in non-GUI mode with a command-line interface
- Schedules test cases

Common API Testing Tools

Table 9-1 lists common API testing tools.

Table 9-1. API Testing Tools

Unit Testing Tools	Integration Testing Tools	Performance Testing Tools
JUnit	JMeter	JMeter
cURL	SOAPUI	LoadUI
Postman	HTTPie	Grinder
Advanced REST Client	Cucumber	Artillery
Mocha	Jasmine	Wrk
Chai	Mocha	Vegeta
TestNq	Advanced REST Client	BlazeMeter
QUnit	NSpec	Locust
pytest	Karate	
Mockito	Cypress	

CHAPTER 10

API Analytics

As the old saying goes: "You can't manage what you cannot measure." This holds true even for the enterprise API programs. API analytics provide data and trends about APIs. API traffic flowing through an API management platform can provide many useful insights to businesses, which can help effectively govern an enterprise API program. An enterprise needs to measure the success of its API program. This can help provide information that can be used by actors in various roles in a wide variety of ways to make the right decision.

This chapter looks at API metrics and discusses how to effectively use API analytics to drive the success of an API program.

The Importance of API Analytics

An API management platform collects operational and business data as traffic flows through it. The data collected is then analyzed to provide metering and monitoring capabilities. The business should regularly analyze this data to improve the API program and channel its investments. Only then can the business reap the benefits of the investments made in its API program for digital transformations. API analytics data can answer the following questions depending on the data collected.

- How has API traffic trended over time?
- Who are the top users of the API—apps as well as end users?

B. De, *API Management*, https://doi.org/10.1007/979-8-8688-0054-2_10

- Which developer app is generating the maximum traffic for the API?
- How many developers have signed up for the API program?
- What is the most recent trend in developer adoption of APIs?
- How has the API performed? How have the back-end services performed?
- What is the API usage pattern across geographical regions?

An API analytics dashboard can provide information about API traffic trends. It shows how APIs are used over time—the peaks and the troughs of API traffic. Aggregated API traffic data can show traffic distribution over a day, week, month, quarter, or year. Average API response time aggregated over time can help you understand API performance during peak and low traffic. API traffic distribution identifies the most popular APIs. Data on an API's users identifies the most popular app. All this information can help improve the quality and performance of APIs and provide valuable insights into API governance.

API Analytics Stakeholders

Stakeholders can use the data collected from API traffic for analytics in a variety of ways. The following are the main stakeholders for API analytics.

- API product owner
- API team
- App developers
- Operations team

APIs are products that you sell to your customers. Hence, as a product owner of the API, the business user would be interested in knowing how their product is doing. Without proper insight, it is difficult to make the right investments into the API program and make it successful. An API program business owner would be interested in getting answers to the following questions.

- **How has the API been adopted?** An insight into API traffic data can provide an answer to this. A continuously increasing traffic trend over a period of time can be a fair indication of the successful adoption of the API. A constant or falling trend in API traffic means that there has been low adoption of the APIs.
- **How many new applications are using the API?** A report on the new apps registered to use an API can help you understand the interests of the developers. The number of new apps registered over a period of time is a good indicator. But just looking at the new app registration data can be misleading because developers may register apps but not use them to invoke the APIs. Hence, it is also important to look at the traffic generated by these apps to measure the real adoption of APIs.
- **How many active developers are there?** A report showing the top developers' app traffic can provide information about the developers who are actively using the APIs.
- **What is the geographic distribution of API usage?** As an API product owner, I would like to know how the API has been adopted across different geographic regions. Depending on the services provided by the

API, its adoption could be concentrated in only a few geographic locations, or it could be widespread. For example, Google Maps APIs have a wide geographic distribution, indicating that users widely adopt it in different locations. If an API is designed to be used worldwide, traffic distribution by geographic region would interest the API product owner to see their adoption in different countries. If traffic comes only from one geographic region, its adoption is limited.

- **How are investments in the API being used? Is the API program bringing in new business?** An API traffic report can help answer these questions for the business owner. An increasing API traffic trend means end users like the API. Depending on the monetization model setup, this would mean an increasing trend in direct or indirect revenue from the API. Custom analytics reports can help drill down to specific business transactions to gain insight into the API's impact.

An API team is the technical team involved in the development of APIs. API analytics reports can provide the following information to help analyze and optimize the performance of an API.

- Traffic
- Response time
- Message payload size
- Errors
- Cache performance
- Back-end service performance
- Developer adoption

With this information, the API team knows how the API program is doing overall, how individual APIs perform, and how to improve the API performance. A higher-than-expected response time may impact the adoption of the APIs due to a poor overall user experience. Hence, the API team must look at the root cause to reduce the response time and improve overall performance. Response caching may help improve response time and be an option for performance improvement. Message payload size is another consideration in improving API performance. Large payloads impact network performance due to bandwidth constraints and can consume more CPU cycles for message processing. Hence, optimizing the message payload size can improve API performance and help drive its adoption.

App developers are the consumers of APIs. These developers are innovating with your APIs and building creative apps that help drive revenue to your enterprise. Their innovative apps help provide better user experiences. By sharing analytics information with app developers, you get better apps. Analytics help developers know how their apps are doing and how much they contribute to your enterprise's bottom line. App developers want to know how they can improve their apps. Ultimately, everyone wants happy end users.

The operations team uses API analytics reports to understand traffic patterns and anticipate when to add back-end resources or make other critical adjustments. An increasing API traffic trend associated with a degradation of API performance may indicate that the underlying infrastructure is reaching its capacity and may need to be supplemented.

API Metrics and Reports

A lot of operational and business data can be collected from API traffic. The metrics can be divided into traffic metrics and developer metrics.

Some of the key API metrics that should be analyzed are as follows.

- API traffic
    - Total API traffic across all APIs
    - Traffic distribution and trends by API proxy
    - API traffic by business or technical assets
    - Top APIs and methods
- Response time
    - Average response time of the API
    - Target service response time
    - Request and response processing latency on the API gateway
- Error rates
    - Error distribution over a period of time
    - Error distribution by APIs
    - Target service error rate
    - Error distribution by HTTP error code: 5xx, 4xx
- Message payload size
    - Average request payload size
    - Average response payload size

The following are some of the key API developer metrics.

- Developer engagement
    - The total number of developers registered with the API program

    - The number of developers with apps
    - The number of active developers
    - Traffic volume trend by developer
    - Traffic generated from developer apps

- Traffic composition
    - Top 10 apps traffic
    - Top 10 developers traffic
    - Top 10 API products traffic

- End-user engagement
    - Geographic distribution of API traffic
    - API traffic distribution by device: device type, OS families, agents, browser type
    - App error rates

Custom Analytics Reports

Default analytics data captured by the API management platform from API traffic may not be sufficient to provide all business insights. You may need to capture certain custom data from the message payload and derive useful analytics information. Many API management platforms provide the facility to extract custom data from messages and log it into their analytics database. This data may be extracted from message headers, query parameters, or payloads and used to create meaningful custom analytics reports. For example, in a hotel reservation API, a business might be interested in knowing the distribution of reservations by city or hotel. Such information can help businesses take actions that result in better customer satisfaction and grow business across cities.

Ensuring good API performance and helping highly engaged developers build apps with your APIs is key to the success of an API program. API analytics provide insights into metrics that should be monitored regularly to ensure the success of an API program. A dip in API traffic can mean user interest is shifting away from the API, the reasons for which could be many. It could be due to the API's poor performance or customers moving to services provided by other competitors in the market. Business owners should critically look at API analytics reports regularly and reflect on how they should further fuel and tweak their APIs to make them more competitive and popular in the market. Proper implementation of API analytics holds the key to the success of an enterprise's API program. API management is incomplete without the proper insights provided by API analytics.

CHAPTER 11

API Developer Portal

The success of an API program for an enterprise depends on the proper planning to build the right API at the right time to meet consumers' current and growing needs. APIs that power the digital business should be built correctly with a clean, well-documented interface and published and socialized with a developer community that can quickly adopt APIs. A good API developer portal easily onboards developers onto the API program.

This chapter looks at the role of an API developer portal in the API lifecycle and what should be the features of a good developer portal so that it can attract developers and facilitate their onboarding onto the enterprise API program.

Need for Publishing and Socializing APIs

A well-built API does not fetch the desired business benefits unless publicized. People—especially developers—looking to build apps using APIs need to know about it. So, an enterprise needs to have a mechanism to publish the details of the APIs and provide a platform for the developers to easily find and use the APIs. Developers need to know the details about the API.

B. De, *API Management*, https://doi.org/10.1007/979-8-8688-0054-2_11

An API should be well documented to provide information about the endpoint, the input/output parameters, the SLAs, the monetization model/rate plans, and other information. The API provider needs a social enterprise API platform to publish information about the APIs, whether the API is for internal or external use.

It needs to be marketed well. API providers need a platform to market their APIs. This includes a powerful search-driven catalog that offers social features such as ratings, reviews, likes, and more. An API must be published in a catalog with appropriate descriptions and tags to easily search for potential consumers.

After developers have found an API in a catalog, they want to know its fitness for their app development. This is where developers browse through API documentation, blogs, and forums to read user feedback on the API and evaluate it. They would like to know how interested the community is in the API to better understand the level of adoption and support for the API. An active community allows developers to ask questions and get honest feedback from fellow developers who are using the API. Good feedback in forums drive faster adoption.

The Importance of the API Developer Portal

A developer portal provides the platform for an API provider to communicate with the developer community. It communicates static information about the API, such as documentation and terms and conditions for use. It can also include dynamic social content the developer community contributes, such as forums and blogs.

Creating a good API is only a small step in building a successful API program. API providers need to expose and publicize information about the API, provide documentation to educate developer communities about the API and provide a platform to easily register developers and their apps. Developers and users of the APIs should be able to provide feedback, get support, and make new feature requests to let the APIs evolve. App developers should also be able to submit and share their own content for others to use.

An API developer portal is a single point of information for an app developer looking to use APIs for building an app. In addition to providing documentation for the API, the portal should provide a platform that allows users to easily play around with and test the APIs; this helps developers better understand its usage in building apps. Embedded API test consoles and smart docs generated from API specifications can be used to test the API interface.

A developer portal should provide developers with analytics information for API usage. App developers should be able to monitor the API usage pattern for their apps. API analytics information can include traffic trends, API performance metrics, and error rates for the API and apps.

Supporting App Developers

App developers are the real users of the API. Innovative apps built by app developers increase API adoption and usage. Hence, as an API provider, it becomes even more important to effectively support the app developer community to accelerate the adoption of your API. An API provider should support app developers to drive the API's social adoption. The support provided can be in various forms.

- Good documentation for users to easily understand the API interfaces
- A test bed to play with the API and understand its behavior
- SDKs and code samples that developers can readily use in their apps to invoke the API

- A Q&A forum for developers to help each other by answering questions asked by others
- An indexed forum to search for errors, issues, or questions and get immediate answers to already-solved problems

An API provider should put much effort and time into building a thriving community. The right investments in building the app developer community with the rights folks can pay enormous dividends later and make the API program successful. An API developer portal should provide the following social collaboration features to support the developer community.

Invitations

Invitations are a popular way to socialize your APIs. They are an easy and effective way to build a community for API users. A developer portal should facilitate sending invitations that create a community of interest around the API. Any user—an API or app developer or a business administrator—should be able to invite others to start using or following an API. You can encourage people to invite their contacts, too. This can build a huge social community connected to the API.

Social Forums

A social forum lets app developers share their experiences with using APIs. It can connect developers who are building apps with the APIs. They can discuss best practices for using the API, any limitations, and how to overcome them. They can post their comments and ideas, ask questions, and raise support tickets with the API provider. The view available to an app developer can depend on the assigned role. An administrator might be able to see all issues logged and all unanswered questions, whereas an app developer may only see the answered questions and the check status on the issues they logged. As the community around the API matures, the forum might act as a platform where API users and app developers answer questions or make comments on questions asked by fellow users.

An enterprise API platform needs to be social. App developers and API users should be able to follow APIs, apps, business organizations, developer groups, or other users. A personalized dashboard for each app developer should provide them with an aggregated view of all items of interest. It should provide a centralized dashboard where they can track what's happening with everything they are interested in.

Federated Developer Communities

The success of an API initiative depends on its adoption by the developer community. A developer portal allows developers to sign up for the API program and get access to the API. The portal helps API providers build their own developer community. But a federated developer community might be a better idea. With a federated approach, developers of other API providers who are partners or are like-minded may want to share the same API keys with developers. So, if a developer signs up with a company's API program and obtains an API key, the same API key can be used to access APIs provided by other company partners.

An enterprise API program should support the concept of an API provider federation. This brings together communities by providing developers with access (through proper authorization) to any API from any provider using a single API key, which helps API providers easily extend the reach of their APIs to a wider community of developers. However, this must establish a deeply federated trust and permissions model between the API providers. The model should allow API providers to opt in or out of the federation model and to choose the partners with whom they want to federate.

Developer Portal Users

A developer portal provides information about an enterprise's APIs for consumption by API consumers. Accordingly, there can be different types of users for the developer portal. Primarily, there are the following types of users for the developer portal.

- **App developers** use APIs to build apps. They refer to the API portal to learn more about the APIs they can use to develop apps. They look for API documentation and a sandbox environment to try the APIs. They register for an account in the portal, register their apps that use the APIs, review the terms and conditions for API usage, interact with other developers in the community through forums, and view statistical information about their app usage on a dashboard.
- **API consumers** use APIs to integrate with their services, get access to data, or build applications. These consumers are generally business partners or internal applications. They use the developer portal to discover the available list of APIs, their functional and non-functional capabilities, security requirements, and more.
- The **API team** provides the APIs. They create the developer portal to publish information about their APIs for the developer community. The API team sets up the portal and the workflow for developers to register and obtain an API key. The workflow may be simple automatic approval or involve manual verifications and approvals. The API team sets up the API portal to do the following.

- Automatic or manual approval for API key generation
- Publish and maintain API documentation
- Provide and maintain a forum for app developers to connect with other developers in the community
- Provide a test bed for app developers to test the API interface through an embedded test console
- Provide contact and support for app developers
- Enforce a role-based access control mechanism for developers to access various features in the portal
- Customize email notifications sent to administrators and developers for user creation, app registration, and approval

- The **API testers** and quality assurance team validate that the API information published on the developer portal is accurate. They ensure that the functional and non-functional capabilities of the APIs are documented correctly. They validate that all mandatory and optional parameters, error codes, and security information to access the APIs are documented without errors on the portal.
- The **API product owner** is responsible for productizing the APIs. They are responsible for identifying the APIs to be built based on market research and user stories. They work with sales, marketing, and other stakeholders to create an API product that will sell. The product owner looks at the information published in the portal to ensure that APIs align with the

business objectives. They ensure that the developer portal provides adequate information to facilitate the adoption and consumption of APIs.

They also refer to the portal to get insights about the API usage, performance, and adoption. They are responsible for understanding what the app developers want and how they use the APIs. They translate the business requirements into terms that the API team can use to build APIs that will sell. The API product owner would be responsible for the following.

- Define how APIs are packaged and published as a product in the portal
- Define the pricing and billing plans for the published API products
- Define the process and rules for app onboarding for API consumption
- Validate the API adoption and usage trends and make recommendations for strategic decisions based on the insights gained.

- **Technical writers** ensure that all information about the API is documented clearly in the portal. They ensure that the API documentation is clear, accurate, and up-to-date so that API consumers can easily understand and use the APIs.
- The **legal and compliance team** ensure that the API developer portal provides all information about the terms of usage and data handling policies. They verify and ensure that the APIs meet all compliance and regulatory requirements as documented in the portal.

API Developer Portal Features

As an API provider, it is important to understand the features that the API portal should have. The portal should attract app developers and provide all the necessary information they might want to start using the API. The following are some features to consider while building or customizing a developer portal.

- **User registration and login**: The app developer should be able to easily sign up for the API program and start using the APIs. The registration process should be simple and easy. Requiring a lot of information to register or a complicated registration process may annoy developers and hold them back from signing up for the API program. Hence, the developer registration form should be simple and easy.

  A minimalistic approach to user registration is recommended. When a developer registers, the approval process can be automatic or manual. In either case, the developers should be sent an email confirming registration. The administrator should also be notified of developer registration and provided a link to approve if required. In a manual approval process, an email should be sent to the developer once their registration request is approved. The login process after the registration should be easy but secure.

- **User management**: A developer portal administrator should be able to create and edit users. Administrators may directly create developer accounts through the portal. Upon successful registration, the portal should email the developer that the account has been created.

The administrator should be able to modify the developer's status from active to blocked if required or update a developer's profile information.

Role assignment is yet another aspect of user management. Admins should be able to assign roles to registered users to control the privileges and access rights of the user based on custom roles and signed-in and anonymous users.

- **API documentation**: The portal should be the source of all information about the APIs. It should provide all documentation for the API, such as interface specifications, FAQs, tutorials, examples, and sample code. Getting started and how-to guides on using the APIs accelerate API adoption. Including request and response messages using real-world examples helps developers easily understand the API interface.

  API documentation can also include a reference guide explaining common vocabulary, data formats, best practices, HTTP response codes, and error messages.

- **Interactive API explorer**: A developer portal should provide an interactive API test console for developers to test the APIs and let them explore and play around without writing any code. Developers can use the explorer to submit a request to the API and view the response. A smart API document lets developers learn how to easily use it.

- **Community management with forums and blogs**: It features community-contributed content, such as threaded discussion forums and blogs that describe the developers' experiences, building an engaged developer community. Developers can get assistance to use the APIs and build innovative apps by collaborating with other users.

- **App registration and key management**: When app developers want to create an app using an API, they need to get an API key. For this, developers need to register their apps with the API provider in the portal. The portal should allow developers to register their apps.

  The approval for the app registration can be automatic or manual. In an automatic approval, the API key is generated immediately upon registration. The approval process can be manual if any background verification needs to be performed before approval. In a manual approval, the API key is generated only after the administrator reviews and approves the app registration. An administrator may also revoke keys or regenerate new ones.

- **Email configuration**: The API portal should send email notifications when developers sign up for the API program or register their apps. The API portal administration should provide the facility to configure the email templates with the content and format of the emails. The admin should also be able to configure when emails should be sent to developers.

- **Dashboards**: App developers like to view statistical information about their apps and the APIs used by their apps. They like to know the number of users using their apps, the number of calls made by their apps, and the various APIs and methods used by the apps. The developer portal should provide a dashboard for app developers to view all this information.

- **Support Information**: The API support information in the portal should provide the developers' contact information to reach them in case of any queries or issues with using the API.

  The contact information can be a phone number or an email address. The support page in the portal can include quick API status information. The status could be active, under maintenance, deprecated, or retired. The support page can also include FAQs, notices, or information of interest to the developer community. Notices could cover the latest updates or activities related to the API. "Coming soon" information can provide a list of upcoming API features.

- **Search**: A search facility within the developer portal is a very useful feature. It lets developers quickly search for information. They can search for APIs of interest, specific information within the API catalog, or specific content within the forums or blogs.

- **API monetization**: The API developer portal must provide information about the API terms of service or license agreement. It should publish monetization information like the rates, billing plans, and pricing structures to use APIs. The API providers must also inform developers about discounts and promotional offers to drive API adoption through the portal.

  The developer portal must provide API consumers access to billing history and download invoices. The portal should also document information about usage limits, billing cycles, payment methods, refunds, and cancellation policies.

The Relationship Between a Developer Portal and an API Gateway

The API developer portal is the door to an enterprise's API program. It lets developers sign up and register their apps to use the APIs. An API gateway provides the API runtimes. An API key is generated on successful registration and stored in a database referenced by the gateway for API key validation. Not only that, all app attributes, developer information, and details about the organization are provided as part of the onboarding process and stored in the database that the gateway references for validation purposes.

The portal is a client for the API gateway to store and fetch API-related information. Normally, the portal makes REST API calls over HTTP or HTTPS to communicate with the API platform. For example, when a developer registers a new app, it requests the gateway to send information about the app to the gateway data store. Every instance of an API developer portal must be associated with an API gateway that hosts the APIs and provides runtime support. Both the portal and the gateway can be deployed on cloud or on-premises. A hybrid deployment model in which the portal is on the public cloud while the gateway is on-premise is also possible.

Developer Portal Deployment Patterns

To promote the use of APIs and to grow the ecosystem, API providers need to publish their APIs through a developer portal. An external developer portal is the most obvious choice as it is accessible to the community of developers outside the organization. They look up the available APIs and their documentation to know about the APIs available to build apps, test them, and integrate them into their apps. An external developer portal provides a first-class experience to the external developer community. An external portal is set with external network access and serves as the host of the publishing external facing APIs

But every enterprise also has hundreds of APIs built and used internally. It makes sense to maintain a catalog of internal APIs with all their documentation to reduce API sprawl, increase the reuse of APIs, and have better governance. What better option is to have them published on an internal developer portal? Understanding this need, many organizations have also started thinking and have adopted the practice of having an internal developer portal. An internal API developer portal is generally set up within the enterprise network and is accessible to internal developers within the organization.

Having a common place to publish all internal APIs improves reuse and reduces the cost of duplication. Internal developers can easily discover APIs that are already built from the internal portal. The internal portal can act as a central catalog of APIs that teams can check before building a new one. Having an internal developer portal provides the following advantages.

- Improved discoverability of APIs
- Increases reuse of APIs
- Reduced development time through reuse of already available internal APIs
- Increases collaboration and innovation through the reuse of APIs published in the internal portal
- Reduced API security risks as developers do not need to share API keys over email. They can get an API key by registering their apps in the internal portal
- Sets the right culture from the beginning for publishing API documentation in the internal portal before publishing it externally

CHAPTER 12

API Governance

API governance provides a policy-driven approach that defines and enforces standards and checkpoints throughout the API lifecycle. It encompasses not only the API runtime but also design through development processes. It includes the guidelines, standards, and processes for API identification, interface documentation, development, testing, deployment, running, and operation. Standards and principles defined by API governance provide API quality assurance, such as security, availability, scalability, and reliability. It ensures that the APIs are standardized, reliable, and secure, which is critical for successful adoption.

The Scope of API Governance

API governance encompasses activities, from the API proposal to its adoption through requirements gathering, building and deployment, and operations during general availability. Figure 12-1 shows the high-level phases where API governance is critical.

B. De, *API Management*, https://doi.org/10.1007/979-8-8688-0054-2_12

***Figure 12-1.** API governance phases*

The following describes the phases.

- **API proposal**: This is the first stage, where the organization proposes new API or change requests. This is done due to new business agreements, changes in existing business agreements, or a new change request submitted to the API governance body. Community managers create an ecosystem: talk to partners, competitors, regulators, and independent developers to identify and propose APIs aligned with the business strategy. The result is a backlog of APIs to be built over a period of time.
- **Technical requirements gathering**: After the API proposal, the next step is to gather the requirements and create the specifications for the API. The requirements must state what the API does and how the consumers will use it. API architects and business analysts work together to create the technical requirements specifications of the APIs.

  The requirements specification must state the input and output parameters for the API. It should identify the security requirements to ensure that only authorized personnel or applications can access the APIs. Security requirements must specify the needs around authentication and authorization, data encryption, and protection against various security vulnerabilities.

  The following are important questions to consider while collecting the technical requirements to build the APIs.

- What are the functional requirements of the API? What should the API do?
- How will the API be used? What are the input and output parameters for the API?
- Who are going to be the consumers of the API?
- What should be the response of the API in case of an error? How should the error message be communicated to the consumer?
- What are the non-functional requirements for the API? How should the API perform regarding SLAs, availability, scalability, security, and performance?
- How will the required API functionality be provided? How would business functionality be implemented? Which back-end systems should be integrated for the same?
- How will the API be secured from various vulnerabilities and threats?

API governance process must enforce that all these requirements are gathered using a predefined template, well understood, and signed off by the API provider and product team before the start of the design phase. The governance process for collecting the requirements must define the following.

- When should the API requirements be collected during the API lifecycle?
- Who will be collecting and defining the requirements, and how? What template should be followed to capture and document the requirements?

- What should be the process to review the requirements? What roles should be involved in the requirements review?
- Who will be responsible for signing off the requirements?
- What should be the process to handle any change in requirements?

- **Architecture and platform**: Soon after the technical requirements for the APIs have been defined, the enterprise and API architects need to create the logical and physical architecture for the API implementations. During the architecture and platform setup phase, the governance processes must define and establish guidelines for the following.
    - Goals and objectives for API architecture and infrastructure
    - Constituent of the cross-functional governance team
    - Roles and responsibilities of an API architect, API developer, tester, and administrator
    - Policies, standards, and best practices for API design, development, and usage
    - Policies and standards for authentication, authorization, data format, versioning, error handling, and documentation of the APIs
    - Review and approval process for API design, build, test, and deployment
    - Testing procedures and quality assurance checks during the API development lifecycle

- API monitoring and performance measurement tools and processes to measure the latency, throughput, and error rates
- Strategy for high availability and disaster recovery of the API platform infrastructure
- API delivery and promotion processes
- The process to accommodate changes in API technology, business needs, and industry trends
- Overall enforcement and accountability to adhere to policies and standards throughout the API delivery lifecycle

- **Design and build**: After the API technical requirements are finalized, it is time to design the API interface and the implementation. Governance for API interface design must define guidelines for the following.
    - Which API specifications standards should be used? Swagger, RAML, or any other standards for API interface documentation?
    - Who is responsible for the review and approval of the API specifications?
    - What is the API versioning approach? When will a new version be created, and how should that be communicated to consumers?
    - What tool will be used to automate the API contract design and documentation?
    - What back-end services will be used to implement the API functionality? How should the fields be mapped for the target system?

When the actual build starts, the scrum master, the API team, and all the members of the API program work together in this phase. Test scripts are created, and APIs are validated for compliance with API specifications. API governance during the build phase must define guidelines for the following questions.

- What tools are to be used for the entire API development lifecycle?
- Which source code repository must be used for configuration management?
- What development standards and best practices must be followed for the API implementations?
- What is the review process? What are the checkpoints to ensure the quality of APIs?
- Which policies must be implemented for APIs?
- Is there isolation between the non-production and production environments?
- How should the API interface lifecycle be managed?
- What is the promotion process, from the lowest development environment to production and eventually to the retirement of the APIs?

- **Testing**: Once the API is designed and implemented, the API testing cycle must ensure that the API is working as per the defined API interface and design. The testing must validate all the functional and non-functional requirements are met. API governance must define the right API test strategy to ensure the quality of the APIs. The API governance process must define the following.

- What testing approach should be followed for API testing? It must define the different types of testing to ensure quality - viz. unit testing, API interface testing, integration testing, functional testing, performance and load testing, security and penetration testing, and acceptance testing.
- What tools should be used for performing different types of testing for the APIs?
- Which team should be responsible for executing the different types of test cases?
- How and when should each type of testing be performed? Should it be automated using CI/CD pipelines or manually executed?
- Which environments should be used for the different kinds of testing?
- How would the test results be reported, and what should the defect-tracking process be?
- Who should sign off for the API testing results to ensure quality?
- **General availability**: After the implementation is done and the APIs are deployed, they must be published to the developer portal for API consumers. Making it generally available should be done in a controlled manner to ensure that the published service-level agreements (SLAs) are met while they are adopted widely. The governance process must lay out the approach for publishing the APIs and making them available to a wider group of consumers. Newly built API may be first released for internal consumption, followed by a beta release before making it generally available (see Figure 12-2).

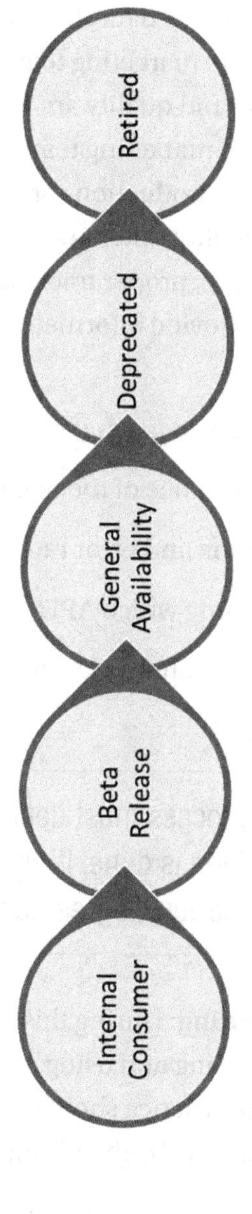

***Figure 12-2.** API release process*

Before publishing an API, consider commercial questions, such as how to monetize the API. Since APIs may expose data to the consumers, the terms and conditions for using the APIs and the associated data should be finalized with the legal team. The marketing team should review and ensure brand use and quality are satisfactory. After commercial, legal, and marketing teams approve, the API can be deployed to the production server and released for beta or general availability. After an API has been made available for general use, proper tracking, and metrics must be provided to provide information that answers the following questions.

- Which API is deployed to what environment?
- What is the performance of the deployed API?
- What are the uptime and error rates for each API?
- Which apps are using which API?
- What are the usage patterns for the API by app, geography, and time?

Note The API governance process must define all the API metrics to be tracked and how the tracking is done. It must define the necessary steps to take in case of service-level agreement violations.

- **Adoption and sunsetting**: During this phase, developers start exploring and using APIs to build apps around them. API governance should facilitate the easy but secure signup and onboarding of developers and their apps. The governance process should monitor how developers perform and use the APIs. Some important metrics to look for must answer the following.

- What is the version of each of the deployed APIs?
- What are the top 10 APIs being used?
- Who are the top 10 consumers of each API?

While sunsetting an API version, all API consumers should be communicated about the release cycle and the versioning. The API documentation page should provide release cycle and version availability information. Consumers should also be notified about the same via email or other notification channels like SMS and WhatsApp. This is important to drive transparency and trust. Companies like Twilio, Okta, and Stripe establish service agreements and drive customer trust by clearly communicating their release cycle and versioning on their API documentation.

Note This step should cover mechanisms that address any API usage issues that developers report. When new versions of an API are introduced, the API governance process must address how to sunset and retire older versions with minimal to no impact on the apps still using them.

The Aim of API Governance

API governance must address the following.

- Governance at the time of the API proposal (new/updates) must ensure that the identified APIs align with the business strategy and meet requirements. It is important to ensure that no existing APIs have same functionality. This prevents duplication and reduces confusion among developers looking for APIs to build certain functionality. The business and other stakeholders must approve funding for the API development.
- API design and development time governance must ensure that the API software quality is maintained. It must ensure that all APIs are protected with adequate security against the most common vulnerabilities. It must also address API versioning strategy and focus on development standards and best practices to be followed. Appropriate reviews and checkpoints must be enforced to ensure the quality of the API.
- API governance must define the right API testing strategy to ensure that APIs deliver the necessary level of security, reliability, and governance. The testing strategy should also ensure that APIs meet the regulatory standards and don't introduce side effects on other related APIs.
- API runtime governance must look at API deployment, monitoring, and dynamic provisioning to guarantee API runtime quality.
- API governance must ensure that the API provider and the consumer follow the service-level agreement.

The Benefits of API Governance

API governance processes and guidelines streamline API workflows and improve productivity. It provides guidance to build APIs that consumers love to use. The resulting APIs are more stable, secure, reusable, and, more importantly, aligned with the organizational business goals. The governance processes also cut risks by ensuring SLA and regulatory compliance adherence. Proper API governance also reduces API sprawl and improves quality and security. The following are some of the key benefits of API governance.

- Consistency and standardization
- Streamlined development processes
- Reduced cost for API delivery
- Enhanced API quality
- Reduced duplication
- Improved productivity for API delivery
- Improved time to market
- Better customer experience
- Alignment to compliance and legal requirements
- Enhanced security and reduced risk
- Higher scalability and flexibility
- Transparency and accountability
- Efficient change management

An API Governance Organization

For an effective API governance and to efficiently define and roll out the governance processes and policies, an enterprise must set up an API governance organization. This governance organization must have representatives from the API governance board, enterprise architecture group, and business sponsors. The governance organization is responsible for all the governance activities and key decisions. Members of this organization work and communicate closely with the line of business (LoB) teams developing the APIs to educate them about the API governance processes, guidelines, and best practices, as shown in Figure 12-3.

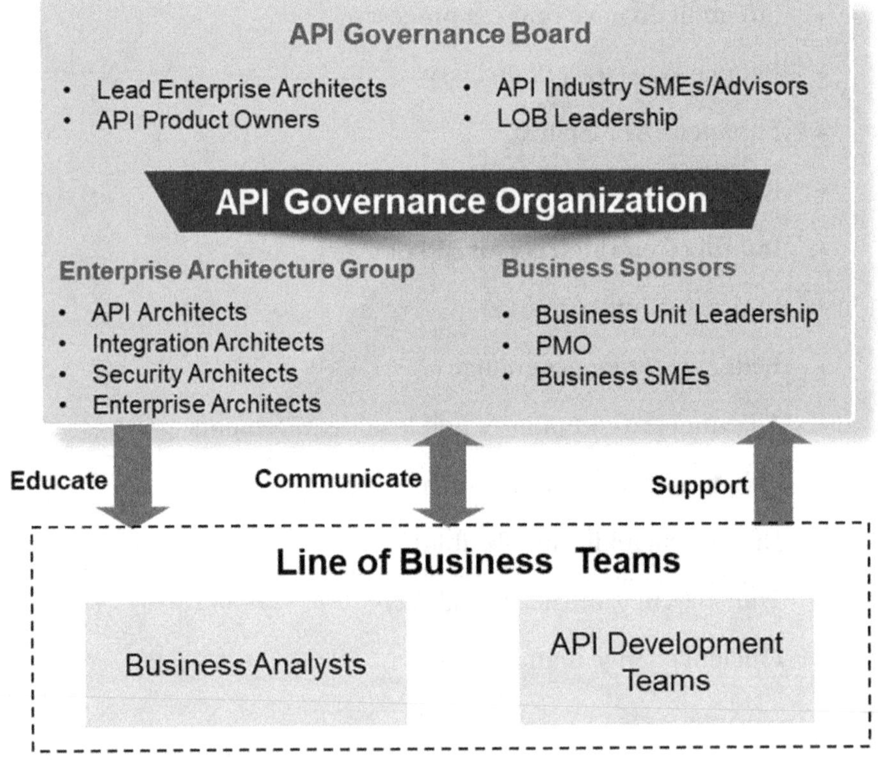

Figure 12-3. *API governance*

Steps to Set up Effective API Governance

The following steps to setup an effective API Governance strategy will increase API development productivity, reduce friction between teams and improve customer experience with API usage.

1. Make a detailed inventory of existing APIs to get a complete view of the API landscape within the organization. Understanding the use cases supported by these APIs lets you know how the APIs are aligned with the business goals.
2. Define API governance processes and policies with the stakeholders in the API program for the entire API lifecycle. The defined policies and processes must be documented and made available to all involved with the API program in the organization.
3. Advocate and explain the governance processes and policies and their benefits to all the teams implementing them. This promotes self-sufficiency and establishes the right culture and environment to drive the organization's adoption of the governance framework.
4. Monitor and iterate through the API governance processes to improvise them. Start by applying the governance standards with a small team. Monitor the impact, identify areas of improvement, and iterate progressively. Aim to improve the policies and expand their impact with each iteration.

An API Governance Model

The high-level API governance activities, checkpoints, preconditions, and the roles required for each of the phases of the API governance model are described in Tables 12-1 to 12-5.

Table 12-1. *API Proposal*

Title	Description
Input	• New API requests made by business analysts and solution architects. An outline solution document for the new API is to be submitted for review. • Solution architects can make API change requests, and submit an outline solution document for the API.
Process	For new APIs • New API request/business agreement to be submitted for review. • API details will be completed in a template that captures the API requirements. It should highlight the use cases related to the API. This evaluates the alignment of the API to business needs. The template must also highlight the information model and the related entities that are used by the API. This explains the business assets that are API-enabled. The service interface definition of the API should also be documented at this stage. • Design lead, tech architect, and solution architect review the submitted API proposal. The architecture review board should approve the proposal. The approval process can be similar to an existing SDLC. A lighter version of the existing approval process can be followed for API proposals. • A governance review by the architecture review board (ARB) of the new API proposal decides whether the API should be built. For API change requests • Business analysts/solution architects submit a change request for an existing API. • API details will be completed in the same template as a new API. • ARB governance review of the API change request decides whether the API should be built.

(*continued*)

Table 12-1. *(continued)*

Title	Description
Output	• *API profile template* document with API specification for new APIs. • Updated API profile template for API change requests. • A new project (for a CR, there is a new version of the project) for the creation of an API.
Checkpoint	• Fortnightly or monthly governance reviews are organized to review new API requests or change requests. The frequency may change depending on the business needs for the APIs.
Exit Preconditions	• Resourcing availability for API development (an API team to be formed). • The ARB or API governance body should review and approve an API spec. • Funding for API development should be approved by business and other stakeholders.
Actors and Roles	• *API business owner*: Responsible for establishing and validating the API's business needs and the funding approval requirements. • *API product owner*: Responsible for interfacing with various API delivery teams to ensure the quality and delivery of the APIs. They must ensure that APIs are built to meet the business requirements. • *API spec lead:* Responsible for the creation of API specifications. • *API architect*: Responsible for the technical architecture of the API solution. • *API leadership team*: Responsible for validating the business requirements and providing funding to build the API.

(continued)

***Table 12-2.** Technical Requirements Gathering*

Title	Description
Input	• API profile template
Process	• Create API specifications document from the business requirements. • Define data mappings between API interfaces and back-end services. • Requirements should be stored and/or updated in a central requirements management tool.
Output	• API specification and data mappings document
Checkpoint	• Review with the business analyst and the API architect, and sign off the API specification.
Exit Preconditions	• Governance guidelines and rules followed • API profile requirements are updated in JIRA
Actors and Roles	• *API business analyst*: Gathers the business requirements for API enablement and identifies the services to be exposed as APIs. • *API solution architect*: Works with the business analyst to define the API specification document and data mapping to back-end services. • *API spec lead*: Defines the API specifications and works with the business analyst and solution architect. • *API project team*: Informed about the new API requirements at this stage. Review the API specifications. • *API governance committee*: Ensures that the process is followed, criteria are met, and quality is maintained. • *Scrum master*: Conducts a spec jam.

Table 12-3. Design and Build

Title	Description
Input	• Approved API specification and data mapping documents • Business requirements document

Process	In the API design and build phase, the API team consists of a scrum master, API architect, API designer, API developers, and DevOps team, who build the API per specifications and business requirements. API development is done in two to three weeks sprints using the agile development methodology. The high-level activities are as follows.
	• The *scrum master* grooms the requirements and fills the action log in a requirements management tool like JIRA.
	• The *API development lead* reviews the API specifications, captures comments, and updates action logs.
	• The *API teams* are responsible for the following.
	  ◦ Reviewing the specification, updating the business agreement (after revival), and updating action logs
	  ◦ API implementation
	  ◦ Committing to SCM
	  ◦ Code review
	  ◦ Demoing to the client and validation by the client
	  ◦ Publishing deployable artifacts to the repository
	  ◦ Updating developer portal links
	  ◦ Publishing information on the developer portal for API subscribers

Output	• Completed action list captured during previous discussions • Follow-up action plan created in action log • Reference implementation running in development • Artifacts uploaded to a repository like GitHub • Developer portal updated

(*continued*)

Table 12-3. *(continued)*

Title	Description
Checkpoint	• Implementation should be compliant with the API specification document (mappings are validated)
Exit Preconditions	• Final review (config review, demo to the client) • Governance guidelines and rules followed • API conformant to design guidelines • API versioning policies followed • Any deviations are documented
Actors and Roles	• *API program manager*: Responsible for the overall program delivery of the APIs. • *API architect*: Architects the API solution and defines the API REST interface. • *API designer*: Designs the API interfaces and API proxy configurations to be deployed on the API gateway. • *API developers*: Configures API proxies in the API gateway. • *API DevOps*: Builds a DevOps framework to support CI and CD for API enablement.

Table 12-4. Testing

Title	Description
Input	• Approved API specification and data mapping documents • Business requirements document • Test Strategy • APIs deployed on non-prod environments
Process	In the API testing phase, the API testing team works to validate and ensure that the APIs are built as per the API specifications and business requirements. The API test team executes the test cases using the right and approved API testing tool. API interfaces are tested to validate that they work as per the specifications. The testing must validate the API behavior for mandatory and optional parameters in the request and response. Appropriate error must be thrown for missing mandatory parameters in the API request. Once the interface has been validated, API testing should test for end-to-end integration and functional testing. Performance and load testing should be done with the APIs deployed on a production-like infrastructure by simulating real traffic for normal and peak times. Defects and issues found during the testing cycles must be reported and tracked till closure. • Creating test plans and test cases • Executing test cases of API Interface testing • Executing integration test cases for end-to-end functional testing • Executing API security and penetration test cases. • Raising defects for issues observed during the testing. • Executing performance and load testing to validate non-functional requirements.

(*continued*)

Table 12-4. (*continued*)

Title	Description
Output	The output of API testing should provide a clear understanding of the quality and performance of the APIs. The output should include the following. • Test execution results for functional, security, performance, and load testing • Prioritized defect list • Detailed and summary test report of overall testing results indicating the number of passed and failed tests • Performance metrics with response time, throughput, and latency for each API • Security findings with vulnerabilities discovered. • Logs and debug information for the reported issues to troubleshoot and resolve them
Checkpoint	• API testing should be conducted at different stages throughout the API development life cycle. Unit, integration, and regression testing should be automated and integrated with CI/CD pipelines to be executed frequently with every code drop and release. • Security and performance testing should be done for the release of every new API or new version.
Exit Preconditions	• All API Test cases are documented. • All test cases are executed. • Test results and reports are documented. • Defects for unresolved issues logged. • API test governance guidelines and rules followed.

(*continued*)

Table 12-4. *(continued)*

Title	Description
Actors and Roles	• *API program manager*: Responsible for ensuring the quality of API program delivery. • *API designer*: Clarifies any doubts about the API design to facilitate testing. • *API developers*: Executes unit test cases and resolves issues reported at different stages of API testing. • *API testers*: Creates automated and manual test cases. Execute test cases to test API interfaces and business functionality. • *API DevOps*: Integrates API test suites with CI and CD pipelines for automated API testing.

Table 12-5. *General Availability*

Title	Description
Input	• API interface definition in the repository • API test console availability • Developer portal updated • Pre-prod environment running reference implementation • API config uploaded to SCM or repository
Process	The following activities are performed during the general availability phase to publish the APIs. • API deployment from the repository to sandbox and production • API documentation published on the developer portal for API subscribers • API health monitoring is set up • APIs are released to consumers for testing and feedback • App developers access APIs and create apps using the APIs

(continued)

Table 12-5. *(continued)*

Title	Description
Output	• APIs deployed to sandbox and production environments • API documentation is updated in the developer portal • Apps built using the APIs
Checkpoint	• Check the API's running status • Check API documentation and test console in the developer portal • Check API analytics for API traffic and performance • API health monitors are configured
Actors and Roles	• *Project team*: Responsible for overall API delivery. • *API support team*: Support to resolve reported issues. • *Operations/run team*: Deploys APIs and monitors their health.

Table 12-6. Adoption

Title	Description
Input	• The number of developers signed up • API traffic reports • The number of hits on the developer portal • The number of mentions on social networks • The number of blogs and forum posts
Process	• During the adoption phase of an API, it is important to have a plan that facilitates easy onboarding of developers and apps and tracks the usage of the API. For this, the following activities need to be performed. • Develop an adoption plan and identify targets. • Target and inform specific development communities about the availability of the new API. • Target/organize hackathons to support adoption. • Track/follow up with members who are in the member adoption forum. • Update the adoption list, developer portal, and API website. • Ensure the publicity of API through various developer channels. • Identify and inform other ecosystems of API availability. • Conduct webinars driven by members to share experiences in adoption.
Checkpoint	• The number of developers and apps onboarded • The number of active developers and apps • API traffic patterns • The number of API issues reported from different channels
Actors and Roles	• *API operations team*: Facilitates the developer onboarding and monitors API traffic. • *API support team*: Resolves issues reported about the APIs.

API Governance Best Practices

API governance is important for building consistent, secure, cost-effective, high-quality APIs that developers and consumers love to use. The following are some of the best practices to be considered for rolling out API governance within your organization.

- **Establish clear objectives**. Define a clear objective for your API governance. Establish what you want to achieve for your APIs and how API governance can help. Your API governance must aim to establish consistent design standards and best practices for API development. It must define and enforce security measures to protect the APIs. Governance must ensure that the APIs are reliable and stable with minimal downtime and disruptions.

  Governance must also focus on building scalable and interoperable APIs that allow seamless system integration. The other objectives of API governance should ensure good API documentation and a robust versioning strategy to allow smooth upgrades and compliance with industry standards and regulations. All the objectives for API governance should be aligned to meet the business objectives and goals.

- **Standardize API design**. A standardized approach to API design makes APIs easier to understand and use. API governance must define the guidelines and standards for API resource naming, data formats, and error messages to be used.

- **Set up strong governance practices**. API governance must define details of processes to be followed at each stage of the API lifecycle. Checkpoints and validation rules must be defined with a RACI matrix for all stakeholders for each API lifecycle stage, from planning and design to general availability and retirement.
- **Implement non-disruptive versioning strategy**. API governance must set the guidelines for API versioning to enable smooth upgrades. The versioning approach should be backward compatible to enable consumers to upgrade without disruption. Versioning can be implemented using the version number in the URL or headers. While upgrading APIs to a newer version, appropriate deprecation and end-of-life information should be passed to the consumers of the older version. All processes and guidelines for new version upgrades and deprecation should be laid down in the governance policies.
- **Implement robust API security**. API governance must prioritize API security and define guidelines for implementing a defense-in-depth approach to secure APIs and back-ends. Guidelines must include measures for authentication and authorization for API access. Sensitive data should always be protected using data encryption and privacy policies. Security guidelines must state approaches to protect APIs against OWASP's top 10 threats.

- **Set up traffic management policies**. API traffic must be throttled at the API gateway to project back-end systems from unexpected load and DoS attacks. Rate-limiting policies improve an API's performance and availability and thus conform to the published SLAs.
- **Automate API lifecycle tasks**. Automation reduces manual errors and improves efficiency. Automating API testing, deployment, and promotion tasks using available tools is advisable. Even tasks to publish the API documentation to the developer portal should be automated to keep the documentation in sync with the actual implementations. Governance processes and tasks should also regularly improve based on feedback, lessons learned, and industry trends.
- **Set up API monitoring and analytics**. Governance guidelines must define the approach and mechanisms to monitor the health, performance, usage patterns, and errors of the deployed APIs. Regular monitoring eliminates bottlenecks and identifies anomalies. Operations teams can take corrective actions to optimize and improve API performance.
- **Publish API documentations**. API governance must provide guidelines to create user-friendly documentation for APIs and publish them through a developer portal. Guidelines to keep this documentation updated with the actual implementation must also be provided.

API consumers can benefit largely from documents to get started with API and resolve commonly faced issues. Forums on the developer portal, sample code, and interactive tools are other forms of API documentation that should be considered while publishing APIs.

API Governance Challenges

While API governance is important to deliver high-quality APIs and build a thriving ecosystem, implementing an effective API governance model has its own challenges. These challenges can vary depending on the size of the organization, the industry, and the technology stack. Some of the common challenges are as follows.

- **Resistance to change**: Employees and teams may resist adopting new governance practices, especially if they perceive them as burdensome or disruptive. Hence, implementing governance needs high levels of communication and training to demonstrate the benefits of the suggested changes and best practices.

  Teams should be involved in the governance design. It needs a cultural change. Senior management must first buy into the benefits of implementing the changes required. Afterward, they must drive and advocate its adoption across different teams with clear communications and directives. There must be dedicated resources and team members' commitment to continuous improvements.

- **The complexity and scale of the API ecosystem**: Rolling out API governance across the different units of organization can be challenging for big organizations with many APIs. As the number of APIs and their consumer base increase, managing and tracking their usage becomes difficult. This can lead to inconsistency in API design and functionality.

  Ensuring that API teams across different business units follow the same best practices and processes for API implementation and delivery is not easy. Comprehensive and up-to-date documentation and clear communication channels for changes and updates provide guidance to adopt the new changes. APIs must be categorized and organized with clear taxonomy and detailed documentation to manage them effectively.

- **Resource constraints**: Organizations with limited budgets and resources might struggle to allocate dedicated personnel and tools required to implement the governance guidelines. Implementing effective governance requires specialized technical knowledge and skills to manage the APIs, which may be difficult to find. People in organizations need to be motivated and upskilled to bridge the gap. Demonstrating the value of API governance in terms of reduced risks and improved efficiency motivates more individuals to get skilled and step forward to advocate and roll out the new governance policies.

- **Measuring Success**: Defining key performance indicators (KPIs) and metrics to measure the success of API governance efforts can be challenging, especially when the impact is not immediately quantifiable.
- **Vendor lock-in**: When an organization tries to roll out changes proposed or mandated by API governance guidelines, vendor lock-in sometimes becomes a major hindrance. Heavy dependence on a specific vendor or third-party APIs makes it difficult to switch providers. In such cases, an exit strategy with a fall-back plan must be defined to reduce vendor dependencies.

Conclusion

Effective API governance is critical to the success of an API program. It builds high-quality APIs more efficiently and reduces overall time to market. However, setting up the right governance model and making it operational across the organization is difficult. Some challenges need strong leadership support and the right organizational culture to overcome. Setting up the right governance model is an iterative process. No set governance model works the same way for all. So, start small with an open mind to learn from mistakes and improvise the processes and policies for API delivery and lifecycle management. Adopt the best practices for API governance for a head start.

CHAPTER 13

Building an Effective API Strategy

An API strategy is about aligning APIs to meet business goals, what technology to use for building secure and scalable APIs, and how to build an engaging ecosystem and grow it with partners and developers using the APIs. Having an API strategy is necessary to reap the business benefits of APIs. This chapter looks at the need for an API strategy, the essential components of an effective API strategy, how to align it to the business objectives, and finally, an approach to build a string API strategy from scratch.

API Strategy Needs and Components

A robust API strategy is the cornerstone and bedrock for all successful initiatives for enterprise digital transformation. It helps businesses do the following.

- Offer more value to customers at a faster pace
- Build a robust and scalable platform and architecture for APIs
- Develop APIs that meet the business and consumer needs
- Secure APIs to protect data and systems from potential security threats

B. De, *API Management*, https://doi.org/10.1007/979-8-8688-0054-2_13

- Grow partner ecosystem with new and long-term partnerships
- Empower and delight users with new experiences

A well-defined API strategy must include strategy for the following.

- Aligning API to business and product goals
- Building a scalable API platform
- Creating a robust and secure API architecture
- Setting up an effective API governance
- Identifying and defining API analytics and metrics
- Actively managing API monetization models
- Building and growing the API ecosystem

Aligning the API Strategy to Business Objectives

The API strategy must be closely aligned with the business objectives so that the ever-growing and ever-changing customer demands can be met easily using APIs. The best approach is to have an "outside-in" view to understand business needs and customer pain points.

APIs must be designed to meet customer needs and business objectives. The API strategy's business goals may vary but must address the following.

- Increasing revenue channels
- Reducing time to market
- Expanding product offerings

- Improving operational efficiency
- Improving customer experience and loyalty
- Increasing partnerships with ecosystem partners
- Decreasing integration and onboarding costs
- Bringing innovation

Align API Strategy with Business Sponsor Goals

The business sponsors must see the business value of implementing the APIs and be ready to support the API program. Focusing API strategy to solve real business problems rather than being only a technology modernization initiative helps to get buy-in from more organizational stakeholders.

Make APIs an Organizational Initiative

For an API program to be successful, it must be viewed as an organizational initiative rather than just an IT initiative. A successful API strategy requires the entire organization to adjust to new ways of working. Organization leaders must foster cross-team collaboration. Executives and management must drive organizational and cultural alignment across departments and business units. All groups and departments within the organization must share the overhead and burden of alignment to adopt APIs. Everyone in the organization must buy into the benefits and outcomes of the API program and be motivated to implement the required changes.

Involve Stakeholders at All Levels in the API Program

API strategy must involve stakeholders from all levels in the organization. Business leaders can identify the new service capability needed to meet the business goals. They also need to understand the technologies needed to build the capabilities. Enterprise and technical architects can tell how such capabilities can be technically achieved by exposing services from current monolith applications as APIs or by integrating with other applications and services within or outside the organization. The delivery team can design and implement the required APIs by following the industry's best practices and standards. API evangelists and marketing teams can promote the APIs to build an ecosystem and grow the business with partners and consumers. A collaborative approach helps resolve all impediments in the successful delivery of API products.

Building a Strong and Effective API Strategy

Let's look at how to build a strong and effective API strategy. An effective strategy must cover all business, technology, and processes to build APIs. Next, let's look at the different aspects under these three categories: defining an API business strategy, setting up governance and processes, and defining and setting up an API technology strategy.

Defining an API Business Strategy

Identify Use Cases

To align API strategy to business goals, start the API program by identifying the use cases that address customer problems and pain points. Identify APIs required to solve the problems, understand the inputs and outputs required for the use cases, and design APIs accordingly. Adopt a product mindset to build the APIs. When the APIs are implemented, they should provide a better customer experience with new and innovative products and services.

Prioritize Use Cases for API Implementation

There may be multiple use cases for API implementation. It is important to prioritize these APIs and define an implementation roadmap. APIs that are easy to build and can yield maximum business benefits should be at the top of the priority. **Readiness to execute** from a complexity and business readiness point of view and **strategic attractiveness** from a business value and impact point of view are the main parameters to be considered for prioritizing APIs. Building such APIs gets executive attention and gains the confidence of the API stakeholders across the organization.

Determine the Core Capabilities and the Value Added by Partners

Not every capability required to provide a service needs to be built in-house. Partners could provide some of the required capabilities. It is best to collaborate with them and leverage their services. This reduces overall time to market. The focus should be on the core business capabilities that can be provided in-house and value-added use services from partners. Select the partner based on the functionality provided by their APIs and their service SLAs. The core service SLAs should not be compromised due to the SLAs of the partners.

Define a Strategy to Drive Adoption and Grow the API Ecosystem

For an API to be successful and generate business value, it needs marketing and campaigns to drive its adoption. Start with finding consumers who are ready to invest time and innovate for the pilot APIs.

These partners can expand your APIs' reach and build an ecosystem with their partners. A thriving API ecosystem holds the key to the success of API programs. Hence, efforts must be put into building and growing that ecosystem with app developers, business partners, and customers. The following steps can grow the API ecosystem through a healthy partnership.

1. Identify the potential partners and end users of the APIs.
2. Adopt an outside-in approach to focus on meeting the customer experience and needs with the APIs.
3. Productize APIs to market them as products with defined SLAs around availability and performance.
4. Monetize APIs with the right monetization model that can increase API consumption and support business growth.
5. Promote the value of APIs to the consumers.
6. Provide training on the usage of APIs and API products.
7. Build a self-sustaining community that encourages API providers and consumers to collaborate. Engage with partners and co-create values.
8. Drive API consumption and adoption through marketing campaigns and hackathons.
9. Set up a developer portal to ease API developer registration and onboarding.

10. Publish API documentation and sample API codes, consoles, and sandbox environments for app developers to try and play with the APIs.

11. Encourage feedback about APIs from app developers and other API consumers.

12. Monitor the business and API metrics regularly to highlight successes, spot anomalies, and take corrective actions.

Devise a Monetization Strategy for the APIs

Once the APIs have been prioritized, businesses must focus on deriving the potential business value from the APIs. They must think about the monetization strategy of the APIs. Businesses must consider how the developers and end consumers will benefit from the APIs, which lets you understand how much consumers would be willing to pay for API usage.

Charging fees strategically for the APIs using the right monetization model helps businesses increase their overall revenue. Developers, who are the consumers of the APIs, would be charged for API usage. Different models can be adopted for charging based on the data or the service provided by the API. To come up with the right monetization model, consider the following.

- What is the value delivered by the API to its consumers?
- What is the price the consumer would be willing to pay for using the APIs?
- What is the financial cost to maintain the APIs, and how to recover it?
- What is the price offered by competitors for similar services?

There are broadly two types of API monetization strategies.

- The developer pays the API provider for using the APIs.
- The API provider gives a financial incentive to app developers.

The following monetization models can be applied to a "developer pays" strategy.

- Pay as you go
- Freemium
- Tiered
- Transaction fee

The following monetization models can be applied to a "developer gets paid" strategy.

- Revenue sharing
- Affiliate
- Referral

These monetization models are covered in Chapter 8.

Setting up Governance and Processes

Build an API-First Culture

Building an API-first culture is difficult and requires everyone to buy into the philosophy and needs senior executive support. API education for senior leadership and key team members accelerates API adoption. Set up workshops to explain the importance and build awareness of API within the organization. All business and IT stakeholders must participate in such workshops and foster a co-innovation mindset to build new use cases and products using APIs. Engineers, developers, and testers must be trained to design, build, and maintain APIs. All API programs must have executive sponsorship to adopt the API-first culture and mindset successfully.

Set up an Effective API Governance Model

API governance defines and establishes the policies and processes to build consistent APIs and meet compliance requirements. The governance structure defines the roles and responsibilities of different stakeholders involved in the API program. It involves advocacy to establish the API-first mindset. The right API governance model helps with bringing the needed cultural shift. API governance builds stable, reusable, and secure APIs by following best practices. It reduces API sprawl and ensures that the APIs are aligned to meet business goals and deliver maximum value.

Define and set up an effective API governance model as follows.

- Create an inventory of the existing API landscape within the organization.
- Identify the owners and the different stakeholders of the APIs.
- Define the roles and responsibilities of the API governance processes.
- Establish a Center for Enablement (C4E) committee to define the API governance model across the organization.
- Define the interaction model of the API governance team with other teams. Federated governance can work well in organizations with different Line of Businesses (LoBs) having specific needs.
- Define an agile API delivery model with review checkpoints at critical milestones.

- Define the standards and governance processes for designing, building, testing, and deploying APIs.
- Define API security and regulatory assessment checklists.
- Define the DevSecOps process for cloud, on-premises, and hybrid deployment of APIs.
- Define an approach and policy for API versioning and deprecation.
- Establish protocols and guidelines for support, incident management, and notifications.
- Identify and define key metrics and dashboards to measure API success.
- Evaluate how every API meets the business goals.
- Define the API knowledge management processes.
- Define a partner onboarding and approval process to build and expand the API ecosystem.

An effective and successful API governance saves time and money by advocating consistency and reusability.

Defining and Setting up an API Technology Strategy

Define a Robust and Flexible API Architecture

A secure, robust, and flexible architecture is the cornerstone for building scalable APIs. The API architecture and design must focus on achieving the following.

- A logical and physical API reference architecture with all the required capabilities.
- Principles for API resource identification following a domain-driven approach.
- Pragmatic REST principles for API design with an approach for versioning and lifecycle management.
- A robust end-to-end API security reference architecture for identity, access management, and data privacy uses Basic authentication, API key validation, OAuth authorization, JWT validation, threat protection, and DoS protection.
- Patterns and reusable API policies designed with coding standards and guidelines.
- A framework for caching, logging, exception handling, and auditing. Error handling should be done following a combination of HTTP status codes and message payloads.
- Guidelines for GraphQL queries to optimize API performance.
- Guidelines for using gRPC protocols for internal API communications to reduce latency.
- Best practices for conditional and dynamic routing and orchestration while connecting to backend services.
- Best practices for message transformation and data mapping within the API management platform.
- Best practices for message throttling and traffic management to protect backend systems from unwanted traffic spikes.

- An approach for API platform and service monitoring and alerting to track performance.
- Best practices and guidelines for user-friendly API documentation.
- An approach to bundle and offer a group of APIs as a product and monetize them using the right model.

Select a Suitable API Management Platform

Not every project or organization may need an API management platform. An API management platform provides various features to manage your APIs effectively and efficiently. It provides capabilities to implement security, data and protocol transformation, traffic management, API analytics and monitoring, API monetization, API documentation with lifecycle and ecosystem management, and much more. However, not all of these capabilities may be required by an organization. Sometimes, the development team is well-equipped to build the required capabilities in-house. In such situations, it is important to do a build vs. buy analysis and understand the cost difference between an in-house proprietary solution and a third-party off-the-shelf product.

Once an organization has decided to adopt an API management platform, selecting the right one with the right capabilities is the key to success. The gateway capabilities of the platform are often the most used features. The API team should be able to design, develop, test, deploy, manage, monitor, and even retire the APIs using the platform. The API management platform should provide API analytics dashboards to monitor the performance and adoption of APIs. It should also provide a developer portal to build the ecosystem with partners. The evaluation criteria should include the ability to set up the platform for HA in single or multiple cloud regions, on-premises data centers, or in a hybrid infrastructure.

Set up the API Management Platform

Once the suitable API management platform has been selected, it must be set up for non-prod and prod environments. Depending on the network topology, it might be required to establish a VPN or dedicated interconnect to securely connect the API management runtime nodes on the cloud to the on-prem systems. The production instance of the platform must be set up with high availability and resiliency. The API management platform must be integrated with enterprise monitoring and alerting systems. Also, if the platform is first set up on-premise, design a strategy and roadmap to move it to the cloud.

Pilot with an API Reference Implementation

Walking before you run is a good strategy to adopt any new change. Hence, once the API platform and architecture are ready, it is time to validate it with a pilot implementation that can serve as a reference for the future. A pilot program manages risks and identifies deficiencies before investing considerable resources and money.

For the reference implementation, identify the right potential use cases and prioritize the APIs to be built. Select APIs from the prioritized list that can potentially add maximum business value. Start the pilot reference implementation for those APIs with the following steps.

1. Create an execution plan to build the pilot APIs.
2. Design and build API interface documents using Open API or RAML.
3. Define security models and measures for protecting the APIs.
4. Build the API business logic using the preferred Microservices framework.

5. Create test scripts for automated API testing using suitable frameworks.
6. Implement an API gateway to manage the APIs.
7. Apply security, traffic management, routing, and other policies for the APIs on the gateway.
8. Identify and address all security threats and vulnerabilities for the APIs.
9. Set up automated CI/CD process. Deploy and test APIs using the same.
10. Bundle related APIs into API products.
11. Set up the API developer portal and publish APIs for consumer access.

Define API Metrics to Measure Success

Once a pilot API has been deployed, it is time to measure its success and make course corrections, if any. Tracking the API performance is necessary to avoid any bottlenecks affecting the apps' performance using the APIs and the end-user experience. At this point, you must identify and define the API metrics and the dashboards that should be monitored continuously. Metrics could be different for different stakeholders. Hence, create separate dashboards for key API metrics for business, operations, application engineering, product management, and executive teams.

The following are some key metrics to measure the success of an API program.

API Performance Metrics

The following are API performance metrics.

- Average and maximum API latency
- API throughput—requests per second or minute
- API errors per minute
- Availability and downtimes
- Incidents reported for each API
- Memory and CPU usage

API Adoption and Growth Metrics

The following are API adoption and growth metrics.

- The number of APIs launched
- The number of developers and apps registered for API usage
- The number of partners onboarded for API usage
- Monthly/quarterly/yearly API traffic growth
- The top consumer by API usage
- The time for the first Hello World! API call
- The time to onboard consumers and partners

API Product Metrics

The following are API product metrics.

- The time and cost to build an API
- Operating costs for running each API
- The time to upgrade the API version
- Cost reduction through API reuse
- The direct revenue/profit generated per API

Conclusion

API enablement is the cornerstone of all digital transformation programs. A successful API program needs a well-thought-out API strategy aligned with the business goals and objectives. The API strategy should include technology and program strategy to smoothly roll out APIs across the organization. The API technology strategy should provide a roadmap for platform selection, architecture, design, development, and deployment of APIs. The program strategy must focus on the overall approach for delivering, releasing, and adopting APIs. The API strategy should ensure that APIs are built correctly and have an ecosystem that drives revenue growth.

CHAPTER 14

The API-First Approach for Digital Transformation

API-first is a product-centric approach to building software products that put APIs at the center of all development. It begins with defining the API interface rather than creating it as an afterthought. This approach makes every product functionality accessible to other systems via API. This chapter introduces the detailed philosophy and concepts of building applications with an API-first approach.

The chapter covers the benefits of following the API-first approach. Some of the core principles to be followed, the approach to get started with the API-first journey, and the probable challenges that may have to be overcome for adopting the API-first approach for the digital transformation program are also covered in this chapter.

Introducing the API-First Approach

The philosophy of API-first approach is to bring in a mindset to think about how the consumer will use the application via APIs before even thinking about the business logic of the application. It starts with brainstorming and

B. De, *API Management*, https://doi.org/10.1007/979-8-8688-0054-2_14

talking to stakeholders to think through and understand the application's use cases and how clients will interact with the system. An API definition with expected input and output parameters is created as the first step. The API interface defines the structure and attributes of the request and response to invoke the application logic via the APIs. This approach encourages modularity, scalability, and reusability of an application's components since products are designed around an API from the ground up.

The API-first approach implements highly flexible and decoupled applications since API providers and consumers only need to abide by the API contract defined for the interaction. Business requirements and logic can evolve as long as they stick to the API contact defined at the start of the development.

Principles of the API-First Approach

The API-first approach must follow certain principles to reap its benefits. The following are the main principles to follow for an API-first approach.

- **Build the API as a product**: This principle brings the API to the center and core of all application development. By creating a culture where APIs are considered the product, application developers build APIs that the consumers love and evolve over time.

  APIs should be a foundational part of product design. They must be designed to adhere to certain specifications and SLAs, like the requirements to be met by the product. APIs should be built like LEGO blocks with a standardized definition and documented way to use them. Just like LEGO blocks can be combined easily to build houses and objects of different shapes and forms, APIs should provide a similar capability to build new innovative applications by easily combining multiple of them.

- **Design APIs for the users**: This principle ensures that APIs are deigned to meet user requirements and needs. Think of the end consumers of the APIs and what data or services they need from the API. Keep in mind the persona of the API user to understand how they intend to use the API. Ensure that the API is easy for the end user to use.
- **Create an API interface before any implementation**: This principle allows developers to define how consumers can use the application via APIs. It defines the input parameters and their format to be sent in the request to the application and the expected data in response. It finalizes the contract that the application developer and consumer must abide by. Consumers and providers are loosely coupled with an agreed-upon contract, letting them evolve at their own pace. It also creates a more modular and reusable software architecture that can easily integrate with other systems.
- **Design APIs that meet business needs**: This principle ensures that APIs are designed with a functional knowledge of the application in mind. Understand the business needs of the application and the use cases. Identify the application's users and actors and how they

interact to provide the input parameters. Understand the expected output from the application for the use case. Depending on that, define and design the API interface.

- **Adopt a modular approach to design the APIs**: This principle designs reusable and scalable APIs. A modular approach lets you design APIs at a granularity that can be reused across other applications and services. It also shields the impact of changes in an API on other components of the system. This allows the APIs to evolve gradually without any dependency.
- **Follow a collaborative and an iterative approach for API design**: This principle allows the development of APIs that work for a wider audience with inputs from different stakeholders. Business analysts, product owners, app developers, and end users can provide API design input that meets business and end-user needs. An iterative approach with a proper versioning mechanism ensures that APIs are designed and built correctly. A thoughtful design with a collaborative approach eliminates expensive and time-consuming rework at a later point in time.
- **Consider security in your API design**: This principle bakes security within APIs earlier in the API development lifecycle, right from the design time. Security should not be an afterthought. APIs, by design, must be protected against sensitive data exposure and unauthorized access.

- **Document your APIs to make them easy to use**: This principle ensures that the API contract is well documented to help consumers use them easily and quickly. Documentation should include a description of the API functionality and capabilities, how to use it, and data formats to use. Documentation should be clear and concise enough with examples and use cases.

  Many tools autogenerate user-friendly API documentation from the API specifications and allow consumers to test them through an interactive portal. Good documentation increases the adoption of APIs and expands the ecosystem.

- **Adopt a test-driven approach for building APIs**: This principle creates and executes test cases based on the defined API contract. Testing should be integrated with the product's development lifecycle to test the APIs at frequent intervals. Test cases should be automatically executed using automated test tools. Successful execution of the test cases ensures that the API is functioning as expected and meets the business and end-user needs.

- **Keep performance in mind while designing APIs**: This principle ensures that the API meets the defined and published SLAs. Some of the metrics to keep in mind are latency, throughput, and availability. The API payload should be lean, containing only the required information as needed by the consumer. This ensures optimal network bandwidth usage for transmitting data and improves response time and performance.

- **Define error codes and messages to communicate API errors**: This principle ensures a structured and consistent approach for communicating error information. HTTP provides a different set of error codes to communicate errors. The API-first approach must use those error codes while defining the API behaviors in case of business and technical faults and errors.

Benefits of the API-First Approach

API-first approach for software development has many benefits that make this approach very popular. The following are some of the major benefits.

- **Faster software development**: APIs define the contract for communication by two interacting software components. With the contract getting defined and finalized at the beginning with the API-first approach, the development of the API provider and consumer applications can happen in parallel.

  The applications must respect and adhere to the interface definition of the APIs and develop their applications according to it. This decouples the development teams in their work. The consumer application does not have to wait for the provider application to be developed first. It can be built against a mock service that conforms to the API interface. Even the provider applications development can happen in parallel if they implement the defined API interface.

- **A better developer experience**: The API-first approach advocates and focuses on building APIs as a product. In an API value chain, developers use this product to create a rich ecosystem. Developers would be using the APIs to fetch or update information needed for their applications. Hence, the APIs should be designed to be intuitive and easy to use for the developers.

  An API-first approach designs the interface with the end user and developer in mind on how they would practically use the APIs. An API designed with REST principles and good documentation provides a smooth onboarding experience for the developers with a reduced learning curve. It ensures that developers have a positive experience using the APIs.

- **Improved software quality**: The API-first approach facilitates the development of microservice-based architecture for any application. With microservices, you can build fault-tolerant systems that can withstand the failure of a microservice. This improves product quality and customer satisfaction.

- **Faster time to market**: The API-first approach advocates treating API as the "first-class citizen." Hence, APIs are the focus of all development. This increases the reusability of APIs as the development team looks for existing APIs to integrate into their applications. New features and capabilities can be built without the need to re-architect the application, which speeds up the overall development process and reduces timelines for releasing new capabilities.

The API-first approach also automates many steps in the API development process with various tools. The tools can automate the generation of SDKs, mocks, and API documentation from the API definition file. This significantly speeds up the overall development lifecycle and improves the time to market for new features and releases of applications built using an API-first approach.

- **Consistent and simplified governance**: The API-first approach promotes discoverability and observability. This reduces the possibility of API sprawl, as new APIs would be created only if one cannot be discovered. If something exists, it should be enhanced to meet the business needs. Greater visibility with an API-first approach also brings standardization and consistency in API interface design. The API-first approach simplifies governance by ensuring that rules and policies are applied uniformly across all APIs.
- **Robust security**: Given that APIs are the first-class citizens in an application's design and are transmitting data that may be sensitive, they should be protected with a solid security perimeter. The API-first approach provides visibility into the data classification of information exchanged via APIs. It helps API architects and cybersecurity teams decide how to implement defense-in-depth security for APIs.

  API architects can design and enforce consistent governance and security across all APIs to protect against unauthorized access and OWASP vulnerabilities. API security can be implemented from day one and protect against future unfortunate breaches.

- **Optimized development costs**: APIs provide organizations with access to data and services. Therefore, with an API-first approach, organizations know at the beginning what data and services can be accessed via APIs. This saves cost and reduces investments that would otherwise be required to make that data or service available within the enterprise.

  Instead of investing in setting up FTP servers, creating and maintaining jobs to parse data, and writing services to retrieve data from partners, organizations can use partner APIs to easily access such data and data management services provided by the partners. It saves money on additional infrastructure and engineering resources to maintain data. Thus, the API-first approach helps with refactoring and reorganizing the value chains, saving development costs.

  The ecosystem built with APIs increases the extensibility and reusability of code and saves development costs.

- **Reduced risk of failure**: The API-first approach relies on the principle that APIs are the product. Hence, like any product, APIs evolve gradually to meet the changing customer needs. Thus, risks associated with ever-changing business needs are reduced with the API-first approach. API-first development creates consistent and reusable APIs that decrease the risk of application failures.

Getting Started with the API-First Approach

Starting development using an API-first approach requires planning, strategic thinking, proper governance, and executive support. The following describes the high-level steps to adopt an API-first approach.

- **Brainstorm and understand the API strategy**: For an organization to start with an API-first approach, it is important to understand the services offered and the business strategy. Based on the key service offerings, identify the consumers of the service and the stakeholders within the organization to provide those services. Having identified the services, brainstorm to understand and define the use cases that these services would fulfill and then figure out the kind of APIs to be built to provide these services to the consumers. Define and list the service capabilities to be offered using APIs.

- **Identify key stakeholders**: Building an API-first organization needs a few new roles to be defined and created within the enterprise. An API product owner and API evangelist. An API product owner defines the organization's API strategy, defines the vision and goals of the APIs, and ensures that they meet the business objectives. The product owner liaises with business stakeholders, developers, and other teams to ensure that API development meets the needs of all parties. The product owner lays out a roadmap plan for API development with a prioritized list of features.

  An API evangelist promotes, advocates, and fosters the adoption of API-first principles and practices within the organization. An API evangelist provides education and training to various teams within the organization about the benefits of the API-first approach. The product owner creates and raises awareness about the value and potential of APIs by sharing success stories and case studies to drive API adoption within and outside the organization.

- **Build an organizational culture for an API-first mindset**: To successfully adopt the API-first approach across the organization, it is important to build a culture for API-first. That means everyone across the organization must consider building APIs as a product. Every capability and service to be built and offered must have a user-friendly API interface.

  APIs must be built with consumers in mind and designed with an easy-to-use interface. You need to identify the stakeholders responsible for building the APIs, and they must buy into the API initiative. Having maximum involvement from various organizational stakeholders in building the API would be better. A company-wide buy-in and a vision shared by teams within your organization is necessary to build the culture for developing applications using an API-first approach.

- **Set up an effective API governance**: An API-first approach also needs strong API governance. All APIs across the organization must follow the same standards and implementation processes. A comprehensive style guide must be created for API development, and that must be followed consistently.

Every API design must follow the same conventions for URLs, versioning approach, input/output parameter names, and error codes. Use tools for API interface design and to maintain consistency. APIs must also be secured uniformly using established organizational and industry standards.

- **Accelerate API development with automation**: Once the API interface has been designed and agreed upon by all stakeholders, it must form the basis for implementing consumer and provider applications in an API-first approach. Various API development and testing tools can automate and accelerate the API development lifecycle steps. These tools can use the defined API interface to create skeleton classes for API implementation, generate API documentation, validate API style and versioning, and create test cases for automated testing of APIs.

- **Manage APIs using an API management platform**: As the number of APIs within the organizations grows, it is necessary to keep track of them to avoid duplication and promote reuse. Developers within the organization should know of available APIs. Hence, organizations must maintain a catalog of APIs with proper documentation for their usage.

  Also, enterprises must manage and track them centrally to implement security and get business insights for API usage. An API management platform is the ideal solution for centralized management and tracking of APIs.

- **Publish APIs via the developer portal**: Once the APIs have been built, they should be published on a portal for internal and external consumption. An API developer portal provides the ability to publish the API catalog to consumers. APIs can be categorized into buckets based on business functionality to make them more searchable.

  The developer portal also allows you to provide interactive documentation of APIs that consumers can use to better understand the capabilities of the APIs and how to use them. It provides a test bed to test the APIs against a sandbox environment. The developer portal builds an ecosystem for your APIs and grows the business.

Challenges with the API-First Approach

Adopting an API-first approach is not always easy. It has its challenges that should be addressed early to reap the benefits.

- **Culture change**: Adopting an API-first approach in an organization is often a big cultural change. Everyone in the organization needs to think differently from the traditional approach they are used to. API-first development requires a new way of thinking about software architecture and development processes, which can be challenging for some teams to embrace. Hence, this needs executive-level support to bring organizational-level change in culture, mindset, and processes.

To be successful with API-first development, organizations must invest in building a collaborative culture and adopt an agile delivery approach. They need to break silos and promote cross-functional teams to work together with a common goal of building APIs that all developers love. The API-first approach must focus on understanding the end-user needs and building flexible, scalable, secure, and easy-to-use APIs.

- **Initial investments**: Another challenge with adopting the API-first approach is that it needed initial investments to purchase new tools, frameworks, and platforms to build and deploy the APIs. Enterprises must plan for API gateway and/or API management platforms to securely expose and manage their APIs. Enterprises may need to invest in API design and development tools to build the API. Investments may be required for training to bridge the skill gaps and upskill people on the design and development of API using different technologies.
- **Increased cross-functional collaboration**: Designing a high-quality API interface before implementing the functionality is not easy. It needs a good knowledge of the business functionality. It needs a deep understanding of the business requirements and the user needs. It needs collaboration between various teams and departments to ensure that APIs meet the needs of all stakeholders. All these need strong communication and coordination efforts that add to the challenges of building applications with an API-first approach.

- **Security concerns**: With an API-first mindset, all product capabilities are exposed as APIs. When these APIs are exposed externally, it increases the security vulnerabilities and threats as they become the target for all hackers and malicious attacks. An increase in the number of external APIs increases the attack surface. Hence, proper planning and extensive design must be done to address various threats. One needs to think through all the possibilities of attacks via APIs and implement appropriate security measures to protect the system and its data.
- **Governance**: The API-first approach also needs strong governance and approval processes. API governance standardizes APIs so that they are reusable and discoverable. A strong governance process is needed to make all APIs consistent across the organization and ensure that they are built uniformly following the right standards and processes. Effective governance reduces API sprawl, promotes API quality and security, and ensures that every API—private or public—delivers its maximum value at scale.

If these challenges are addressed early with proper executive support, developers can design and build robust APIs that meet the application's requirements and provide a better user experience.

Conclusion

Adopting an API-first approach has many benefits for the organization. It builds APIs as a product that provides an enriching developer and end-user experience faster and more efficiently. But following the API-first approach is hard, and it needs a culture and discipline to be followed in building the API. However, the effort is worth it as the result is a better product—an API everyone loves.

CHAPTER 15

Build APIs as a Product

APIs are generally seen as a technology enabler to provide a service or business capability or enable easy application integration. However, that does not paint the complete picture of APIs. Organizations offer their core products and services via APIs to expand their ecosystems with partners. App developers are building apps using APIs that connect to enterprise back ends to provide new innovative experiences for consumers. As a result, APIs have become the core of the business, driving value and growth. APIs not only provide access to core enterprise products and act as the mode of service delivery but are being seen as the "product" itself. This is a significant paradigm shift that needs discipline and a cultural change within the organization to reap the real business benefits of APIs and have a competitive advantage.

APIs must be designed, developed, and marketed like any other product. It needs a change in the way of thinking. Organizations must think of API as a digital product for improving customer experiences. APIs must be packaged and sold as stand-alone products with their own business and monetization model. This chapter looks at the benefits of building APIs as a product and how some organizations have been offering their services using APIs as a product approach.

B. De, *API Management*, https://doi.org/10.1007/979-8-8688-0054-2_15

This chapter covers the philosophy of building APIs as a product and discusses the differences between a product and a project mindset for building APIs. The chapter also covers the detailed approach to building APIs as a product and the importance of an API product owner in that journey to drive and use that mindset to deliver a minimum viable product.

The Benefits of Building an API as a Product

Building APIs as a product offers companies more opportunities to improve their revenues through API monetization. Many companies like Salesforce, Stripe, and eBay have opened up their core business using APIs. As per reports from the *Harvard Business Review*, 50% of Salesforce transactions and 60% of eBay's listings are done through APIs. Treating APIs as a product also helps improve their overall quality with consumer feedback. A product mindset forces the organization to prioritize various non-functional aspects like security, reliability, and availability, making APIs as a product more robust, powerful and attractive.

Examples of API as a Product Delivery

Today, many organizations provide their services and data using the API as a Product delivery model. The following are some examples.

- **Google Maps**: Google is providing its Google Map services via APIs that enterprises and developers use to access Google's plethora of geographic data and provide value-added and enriching experiences to their customers.

- **Uber APIs**: Uber provides its car booking services across the globe via APIs. Various travel portals have integrated with Uber via their APIs to provide their end customers with a seamless cab booking experience.
- **Embedded finance**: Many banks and financial institutions across the globe have been providing services like lending, payment processes, and insurance that can be consumed from non-financial platforms.

  Financial services are being integrated into everyday products and platforms to make them more accessible and convenient for customers. This is possible through APIs for payments, lending, insurance, investments, and other financial operations that are exposed by financial organizations and can be integrated into non-financial products and apps for everyday use. Organizations providing these APIs build them as products to provide a seamless integration experience.

These are just a few examples of enterprises and institutions providing access to their core business applications and services via APIs. By selling APIs as a product, companies can monetize their data and services while ensuring certain levels of service quality for their customers using the APIs.

Understanding API as a Product Strategy

Let's look at the characteristics of a "product" to better understand what it means to deliver an API as a product. If you imagine a smartphone or a car as a product, you realize it has the following characteristics.

- It has a specification that defines its features and capabilities.

- It has a development lifecycle for its design, build, test, release, and deprecation.
- It is marketed to promote its adoption among users.
- It evolves with new features and capabilities.
- It comes with an assured quality of service.
- It has a cost or pricing model.
- It has a manufacturer who supports it post-sales with fixes and repairs.

For APIs to be successful, they should be designed and built using the same philosophy and characteristics of a product.

The Difference Between Project vs. Product Mindset

The importance of building API as a product becomes clearer when you look at the difference between a project and a product mindset. Traditionally, in the IT world, most work has been delivered as a project that has a fixed scope, deliverables, timelines, and resources allocated. After the work is done, the allocated resources move on to work on a new project. But, with the shift in customer demands, there is often a need to work on customer feedback and improvise the deliverables. Customers today expect their experience to evolve and become better with the service provided. That brings in the need for continued delivery of services rather than fixed scope delivery from a project—a shift from a project mindset to a product mindset.

Lets look in details at the difference between a project and a product. The following is the definition of a project as provided by the Project Management Institute.

> *A project is temporary in that it has a defined beginning and end in time, and therefore defined scope and resources. And a project is unique in that it is not a routine operation, but a specific set of operations designed to accomplish a singular goal.*

A product is a good or service that solves a customer problem and delivers value. It is built with a customer focus and evolves with multi-directional feedback. It follows a more pragmatic and adaptive approach to providing customer value.

The shift to a product mindset is the need of the hour to deliver better outcomes that address the ever-changing needs and provide higher customer value. This mindset fosters a problem-solving attitude through end-user interactions rather than taking stakeholder orders. It focuses more on delivering values and minimizing waste through continuous, iterative, and incremental development loops. APIs should be designed and developed as a product that adds value and solves real customer problems over time.

Table 15-1 summarizes the differences between a project and a product mindset.

***Table 15-1.** The Differences Between a Project Mindset and a Product Mindset*

Project Mindset	Product Mindset
The project has a fixed scope of delivery with start and end dates	Products solve a customer problem holistically in an iterative manner with an evolutionary approach
The project focuses on building a specific solution or system—what to work on and how to build it to meet a system requirement.	The focus of the product is to solve a customer problem—understand the whys and address the customer's needs.
The project aims for on-time, on-budget, and on-scope delivery.	Product aims to deliver what is feasible, valuable, and desirable to customers.
The project aims to deliver by breaking a big scope of work into smaller pieces.	Product is built experimentally with small incremental goals that deliver value to customers.
The project has key delivery metrics to measure its success	The success of a product is measured based on the customer experience and feedback
The project does an upfront analysis to identify and mitigate all risks	Product development follows a just-in-time resolution of impediments through cross-team collaborations
Project delivery follows rigid governance with strict standards, guidelines, and checklists.	Product delivery follows more pragmatic and adaptive guardrails to ensure compliance with industry and regulatory requirements.

Having understood the value adds that a product mindset brings, let's now look at what it needs to build APIs as a product. The following sections highlight the overall approach to building APIs as a product that consumers will love - starting with a mindset change.

Build the API Product Mindset

Building APIs as a product is a cultural change that needs to foster a product mindset. Let's look at how to build the APIs with a product mindset.

Define API Specifications that Meet the Needs of the Target Audience

API must be designed to meet the needs of its target consumers. Its functionality and value proposition must be clearly defined. API development must, therefore, start by defining its specifications. The API specification defines the contract for using the API. The contract must be user-friendly and easy to understand. It must define the input, output, and mandatory and optional parameters to use the API. Open API specification can be used to define the specifications of the API. The specification defines the contract for using the API and must state all the available capabilities and operations supported by the API, along with the data format for information exchange. APIs should be designed keeping the customer and end-user needs and context in mind. Designing an intuitive, user-friendly, and pragmatic API with a defined specification lays the foundation for a successful API.

Design and Build APIs per Specifications

Like any product, API development should go through all the phases of SDLC design, build, test, deploy, and retire. API design starts with its specification—defining the input, output, and data format for all operations to be supported. The design must also define its access and security policies and follow the right design principles for building REST, GraphQL, or gRPC APIs. API designers also define the technologies and design patterns to be used for the implementation. An API may be implemented using microservice-based architecture for flexibility and agility to make future changes. The design must also cover the availability and scalability needs of the APIs to meet the growing consumer demands. After the design is complete, the API developer builds and unit tests the APIs.

Like a product that can be built using materials or components sourced from various vendors, an API can be built using any language or framework best suited to implement the business functionality. Developers may use Java Spring Boot, Python Fast API, or any other frameworks they choose for implementation. Once implemented, the API must go through a rigorous round of testing. Typical test cycles include API interface testing, integration testing, security testing, and performance testing. Once tested, it is deployed on a production server and made available for consumption.

Promote APIs with Comprehensive Documentation and Marketing Campaigns

APIs need to be marketed to promote their consumption like any product. The most common approach to marketing APIs is to publish them on the company's API developer portal. Organizations can publish the list of their available APIs and their specifications on the developer portal. API consumers can then find them on the portal.

Comprehensive documentation with all the endpoints, input parameters, API key, responses, and potential errors is key. Interactive documentation, with tutorials, allows developers to experiment with the API and promote immediate API adoption.

Another common way to market APIs is through developer hackathons. Such hackathons can spread information about the API through the mouth of developers who want to use the APIs to build innovative use cases to solve real-world consumer problems. It also helps to get honest and direct feedback about the APIs' capability and ease of use.

Improve APIs Based on Customer Feedback and Needs

Organizations must plan to implement the feedback received to improve the APIs and provide a better experience for consumers. New capabilities must be built incrementally and released to market as a new version or variant. With the release of a new version, older versions of the API must be slowly deprecated over time.

Maintaining multiple versions of the same API is a costly affair. Hence, the organization must consciously decide to only have a maximum of two to three versions active at any time. The ideal number of active API versions is two. However, under practical situations, organizations may have to keep more than two versions active for their consumers. Keeping a greater number of versions active means increased maintenance costs and overheads. Hence, organizations must actively plan to deprecate older versions and work closely with their clients to help them migrate to the newer API version. Publishing an EOL date for older versions or incentivizing consumers to move to new versions are common approaches to retiring older API revisions.

Adhere to SLAs Advertised for APIs

Every API released must ensure a certain quality of standards. Response time, availability, reliability, and security are some SLAs that every API must conform to. Organizations must invest in ensuring that APIs meet the advertised or promised SLAs. Consumers have higher confidence and loyalty for APIs that meet the SLAs. Planned outages must be communicated well in advance to the API consumers. Every API must be instrumented and monitored to ensure the highest quality of service. The built-in dashboards provided by most API Management platforms, can be readily used to view and monitor API performance analytics and SLA adherence.

Monetize APIs with the Right Model

Like any other product, APIs must have the right monetization model. Consumers and subscribers should be willing to pay for and feel the value of their money while using the APIs. Not every API may be directly monetized. Indirect and freemium monetization models often increase API consumption and attract new customers.

Choosing the right API monetization model is important for its successful adoption. Arriving at the right monetization model and pricing for usage is non-trivia. The cost of API usage must be derived based on the value it provides to its consumers, either through the data or the service provided. For example, API providers may charge a fixed convenience fee from their consumers for providing a movie ticket or Uber cab booking service, or it can charge based on a tiered pricing model for no. of usage to retrieve important and valuable data.

Provide Warranty Support for APIs

Finally, every API needs to be supported by its provider. App developers, who are the main consumers of the APIs, must be able to report issues with invoking the APIs and get the required support to resolve them. Support can be provided in response to issues reported through a ticketing system, contact center, chatbot, or community portal. API consumers should be able to discuss their issues with other fellow users. Reported bugs and issues should be addressed promptly to win the consumers' trust using the APIs. Whatever the mechanism or platform be, proper support for every API is needed and important for their success, and organizations building APIs must invest in it.

Build APIs as a Minimum Viable Product

Getting valuable feedback early is essential for building good APIs. Feedback from app developers and other API consumers can be used to iterate and improve the API quality. Hence, instead of releasing APIs with all the desirable features in one go, they must be developed as a minimum viable product that focuses on the core value proposition and can be scaled rapidly. Additional capabilities can be added in future releases iteratively. The following principles should be followed when managing the lifecycle of the MVP release.

- Design and build APIs that are easy to use following the RESTful best practices.
- Focus on building the core API capabilities in initial releases and additions.
- Protect APIs using adequate security policies for authentication, authorization, and data protection.
- Automate API testing and deployment using the DevSecOps approach to ensure quality and consistency.

Drive API Adoption with a World-Class Developer Experience

Once an API has been built and deployed, it is important to drive its adoption. Developer experience plays a crucial role in driving API adoption. App developers must be able to easily find the APIs and start using them for their apps. Developers look for good interactive documentation for the API interface to quickly get started with the API. An easy and seamless onboarding experience attracts developers to use the APIs. Ensuring adherence to API performance SLAs through regular monitoring is another important step to drive API adoption.

The approaches discussed in the following sections help enterprises provide a world-class experience to their API consumers and drive API adoption.

Set up a Developer Portal to Publish APIs

Enterprise partners and ecosystem developers must know about the APIs. They need to know what APIs are available, their capability, and how to use them for building new and enhanced customer experiences. The first step toward that is to set up a developer portal and publish API documentation in the portal. The developer portal provides the platform for app consumers to start with the APIs. It significantly improves the time to market with easy access to API documentation, a getting started guide, a test bed, and a playground to build the first "Hello World" app using the APIs. Developers can try out the APIs through interactive documentation against a sandbox environment. The developer portal also provides additional capabilities like forums and blogs to build communities that can drive API adoption. Growing adoption of APIs within the partner ecosystem brings invaluable feedback to improve the APIs and opens doors for new business opportunities with APIs.

Evangelize APIs and Act on Feedback

API teams need to establish the presence of their APIs within the right communities to drive their adoption. Hackathons are a popular way to spread the news and capabilities of the APIs through the word of mouth of developers. Meetups and conferences are other avenues to evangelize API adoption. The enterprise must invest in providing test beds or a sandbox environment for developers to experiment with the APIs. Feedback received directly from app developers can make the APIs better. Hence, significant effort must be invested to understand and address the developer's needs and preferences. Assurance to the developer community with all the necessary support through various channels to resolve their queries and issues with API usage, increase their trust, and thus increase API adoption.

Monitor APIs for SLA Adherence

With increasing adoption, it is important to ensure that the APIs meet certain performance SLAs. An increase in latency or a growing number of 5xx errors are common issues noticed with growing API traffic. Keeping an eye on the APIs' performance metrics helps ensure that the client applications or mobile apps using these APIs are also working as expected. Proactive monitoring can identify potential performance bottlenecks and plan for necessary actions to mitigate them. Hence, enterprises must set up proper monitoring and alerting systems to monitor API performance.

Most API Management platforms provide in-built capabilities and dashboards to monitor the performance of the individual APIs and API products. Creating appropriate dashboards for various stakeholders like business owners, API developers, and platform operators provides the required view of the business and operational metrics to drive API adoption and address challenges with API usage.

Monetize APIs with the Right Monetization Model

Like any other product, APIs must be priced appropriately with the right monetization model. The monetization model must provide value to all actors in the API value chain, including the API provider, app developer, and end user; only then is the monetization of the API successful.

The monetization models can be broadly categorized into direct and indirect monetization models. Whereas the direct monetization model results in cash and revenue growth, indirect monetization delivers value through varied ways like improved brand value, increased customer base, easier partnership, improved operational efficiency, and many more.

Let's focus on selecting the right direct monetization model for pricing APIs. Direct monetization models can be of two types: the subscriber pays or gets paid. In the "subscriber pays" model, the consumers pay the provider for API usage. The "subscriber gets paid" model is a revenue-sharing model where the API provider shares their revenue with the app developer for the traffic routed through their apps.

A "subscriber pays" model can be of various types.

- **Pay-per-use**: In this model, the consumers pay for every invocation of API. There is no minimum or tiered pricing for API usage. Consumers are billed on a periodic (e.g., monthly) basis. Pay-per-use may be a lucrative monetization model, but it has its downside as it deters new users. This model works only when the end user sees value from the API usage.
- **Freemium**: In this model, consumers get to use the APIs for free during the initial set of calls within a period. For example, the first 100 API calls in a month may be free, and calls beyond that may be charged.

Another flavor to this model is that you can use APIs that provide basic features for free, but advanced features may be charged. APIs to view information may be free, but you may have to pay if you want to use APIs to create and update. Many popular APIs have been launched with a freemium model that has helped attract and onboard many app developers.

- **Tiered**: In this model, the consumer is charged at different rates based on the number of API calls made during a period. This model provides different pricing slabs based on the call volume. For example, for the first 1,000 calls, subscribers may pay 10 cents/call. For 1,000 to 10,000 calls, subscribers would be charged at 8 cents/call, and beyond 10,000, the rate per API call would be 5 cents/call.

  An alternative to tiered pricing is based on the slab selected by the API consumer, similar to the old mobile phone plans that allowed a certain number of calls within a pricing slab, and consumers selected that slab based on their usage pattern. For $100, a subscriber gets 10,000 API calls a month; for $500, the subscriber can make up to 100,000 API calls a month. So, the subscriber can sign up for a plan and get billed a fixed amount even if they don't use the entire allowed quota of API calls for their slab. Calls made beyond the allowed limits may be blocked or charged at a premium rate. A tiered pricing model can drive up the API consumption. Usually, tiered pricing is adopted to drive higher usage of APIs.

- **Transaction fee**: In this model, a fixed or a percentage of the transaction fee is paid to the API provider.

Market API Products

Like any other product, APIs should be advertised and marketed to highlight their benefits and value adds. It is important to identify the target consumer segment of the API—be it business partners or app developers looking to build cool apps. Demonstrate how the APIs can help solve the business problems and pain points of the consumers.

API marketing must highlight the developer experience rather than corporate branding. Marketing should focus on the capabilities and ease of use of the API. Investments in marketing must promote the API value proposition, its ease of use, and rich documentation for developers. Build and demo sample use cases highlighting the API value proposition to make an unforgettable experience. Highlight the community support and availability of sandbox environments for trying out the APIs, resolving issues, and experiencing it before use. Marketing and promotions through targeted ads, webinars with influencers, or thought leadership content can also drive API adoption and create a brand for the API. Twillo, Stripe, Google Maps, GitHub, and OpenWeather are organizations that have marketed their APIs well with the right documentation, community support, and clear pricing strategy to drive their fast-paced adoption and growth.

The following are some of the best practices to market APIs.

- Publishing APIs in popular API directories and marketplaces
- Creating content to articulate the business value of API
- Hosting events like hackathons and webinars to talk about your APIs
- Providing informative content to get started with using the APIs and building apps

- Using social media to connect with prospective API consumers and build relationships
- Creating forums to build a developer community for your APIs
- Using launch announcements with countdowns to publish new releases of APIs
- Publishing the API monetization and business models
- Rewarding app developers for building innovative use cases with the APIs

The Role of an API Product Owner

It needs to have a product owner to build an API as a product. An API product owner is a key leadership role responsible for making all the key decisions on how an API should be built to deliver customer value. The API product owner is responsible for defining the end vision and goal of the API. They are the voice and advocate of the API consumer, who understand consumer needs and pain points. They define the functionality that should be provided by the API and the strategy to build it the right way. They assess the impact of the API on the consumers and get their feedback to improve it further. The product owner ensures that the API meets the business goals and is built with values a consumer would be willing to pay for.

In building APIs as a product, the product owner would be responsible for the following.

- Defining the overall product strategy to ensure that the APIs meet the business objectives and market needs
- Managing the stakeholders' expectations, including business executives, developers, marketers, and end users

- Defining an iterative roadmap for building APIs with a list of features to build, their priorities, and enhancements based on business value, user impact, and technical feasibility
- Communicating and evangelizing the vision and value of the APIs with regular updates on the progress to all stakeholders
- Overseeing the release process of the APIs and working with development teams to ensure release schedules are met
- Monitoring and tracking the usage and adoption of the APIs to identify areas of improvement and optimizations
- Continuously gathering feedback from users of the APIs, reviewing market needs, and subsequently suggesting iterative improvements for the APIs

In this journey of API, the API product owner would interact with stakeholders involved in the API value chain. The product owner would interact with the customers and end users to understand their needs, service expectations, and the use case for the API. Based on these inputs, they would help define the API capabilities. The API product owner also interacts with the business and strategy owners to secure funding to build the APIs. They work with the design and build team to define the implementation roadmap and ensure that the APIs meet the business requirements. The API product owner plays a crucial role in building APIs as a product. Throughout the lifecycle, the API product owner liaises with the marketing teams to evangelize and define the API's business value and monetization model. In summary, the API product owner creates and manages the end-to-end roadmap to build APIs as a product that consumers love to use.

To succeed in the job, the API product owner must have a business mindset and possess the following skills.

- Good leadership qualities and collaboration skills
- Good product management skills
- Good knowledge of the business
- Excellent interpersonal and communication skills
- API technology knowledge

Conclusion

Building APIs as a product not only helps to monetize them but also helps to win the confidence and trust of the consumers and app developers. It sets organizations on the right trajectory to reap the benefits of their investments in API programs. However, it needs a change in the organizational structure and culture to bring in the right mindset. An API Product owner plays a vital role. Organizations must be ready to invest and appoint a product owner who can bring in the right leadership to build and launch APIs as a minimum viable product that can later evolve with feedback from developers and end users.

CHAPTER 16

API Architecture Trends in 2023

Today, APIs are the cornerstone of all digital transformation initiatives across the industry. APIs are driving innovations and have become the backbone for new customer experiences. However, customer demands, economic forces, and industry trends are reimagining how APIs should be used to grow the business and remain competitive. This chapter covers some of the top trends in the industry that are adopted as API technologies evolve and enterprises accelerate their APIs and digital transformation journey.

The recent pandemic has forced organizations to significantly change their business model and consumer experiences. The change is evident in every industry, from retail to banking to healthcare, travel, and hospitality. There has been a rise in digital and contactless payments, an increase in e-commerce transactions, and a change in customer expectations. Insurance companies and hospitals have adapted to the demands of virtual visits. While all these changes have been possible because APIs have provided secure channels of interaction, there has also been a change in the way APIs are designed and used to build different use cases.

With the evolution of technologies, new patterns of API interactions have evolved. Microservice architecture has become mainstream for digital application development, enabling enterprises to build highly scalable and flexible architecture using a collection of small and loosely coupled

B. De, *API Management*, https://doi.org/10.1007/979-8-8688-0054-2_16

services that can be deployed independently. Application deployment in containerized Docker environments orchestrated using Kubernetes has helped to build lightweight and portable applications. Developments in serverless computing have allowed developers to focus more on writing optimal code without worrying about server maintenance or scaling server resources to meet customer demands. Developers are now building more flexible and reactive APIs using event-driven architectures. Applications built using event-driven architecture allow systems to emit and respond to events and triggers in real time. This architectural pattern has built high-performance and real-time applications. AsyncAPI has brought the richness of the REST API ecosystem to the event-driven world with machine and human-readable specifications for asynchronous APIs. The rise of technologies like gRPC and GraphQL has built performance-optimized APIs that return the exact amount of information needed for the application to function. APIs also enable enterprises to harness the power of AI/ML technologies. Since these technologies depend on large volumes of data, enhanced security for APIs is the need of the hour to succeed with artificial intelligence (AI) and machine learning (ML). With all these advancements, API-first architecture takes center stage, where APIs are treated as first-class citizens.

This chapter delves into more detail about some of these new and emerging technology trends supporting the growth of the API ecosystem at the time this book was written. Over time, some of these trends may change, and new patterns evolve.

Trend #1: Increasing Adoption of the API-First Approach for Building an API as a Product

Today, APIs have become a key ingredient for all digital transformation programs. The API-driven business model has become a necessity for organizations to remain competitive. Hence, organizations are increasingly exposing their products and services as APIs. These APIs are being monetized and offered as a product. Companies can monetize their data and services and create new revenue streams by offering APIs as products. Companies like Salesforce have generated half of their revenue through APIs. Other businesses and developers consume these APIs to integrate with their applications. Hence, APIs are being designed with an API-first approach, keeping the experience of developers and consumers in mind. The API-first approach prioritizes developer and consumer experience, which is important to sell APIs as a product. The API-first approach focuses on building a software platform using APIs that are easy to integrate with and scale and can be sold as the primary product. To summarize, an API as a product is the business strategy, while the API-first approach is the technical approach to build the APIs that meet the business needs.

Initially, APIs were used primarily for internal application integration to improve business process efficiency. However, the rise of APIs as a product has helped businesses drive revenue and create new business opportunities. According to Market.us, the API management market size is projected to surpass around USD 49.9 billion by 2032, and it is poised to reach a CAGR of 28% from 2023 to 2032. (`https://www.globenewswire.com/en/news-release/2023/03/21/2631010/0/en/API-Management-Market-to-Reach-Valuation-of-USD-49-9-Billion-at-Cagr-of-28-by-2032-Report-by-Market-us.html`)

The rise of the API-as-a-Product trend is evident in many industries like banking, healthcare, telecom, retail, and transportation. Companies like Stripe, a payment processing company, have built their business by offering payment processing services via APIs. Developers can integrate Stripe APIs into their applications for processing payments, and the company charges a fee for every transaction processed using its APIs. Twilio provides APIs that allow businesses to integrate with its cloud communications platform for building messaging and voice applications. The company charges a fee for each message or call made through its platform. AccuWeather and WeatherAPI both provide weather information via APIs to a broad variety of consumers and developers. Their well-documented and easy-to-use intuitive APIs have helped developers build engaging applications by integrating with their APIs that are offered as stand-alone products.

Benefits of the API-as-a-Product Approach

Building an API as a product provides several benefits, as follows.

- Allows companies to monetize their APIs and create new revenue streams
- Improves customer experience and increases consumer satisfaction as they can rely on the published SLAs of the APIs
- Increases innovation as developers can build new applications using the APIs
- It provides more control to the companies to define how their data and services provided via APIs will be used
- Expands the outreach of the API ecosystem through collaboration with partners

Trend #2: Building an Ecosystem with Hyperconnected APIs

Today, organizations embrace an API-first approach to build and provide their data and services as API products. Instead of keeping data a secret, organizations are more willing to share it with their partners to fuel innovation and creativity. APIs are being used as the channel for partnerships to collaborate and innovate jointly. APIs are helping build an ecosystem through safe and healthy partnerships mutually beneficial to API providers and consumers.

The development of ecosystems with APIs is helping organizations to grow their business and stay afloat in the changing marketplace. Organizations now don't have to depend solely on their traditional revenue channels but can grow their business by collaborating with partners using APIs. Companies are trying to build an API ecosystem to open their business models to innovations. API consumers are the participants in this ecosystem. Consumers can be your internal stakeholders, partners, or third-party developers. This ecosystem can improve the customer experience and reduce development costs.

Rideshare apps like Uber use Google Maps APIs to help customers easily book rides for their local transportation. This collaboration is not only generating revenue for Uber but also for Google. APIs created by Uber to book rides through their app are being integrated into other third-party travel apps to provide their end customers with a complete door-to-door travel experience. Thus, a hyperconnected API ecosystem is improving the end-user experience and opening new revenue streams for each ecosystem's participants.

To build a successful API ecosystem, you should first understand your customers' needs. Do not think only of the services that you can provide, but think of how you can collaborate with others to fill in the gaps and provide a holistic customer experience. Design APIs with user experience and needs in mind. Provide good documentation for the APIs to facilitate its widespread adoption. Work with partners that can improve the overall product through quick and efficient API integration.

Trend #3: Enhancing API Security to Protect Against Increasing API Vulnerabilities

While the growing API ecosystem is advantageous for all organizations and helpful in increasing revenues, it also comes with the challenges of new and unknown security threats for the APIs. Organizations need to gear up and protect their APIs against a variety of threats that were not a concern earlier. According to a report published by SALT Security Labs on the State of API Security based on their survey, 94% of respondents have experienced security problems in production APIs, and there has been a 400% increase in unique attackers. APIs are at the core of every modern application, and attackers continue their efforts at unprecedented rates. Hence, today, API security has become the key focus of all organizations. It has become a major business issue and is a C-level decision for many organizations. There is an increasing investment in API security to protect data and services against security breaches so that they bring desired business benefits.

A robust API security is needed to protect sensitive data from leaks and prevent tampering and loss. API Security must also ensure system integrity by allowing access to APIs by authorized users and applications only. Robust API security must ensure data and functionality correctness, reliability, and confidentiality and prevent unauthorized access and potential malicious attacks.

The following are some of the major API security problems that most organizations face.

- Data breaches due to vulnerabilities and injection attacks
- Problems in API authentication
- Misconfigurations in API Security
- Denial-of-service attacks
- Poor logging practices causing accidental exposure of data
- Zombie APIs

There are multiple ways to protect APIs from security breaches. One of the most common ways to secure APIs is to use one or more of the following.

- Dedicated API security tool
- Web application firewall
- API gateway
- Network firewall

Some of the best practices to implement API security are as follows.

- Implement robust authentication and authorization for API access using a centralized OAuth server.
- Use strong authentication mechanisms using OAuth 2.0 and JWT tokens. Use opaque bearer tokens for external client authentication.
- Use OAuth scopes and claims for authorization checks.
- Use TLS/SSL for API communications to encrypt data in transit and prevent eavesdropping and tampering.

- Avoid exposing sensitive information in error messages. Ensure sensitive data is encrypted or masked in logs.
- Protect APIs against brute force and DDoS attacks using rate limits and quota policies.
- Perform schema validations and sanitize inputs to protect APIs from common injection attacks for SQL, XSS, and scripts.
- Conduct API security vulnerability testing early in the API development lifecycle.
- Perform regular security audits and conduct penetration testing to identify security vulnerabilities.

Trend #4: The Adoption of Microservices Is Building a World of Hyperconnected APIs

The adoption of microservices architecture has increased in the last few years as organizations seek to build highly scalable applications with a flexible architecture and increased agility. Microservices architecture builds modular applications that can be deployed, scaled, and managed independently. REST API is the most common protocol for microservice communications. Hence, microservice adoption in the industry is fueling the growth of APIs. APIs enable a highly decoupled, flexible, and scalable architecture using microservices.

Hence, organizations are embracing an API-driven approach to support their microservices architecture. Increased adoption of microservices is fueling an exponential growth of APIs that interact with each other. A world of hyperconnected APIs is emerging, where one API interacts with several others. These APIs can be internal or external and must be governed, managed, and secured. This increases the complexity of API management and brings in the need for newer capabilities that the new-age API management platforms should provide.

Trend #5: More APIs Are Powered by Serverless Infrastructure to Reduce Overhead

Today, advancements in cloud technologies have created the opportunity for organizations to deploy their applications and APIs on a serverless infrastructure and not worry about procuring and maintaining hardware for deployments. With serverless, you do not have to provision and manage your on-prem servers. Application development teams can focus more on building the business logic and APIs rather than on setting up and resolving issues with infrastructure.

Serverless computing doesn't use any permanent infrastructure. It follows an event-driven model, where the infrastructure is provisioned when required to process the traffic. Serverless APIs use a serverless computing backend. This provides the advantage that businesses and developers do not have to worry about server maintenance and scaling them to meet the growing demands. Since the server resources are provisioned only when needed to serve the API traffic, you only pay for the actual resource usage rather than the entire server setup, which reduces the overall cost and improves efficiency. To summarize, the following are some of the key benefits.

- Serverless APIs are cost-efficient because you don't pay for idle time.
- Serverless APIs have reduced maintenance overheads.
- Serverless APIs have higher reliability and availability.

- Serverless APIs do not need to worry about capacity issues.
- Serverless APIs are highly scalable.

An increasing number of organizations are adopting serverless technologies and APIs and have seen significant success in their endeavors. It has helped them with reduced maintenance and development costs and has helped to scale with demand automatically. Serverless APIs have also improved developer productivity with reduced engineering lead time.

While serverless APIs may sound awesome and come with their own benefits, they require a new mindset to design and build them. Also, since today, serverless technologies are mostly provided by public cloud providers like AWS, Google, and Azure through their proprietary service, adopting serverless API comes with the risk of vendor lock-in.

Trend #6: Using GraphQL to Efficiently Fetch Data with APIs

GraphQL was created by Facebook in 2012 and later open-sourced in 2015 to efficiently fetch data from any source and solve problems of over/under fetching data. Traditional REST approaches to fetch data provide far less or a lot more information than what is needed by the client application. Over-fetching can choke the bandwidth at times and impact the overall application performance. There must be a mechanism to specify the exact information or attributes required in the response— neither more nor less.

GraphQL is a declarative query language for APIs that allows clients to ask for exactly what they need and nothing more or less. It allows client applications to describe the type and shape of required data. This approach to data fetching provides the following advantages.

- **Increased flexibility for API development**: GraphQL allows developers to request the data they need. Hence, clients can specify the information they want. This provides increased flexibility in developing more efficient and effective APIs.
- **Improved API performance**: GraphQL prevents over-fetching data and reduces bandwidth requirements. In cases where REST API had to be called multiple times to fetch all the required data, resulting in slower API performance, GraphQL lets you fetch all the required data in a single call to the server. This improves overall network resource usage and application performance.
- **Improved developer experience**: GraphQL allows developers to specify their queries declaratively and ask for specific data. This makes queries cohesive and easier to understand. Related data can be fetched in a single request rather than stitching them from multiple responses if using REST. With GraphQL, you can fetch all the data from one single endpoint. All of these improve the overall developer experience while using GraphQL APIs.
- **Easy to evolve and maintain**: It eliminates the need to version APIs. GraphQL API allows you to easily add new fields and relationships without worrying about breaking existing client code, thus reducing compatibility issues between clients and servers.

Gartner predicted that more than 50% of enterprises will use GraphQL in production by 2025, up from less than 10% in 2021. Today, GraphQL is widely used by many renowned companies, like GitHub, PayPal, Twitter, Meta, Glassdoor, Audi, Airbnb, and *The New York Times,* to name a few.

A growing community is building tools in various languages for GraphQL developers. Though the adoption of GraphQL is increasing, some drawbacks should be considered when designing GraphQL APIs. The following are some of the disadvantages.

- **Caching overheads**: GraphQL uses a single endpoint and POST verb for all requests. Every query acts on the same resource entity. Hence, unlike REST API, where each unique resource URL can be used as an identifier, implementing caching can be complex due to the lack of such an associated identifier in GraphQL.
- **Inefficient queries impacting performance**: While GraphQL allows you to specify the data to be returned in the response, it does lack the ability to specify maximum query depths, query complexity weighting, avoiding recursion, or persistent queries to stop inefficient requests from the client side. This may result in a large data set being returned in response over the network, impacting performance if the client asks for deeply nested or multiple related entities.
- **Challenges with throttling requests**: Since GraphQL uses a single endpoint for all requests, throttling the number of requests for specific requests at the same endpoint can be challenging. It is difficult to define throttling limits based on the query.
- **Lack of monitoring infrastructure**: Most present-day monitoring tools rely on ping services and health check service URLs to probe the health of the service. They rely on the HTTP response codes to determine the health of the service. An HTTP response code of 2xx is regarded as a healthy state. REST services respond with a 4xx or 5xx response code in case of errors.

However, GraphQL always responds with an HTTP status code of 200 OK, even in case of errors. The error information and the data in the response payload are included in the "error" field. Hence, any monitoring tool must parse the response payload to check for success or error to determine the health of the service. This makes it challenging to monitor the health of GraphQL with traditional monitoring tools.

Trend #7: The Rise of gRPC as a Protocol for Efficient Service Communications

Today, organizations build applications using microservices architecture that gives higher flexibility, agility, and scalability. These microservices communicate frequently with each other to fulfill various business functionality. This brings in the need for a low latency and high throughput communication protocol for inter-microservice communications. gRPC is the answer from Google in 2015 for that.

gRPC uses a protocol buffer for data serialization and HTTP/2 for the transport protocol. These two techniques make gRPC more efficient and highly performant.

A **protocol buffer** lets you serialize and deserialize structured data in a binary format that reduces the overall size of the encoded message. Since the data is represented in binary format, it is less CPU-intensive and reduces processing complexity. All these make the protocol buffer more efficient than other formats like JSON and XML.

HTTP/2 communication uses smaller messages framed in binary format. It supports bidirectional communication and allows you to make multiple calls via the same channel. This makes HTTP/2 more compact and efficient for sending and receiving messages.

These techniques make gRPC APIs seven to ten times faster than REST APIs, driving the increasing adoption of gRPC as a protocol for efficient microservice communication. gRPC can become the preferred choice over REST when building high-performance polyglot applications where efficient communication is the key.

Unfortunately, the lack of mature community support and limited web-browser support for gRPC currently deter its adoption at a wider scale in the mainstream. But this will likely change soon as the community support grows with more information on best practices, workaround, and success stories of gRPC implementation.

Trend #8: Enabling Real-Time Communication Using Event-Driven APIs

Event-driven architecture enables real-time communication and seamless integration between different systems and services. It eliminates the need for a consumer service to poll and wait for updates. It uses events as triggers to communicate between services. Consumer services would register with a broker with its interest in a business event and would be notified as soon as that event occurs. This mode of asynchronous communication improves overall scalability by decoupling the communication logic from the business logic. It is commonly used to build microservice-based applications, where each service is a producer or consumer of events. Event-driven APIs combine the strengths of APIs with event-driven architecture.

Event-driven APIs provide the following benefits.

- **High scalability and resiliency**: The event broker decouples the provider and consumer services. Provider service can continue to process the request without being impacted by the state of the consumer services. Also, the events produced can be processed by multiple subscribers. Decoupling of the producer and consumer service improves the application's overall scalability and resiliency.

- **Better performance**: Real-time communications based on an event trigger improve the application's overall performance. Consumers do not have to poll for updates; they are notified in real time via events when an update happens.
- **Improved flexibility**: Decoupling between provider and consumer service avoids any kind of point-to-point integration. It is easy to add new producer and consumer services to enhance the application's functionality without any impact. Also, changes can be made to the provider and consumer implementations, provided they adhere to the event schema definition.

Overall, event-driven API architecture improves the application's scalability, performance, and flexibility, enabling organizations to react quickly to changing business requirements. This is driving the increased adoption of event-driven API despite the implementation complexities. Today API many management platforms have also evolved to provide integration capabilities with event brokers to support event-driven APIs, enabling asynchronous and real time communications.

Trend #9: AI/ML Features via APIs

AI and ML technologies have matured significantly. Organizations are considering adopting and integrating them in their applications to provide a better customer experience. However, setting up the AI capabilities is not simple, and not every organization can afford to build them in-house. APIs have paved the avenues to easily add AI and ML capabilities into the applications and make them more intelligent.

AI APIs can be used for various functions including, but not limited to, facial recognition, speech recognition, image recognition, sentiment analysis, language translation, text summarization, location detection, stock market predictions, future recommendations, and many more. APIs that use AI have unlimited potential to help businesses with creativity, speed, and growth.

AI-based APIs provide the following benefits.

- **Cost savings**: Building and maintaining an AI infrastructure requires significant investment. With AI capabilities available from major and niche providers via API, organizations do not have to invest in manpower and server resources to build the capabilities in-house. This is a huge cost saving for companies using AI capabilities in their applications.

- **Efficiency**: Using pre-trained models helps developers save time and resources on building such models on their own. APIs provide the required capabilities without having to build them from scratch. This fast-tracks the integration of data science and AI capabilities into the applications easily without doing any heavy lifting of building and training your own models. A well-designed AI model can help companies automate parts of the business processes using accurate data-based decisions, thus increasing overall operational efficiency.

- **Scalability**: Many of the APIs to leverage the AI capabilities are provided by large niche vendors as SaaS platform. They manage the availability and scalability of the APIs.
- **Accessibility**: APIs abstract the AI and ML capabilities and make them available to all. Major providers like Google, Amazon, Microsoft, and others are providing these AI capabilities as public APIs that can be accessed from anywhere, and that too at a very attractive price. This is one of the drivers promoting the growth and adoption of AI APIs across industries.

Because of all these advantages, organizations are integrating AI APIs as tools to save on AI infrastructure and development costs and boost business profits.

Also, today, many leading API management platforms have integrated AI capabilities for intelligent routing and provide BoT and anomaly detections for enhanced security.

Trend #10: Managing Internal APIs Using a Service Mesh

With digital transformation underway, organizations are rearchitecting their existing applications and building new applications using microservices. These microservices communicate using APIs. Even though these are mostly internal communications, the APIs must be managed and secured. A service mesh is an alternative to an API gateway to manage internal API communications.

Service mesh is used for managing interservice communications in a microservices architecture within the boundaries of the corporate firewall. A service mesh like Istio, Linkerd, and Consul provides capabilities to implement security, traffic management, load balancing, routing, service discovery, networking, and monitoring for the internal APIs in a non-invasive manner. Its primary goal is to provide secure, fast and reliable service-to-service communication within a cluster.

Service mesh architecture has two components: the data plane and the control plane. A sidecar proxy is deployed alongside each service in the data plane, controlling the ingress and egress traffic. These are lightweight reverse proxy processes deployed in a separate container. Sidecars intercept the traffic and execute the security and communication policies defined by the control plane. The control plane provides the management capabilities of the service mesh. It allows easy traffic management, network resiliency, security, and custom telemetry data for each service. All these can be done by adding policies at the control plane level.

In brief, with the growing adoption of microservices for building flexible and scalable architecture, service mesh adoption is also increasing for managing and securing interservice communications.

Trend #11: Multiple API Gateways Are the Norm Going Forward

Companies today are adopting multiple gateways to bring more value to their business. The following are some of the key reasons behind this adoption approach.

- Diverse security requirements for internal and external API traffic
- Multi-cloud and hybrid deployment models
- Central vs. local governance for data and privacy regulations and culture
- Close the gap of growing API management requirements.
- Separate infrastructure for non-prod and prod environments

Diverse Security Requirements for Internal and External API Traffic

The security requirements for internal and external APIs are different. External APIs are exposed to ecosystem consumers and hence have increased cyber security threats. They also have more stringent compliance requirements. On the other hand, internal APIs may have a higher level of trust when consumed by internal applications. These internal applications may need some flexibility to test and innovate with the APIs. These differences in security paradigm often drive companies to have separate API gateways to manage external and internal APIs. A separate gateway comes with the advantage that in case of a breach or security attack on one, the other can continue to function without bringing all APIs to a standstill.

Multi-cloud and Hybrid Deployment Models

Today, organizations are adopting the cloud for digital transformation while many legacy systems are still on-premise. Companies have adopted a multi-cloud strategy to adopt the best of all clouds. As a result, many organizations have their application and data spread across hybrid cloud and multi-cloud infrastructure across a country or several global regions. Countries may have different regulations requiring them to enforce regional traffic management for the APIs. Such heterogeneous and distributed IT environments and regulatory requirements have driven organizations to adopt multiple API gateways to build, deploy, and manage their APIs in different geographic regions. This kind of setup improves performance, availability, and security.

Central vs. Local Governance for Data and Privacy Regulations and Culture

Large multinational organizations have different business units with operations in different countries. Each business unit and country may have different needs and requirements. Adopting a decentralized approach for building and managing APIs for each business unit is often a better approach from a governance and operational perspective. It gives the agility and flexibility to grow the business against centralized governance. Decentralized governance with a separate API gateway gives each business unit the autonomy to build, test, deploy, and manage their APIs. Multiple API gateways ensure compliance with regional data and privacy regulations.

Also, organizations that have grown through mergers and acquisitions have owned and managed multiple API management platforms originally set up within the organization before the acquisition. It is not easy to manage and maintain multiple platforms. So there are often efforts to consolidate the API management platforms. However, it is not an easy task partly because of the internal resistance to change and because migrating APIs from one platform to another is not straightforward. Hence, the co-existence of multiple API management platforms for some time becomes inevitable in such scenarios.

Close the Gap of Growing API Management Requirements

An API management platform is expected to provide full lifecycle support for designing, building, testing, deploying, managing, and operating APIs. API gateway is at the heart of every API management platform. It is expected to cover broad capabilities like security, traffic management, routing, load balancing, protocol mediation, transformation, monitoring, and visibility. There are many API management platform vendors in the market. However, not all vendors have the same maturity levels in their product offerings to meet the enterprise requirements. So, if an organization had started its API journey with a vendor product that was at its inception with limited capability support, they might soon see the need to migrate to or adopt a more mature API management platform as they outgrow the capabilities of the existing gateway. In such scenarios, they may continue to use the existing gateway for internal use for limited use cases and add a new platform to fill the gaps.

Separate Infrastructure for Non-Prod and Prod Environments

A separate infrastructure for non-prod and prod environments is common in many organizations, and keeping the infrastructure and environments separate for non-prod and prod setups is highly advisable. This provides an added level of security by restricting access for developers, testers, and operations teams to the production environment and protects from any inadvertent configuration changes. Even the non-prod environment may have separate infrastructure setups for Dev, SIT, and UAT environments with segregation of network boundaries. Due to all these reasons, it may be required to set up separate API gateways for different stages of the API lifecycle. This also prevents confusion on which endpoint to use for which environment.

Trend #12: Increased Focus on the Developer Experience

The *developer experience* describes an application developer's overall perception while using the APIs. It starts with understanding the API interface from its documentation, the onboarding process to use the API, trying and testing it using various tools, and the overall support to resolve any issues. Developers expect a completely frictionless and enjoyable experience while integrating the APIs into their applications. The developer experience must address the trust, education, tools, and usability of the API.

The Importance of the Developer Experience

A rich developer experience is needed to create a thriving API ecosystem and foster innovation with collaboration.

As the API economy expands, the experience of the developers building applications using the API becomes increasingly important. This is so because, without good experience, developers abandon the API. If an API is hard to discover or poorly documented, making it difficult to understand or is poorly maintained with no adherence to the defined SLAs, developers drop it for a simpler and easier-to-use API. That means few apps might be built using the APIs, thus reducing revenue growth opportunities. Developers abandoning APIs can have tangible business consequences. It is important to note that good developer experience is important not only for external APIs but also for internal APIs. A poor developer experience with internal APIs can negatively impact productivity and time to market.

Building a Rich Developer Experience for APIs

The following are some tenets to keep in mind that boost the developer experience for APIs.

- Identify the users who are going to be interacting with the APIs.
- Design and build sound APIs that are simple to use and solve a business problem.
- Publish APIs on a developer portal or API marketplace to make them discoverable.
- Provide an easy onboarding path for developers to use the APIs with a simple signup.
- Provide clear and thorough documentation for the APIs that is complete, up-to-date, and easy to follow.
- Provide a test bed for the developers to try the APIs against any sandbox environment.
- Provide a getting-started guide to help developers build their Hello World! app with APIs. A developer is happy if they can successfully use the API from their app within 5 minutes.
- Provide code samples in different programming languages.
- Provide exceptional support to developers for resolving queries and issues with API usage. Make it easy for them to raise tickets or chat to get support when encountering issues with your APIs.

- Build an active community or forum for the developers to share their experience with API usage and learn from others about the use cases they are building with the APIs. Stack Overflow, Slack, Discord, and Twitter can be used for community building.
- Measure and track the parameters for developer experience and make changes as required to improve them. KPIs for the developer experience include developer onboarding time, the time to the first Hello World!, request throughput, average and max latency, developer signups and logins, and active apps.

Using the preceding approach, you can build a great experience for your APIs that developers enjoy and love. Happy and satisfied developers are likelier to recommend the APIs to others in their community, integrate them into more apps, and build new capabilities around them. Overall, a happy and fruitful developer experience holds the key to the growth and success of your APIs and expands the ecosystem.

Trend #13: The Rise of the API Marketplace

An API marketplace is a platform that aggregates APIs from different providers. It allows multiple API providers to upload and publish their APIs. At the same time, an API marketplace enables API consumers and app developers to discover and integrate the APIs into their apps. API consumers can easily find APIs of their choice and build more powerful and user-friendly apps. Publishing APIs on the marketplace helps the provider increase the visibility and accessibility of their APIs. With a common platform for providers and consumers, it has the potential to boost the production and consumption of APIs and grow the ecosystem of APIs faster.

The Difference Between an API Marketplace and an API Portal

An API marketplace may sound like an API portal because of the similarities in their capabilities. However, there is a big difference. The API portal is set up by the API provider and deployed in an infrastructure of their choice. The entire responsibility of setting up, maintaining the portal, and publishing the APIs lies with the API provider. The portal provides capabilities to publish the interactive API documentation as a searchable catalog, onboard app developers and register their apps, test bed to try out APIs, access control, and many more features. However, all of this is limited to a single API management platform that the API provider owns.

On the other hand, the API marketplace brings multiple API providers and consumers to a common platform. It is a platform that offers a collection of APIs from different providers. App developers or API consumers can use this platform to search for an API from any of the listed vendors that meets their needs. It is a central hub connecting API providers with developers, encouraging increased collaboration and innovation.

The Advantages of an API Marketplace

Integrating API providers and consumers on a common API marketplace platform provides the following benefits.

- A better developer experience with searching APIs in a single place
- Collaboration from more API providers and consumers helps get constructive feedback to enhance the APIs

- Incentivizes and promotes healthy competition between providers of APIs with similar functionality to improve the API capability and developer experience
- Builds and grows the ecosystem around APIs with accelerated application development by leveraging third-party services

APILayer, Celigo, Integrately, and RapidAPI are some of the popular API marketplaces to list your public APIs. Companies increasingly use the API marketplace to publish and monetize their APIs and expand into new markets. It holds the answer to how to increase the value of APIs and achieve business goals.

Trend #14: API Monetization Is on the Rise

Organizations that have built APIs for digital transformation are increasingly looking at monetizing the APIs. Although a rising trend in API monetization has been observed across all industries, it is more prominent in the financial, telecom, and healthcare sectors.

Different monetization models can be adopted depending on the business use case. However, the most popular and successful models include the developer pays, the developer gets paid, and indirect monetization.

Conclusion

This chapter explored the dynamic and ever-evolving landscape of API development and management. The trends discussed here highlight APIs' transformative power in shaping how businesses operate, how software is developed, and how data is exchanged in our increasingly interconnected world.

From the imperative of API security to the shift toward microservices architectures and the rise of GraphQL, it's clear that APIs have become the backbone of modern software ecosystems. Organizations are embracing these trends and innovating in response to them. Organizations are also embracing serverless technologies and containerization on a multi-cloud platform to build scalable APIs. API management platforms are also being rearchitected using cloud-native technologies to handle the growing API traffic volumes. The evolution of artificial intelligence and machine learning has given a new direction to API use.

API management platforms are a strategic necessity today. They provide deeper insights into developer experience with advanced analytics using ML technologies. Advances in API lifecycle management capabilities highlight the growing maturity of the platforms. Leading API management platforms use AI/ML to provide greater automation, efficiency, and security. As businesses seek new revenue streams and partnerships, API monetization, and event-driven architectures are emerging as key strategies.

As time progresses, staying vigilant and adaptive as the API landscape evolves is crucial. It is essential to recognize that these trends are not isolated developments but are related and interconnected threads in the fabric of digital transformation. All developers, architects, and business leaders need to truly understand these trends, and the ability to navigate this complex API ecosystem is a strategic advantage. API development and management journey is ongoing, and those who embrace these trends with agility and vision are at the forefront of technological progress.

Index

A

B. De, *API Management*, https://doi.org/10.1007/979-8-8688-0054-2

B

C

D

G

H

I

N

O

R

U

V

W

X, Y

Z

Printed in the United States
by Baker & Taylor Publisher Services